Trade and Economic Contacts Between the Volga and Kama Rivers Region and the Classical World

Andrey Bezrukov

BAR International Series 2727
2015

Published in 2016 by
BAR Publishing, Oxford

BAR International Series 2727

Trade and Economic Contacts Between the Volga and Kama Rivers Region and the Classical World

ISBN 978 1 4073 1382 5

BAR Publishing is the trading name of British Archaeological Reports (Oxford) Ltd.
British Archaeological Reports was first incorporated in 1974 to publish the BAR
Series, International and British. In 1992 Hadrian Books Ltd became part of the BAR
group. This volume was originally published by Archaeopress in conjunction with
British Archaeological Reports (Oxford) Ltd / Hadrian Books Ltd, the Series principal
publisher, in 2015. This present volume is published by BAR Publishing, 2016.

Printed in England

BAR
PUBLISHING

BAR titles are available from:

        BAR Publishing
        122 Banbury Rd, Oxford, OX2 7BP, UK
EMAIL   info@barpublishing.com
PHONE +44 (0)1865 310431
FAX   +44 (0)1865 316916
        www.barpublishing.com

CONTENTS

FOREWORD

The author of this volume is my colleague and formal post-gradual student. After Andrei Bezrukov completed his post gradual study in the Department of Classic Archaeology of the Institute of Archaeology, Russian Academy of Sciences (IA RAS), he returned to the Department of Ancient and Medieval History in the Magnitogorsk State University (now Nosov Magnitogorsk State Technical University). In Moscow his teachers were the Corresponding Member of RAS Pr. G. A. Koshelenko and Pr. A. A. Maslennikov. Together with Andrei Bezrukov we have worked at many sites in the Ural Region, the Bosporus, Colchis (Dioscurias), etc. Twenty five years ago we started to work in the Phanagorian Archaeological Mission of the IA RAS led by Pr. V. D. Kuznetsov., where we are working till now. Although A. Bezrukov inseparably linked with excavations at Phanagoria, the study of transit trade in the Volga and the Kama Region and imported items from Greek centres of the North Pontic region, Rome and Byzantine Empire found there remain to be his general scientific interest. I was a supervisor of Bezrukov's PhD with my pleasure. I am under a debt of gratitude to the Director of the Department of Field Studies, IA RAS, Pr. A. A. Maslennikov, who was the official opponent under the defense of Bezrukov's dissertation. Also I appreciate sincerely the help of my Chelyabinsk colleagues Pr. A. D. Tairov and Pr. S. G. Botalov, who gave us many pieces of advice.

Present book brings useful information on the imported goods and items found on the territory of the Ural, the Volga and the Kama Regions, as well as the publications and descriptions of the artifacts. The imported items are regarded by the author as the evidences of economic, political and cultural contacts between the tribes of the Eastern Europe and the ancient states in the West and the East. The author's special consideration is given to the possible equivalents of exchanges and trade links between the tribes of the barbaric hinterland and ancient civilizations.

The Volga and the Kama Region is of the specific interest. This is an important road junction – the crossing of the main caravan roads with the waterways. Penetration of a certain group of imported items there could be related to migration of nomadic tribes of the Sauromatians, the Sarmatians, the Alani, the Huns and other unions. Besides, a few branches of the Silk Road ran across the region. Recent discoveries gave very new information on finds of imported items. Among them, for instance, there is a very impressive "Roman wine kit" containing silver and bronze jug, a scoop, a strainer, a bailer, and a tumbler, found in the Magnitny necropolis near Magnitogorsk in 2010 (see Botalov & Ivanov 2012), a few Late Roman phalarae with depictions of two generals or warriors from the site of Ufa II and numerous antique and Byzantine jewellery items from Bashkir Trans-Urals, which arrived with the Huns (see Garustovich & Ivanov 2010), etc. A. Bezrukov introduces the reader with a large part of imported goods (including unknown and little known) which arrived to the barbarian provinces of the Volga and the Kama Region though direct exchange or as gifts and war trophies. Even for this reason, his book should be warmly welcome.

Pr. Mikhail G. Abramzon

PREFACE AND ACKNOWLEDGEMENTS

The subject of the present research was determined in the course of studying of the archaeological data obtained during excavations of the ancient cities of the North Black Sea region, as well as the barbarian settlements of the Don and the Kuban Rivers Regions.

The historical tradition, common for the national and global practice, urges the researchers, as we see it, to rely on the available written sources to reconstruct the processes which took place in the civilization centers and on the adjacent territories.

The deep «illiterate» periphery of the territory inhabited by various barbarian tribes remained, normally, a «twilight» semi-fantastic zone in the interpretation by ancient or medieval narrators, or was considered a platform mostly for archeological surveys.

In this regard, production of papers of this kind is quite logical. They attempt at identification and description of certain historical realities on the basis of complex analysis of narrative, archaeological, numismatic and other evidences, and thus, today they represent the only actually possible solution for historical research of the territories inhabited by peoples of scriptless civilizations.

The present paper uses all materials available to contemporary historians to reconstruct one of the most important kinds of socioeconomic communications – the trade contacts between the peoples of the Volga and the Kama Rivers Region and the states of the ancient times and the early medieval period.

As far as we know, no complex research of this kind has been undertaken in respect of the Ural and the Volga Rivers Regions. The ancient imported objects found in the steppe and forest-steppe areas of the Volga and the Kama Rivers Region attracted the attention of historians and archaeologists and were used, first of all, for characterization of the commercial links of the population of individual regions with the ancient state formations of Eastern Europe, as well as the level and forms of their organization in the process of intertribal exchange and international trade.

There were also attempts to reconstruct the routes of the imports arrival to certain areas of the Volga and the Kama Rivers Region. However, on the whole, the trade and economic contacts of the population of the steppe and forest-steppe zones of the Volga and the Kama Rivers Region with the ancient world remained out of focus of either domestic or European specialists. We need to mention that the main papers on which we relied were highlighting either the historical and artistic aspects of the subject (Tolstoy I.I., Kondakov N.P., Matsulevich L.A.), or its archeological side (Rostovtsev M.I., Rau P.D., Rykov P.S., Grakov B.N., Shelov D.B., Moshkova M.G., Skripkin A.S., Botalov S.G. et al.), or the papers were related only to numismatic studies (Zaikovskiy B.V., Kropotkin V.V., Leshchenko V.Yu.).

In our opinion, this circumstance defines the timeliness of the subject of the present research.

The academic interest of the present paper lies in the fact that the comprehensive analysis of objects of imported origin taking into account the results of archaeological studies will allow to provide a more precise and complete description of the main mechanisms of trade and economic relationships between the societies which occupied different levels of socioeconomic and political development.

One of the most disputable is the question: which imported objects reached the local tribes due to direct trade exchange and which ones were gained as the result of combats with Roman squads on the Empire's frontiers or as gifts for participation in internal wars of the Bosporan tsars – this is extremely difficult to define.

We believe our research will allow us to state quite confidently that a large part of imported objects was brought to the barbarian provinces though direct exchange or as gifts and war trophies; we make a reservation that penetration of a certain group of imported products could be attributed to migration of some nomadic tribes.

Probably, this position can be accepted as a relatively justified one, in the general context of the present research subject, but in individual parts of the paper the highlighted socioeconomic mechanisms will have a specific nature.

For instance, the nomadic tribes of the Sauromatians, Sarmatians, Alani, Huns and other unions came to possession of imported items originally as exchange products, trophies, military or road recompense. Further, one can propose with a large extent of probability that the items travel with the tribes for significant distances, on itineraries which sometimes had no relation to the Silk Road or other routes. Then, sometimes after a long period, the items were laid into graves, usually, of the noblest nomads.

As for the settled population of the Volga and the Kama Rivers Region, it makes sense to speak about the trade exchange which actually took place on the banks of the Itil river in the late ancient and early medieval period.

These remarks relate to general methodology and provide definite highlights of the historical process which took place on the territory under review. They do not have categorical nature, because the subject chosen by us for the research is quite versatile, and at present it is not possible to reflect all its aspects unambiguously, considering the modern base and the accumulated materials.

In the historical, cultural and economic processes in the Volga and the Kama Rivers Region the dominating role belonged to the external and internal cultural, economical and political links and interactions; besides, we should not ignore the military and political history of the nomadic Iranian – and Turkic-speaking tribes and the related conquests, internal wars, migrations and massive movements of different population groups.

The sets and individual finds of imported objects and coins discovered in the Volga and Kama Rivers Region are generally typical also for other barbarian territories (the Don River Region, the Kuban River Region, the Dnieper River Region), thus evidencing the similarity of the trade exchange process mechanisms.

In terms of quantity, as shown further, inexpensive decorations prevail; also wide-spread were red-clay pottery and red-varnish ceramics, Italic and Gaul-Roman bronze utensils, Roman and Byzantine silver vessels, mirrors, coins, while there were almost no Italic ceramics, decorations, weapons or armature.

A special role belongs to papers dedicated to analysis of trade communications and itineraries of the Silk Road, the fur road and other roads (Lubo-Lesnichenko E.I., Mukhamadiev A.G., Treister M.Yu., Shilik K.K., Kopylov V.P., Rashke M.G., Mamleeva L. A., Tairov A.D. etc.).

At the initial stage of our work we gave preference to the statement which said that the comparison of the written, archaeological and numismatic evidences proved that almost all main trade communication routes in the specified regions ran along the valleys of the Volga, the Kama and the Ural rivers, as well as along the water sheds of their large tributaries.

However, during the research it became obvious that in the steppe and forest-steppe zones of Eurasia, on the territories under review, in the ancient times and during the medieval period land roads were mainly used for commercial communications, as it is demonstrated by the relationships of the Caucasus and the Kama River region, starting from the Ananino period.

Thus, the main objective of the present paper is to generalize and systematize the accumulated written, archaeological and numismatic materials which reflect the trade and economic contacts of the region.

This book is mainly based on the thesis paper which I supported in December 2005 at Chelyabinsk State University, although the book contains significant amendments and necessary clarifications which are quite numerous in the present paper and were not included into the original dissertation in Russian.

The above deviation from the original Russian text is justified by the bibliography made as complete as possible for today, the new archaeological discoveries in the Volga and the Kama Rivers Region, as well as by broadening of the research scope with inclusion of data about the imported objects found in Northern Kazakhstan and in the Upper Volga River Region.

The novelty of this paper lies in the fact that for the first time in the national historiography (as far as we know, this issue was hardly considered by foreign researchers) the author generalized and systematized the significant volume of narrative, archaeological and numismatic materials related to studies of the ancient imports and trade routes in the peripheral barbarian territories of Eastern Europe (the Ural, the Volga and the Kama Rivers regions), from arrival of the first imported items till the early medieval period.

The scientific and practical meaning of the research is characterized by the possibility, based on the new conclusions, to readdress the traditional opinions on the matters related to trade and economic relationships of the barbarian hinterland territories with the ancient centers.

I must say warm words of gratitude to all the people who helped me and made invaluable contributions to drafting of the book and structuring of the major part of its content.

First of all, I would like to thank Prof. Mikhail Grigorievich Abramzon, Director of the Institute of History and Philology of Nosov Magnitogorsk State Technical University, and Gennady Andreevich Koshelenko, Formal Head of Classical Archaeology Department and Associate Member of the Russian Academy of Sciences.

I would like to say a few words about Prof. Mikhail Grigorievich Abramzon. Without his guidance and support I would never be able to produce this paper at the doctoral thesis level.

Mikhail Grigorievich is always available for his colleagues and students; he spends a significant portion of his precious time on reading and correcting texts and other academic papers aiming at providing maximum assistance on various aspects of the scientific research activity.

He criticized, advised, proposed final wordings, helped with search and collection of new literature on the subject. M.G. Abramzon is undoubtedly one of the leading specialists in ancient numismatics combining skills of a field scientist with high level of analysis. It is a great honor for me to know him personally, learn from him and work together.

I would like to express my special thanks to Dr. Elias K. Petropoulos for his recommendation and the idea to present my study as a complex, taking into account the available narrative, archaeological and numismatic materials related to various aspects of the topic. Elias K. Petropoulos provided me with advice, suggestions and comments during my work, and his opinion was very important to me. I appreciate his recommendations and valuable references to academic literature, his comments on interpretation of archeological and written sources in the course of preparation of my manuscript, as well as his belief in success.

I also express warm thanks to Alexander Alexandrovich Maslennikov, archaeologist, Doctor of Historical Sciences, and his colleagues from the Institute of Archaeology at the Russian Academy of Sciences in Moscow with whom I often discussed various aspects of Greco-barbarian contacts using the example of the North Black Sea Region, the Don River Region and the Kuban River Region.

Finally, I would like to say words of gratitude to "British Archaeological Reports, International Series" and my colleague Dr. David Davison, the publication director, for his active support of the publication of this paper in English.

Andrey Bezrukov Assist. Professor at the Department of World History of the Institute of History and Philology of Nosov Magnitogorsk State Technical University

INTRODUCTION

§ 1. GENERAL NOTES

It is an important and challenging issue to perform an analysis of trade and economic relationships of the Volga and Kama Rivers Region, the peripheral areas of the Eastern Europe, with the Roman Empire and Byzantine Empire, relying mainly on the study of objects of Roman and Byzantine origin found on the territory covered by our research. The solution of this problem will lead to a fuller appreciation of the peculiarities and the character of mutual relations between the ancient world and the remote areas inhabited by barbarians.

Identifying the stages of the development of trade relations between ancient cities and the barbarians, determining the variety of the imported goods, which came from many ancient states and in different chronological periods, will allow us to have a new perception of some aspects of the political and commercial expansion of the ancient states into neighboring areas, nations and tribes. Furthermore, it will help to consider the level and forms of interaction during intertribal exchanges and international trade of numerous tribes and nations with western and eastern cities and states.

Taking into account that the main part of the imported products found in the Volga and Kama Rivers Region are of Roman origin, special attention in our book is given to the research of the trade relations of the Roman Empire and then of the Byzantine Empire with the remote areas. With regard to this topic, the majority of researchers have always focused particularly on the eastern links of the above mentioned Empires because the Atlantic coast was a natural boundary in the West, whereas the vast eastern territories were distant from the areas where Roman legions could reach, and only merchants and trading caravans were able to make their further way there. At the same time, very little consideration was given to north-eastern contacts, and the vast steppe and forest-steppe zones of the Eastern Europe were neglected.

The essence and trends of the early trade relations are evidently among the most sophisticated and topical aspects in the ancient history of the peripheral area of the Eastern Europe, on the whole, and the Volga and Kama Rivers Region, in particular, considering scanty written testimonies. The trade relations could be determined by various aspects of the society life, such as trade exchange of raw materials, livestock and goods; cultural interchange and so on. It should be noted that the drift of some population groups from the neighboring regions, migration of strong nomadic tribes influenced the life the people led on the territories under examination.

The history of the population in the steppe and forest-steppe zones of the Eastern Europe in the late BC – early AD centuries comprises a number of important and sophisticated issues which have been poorly analyzed so far and undeservedly neglected. The researchers might have failed to handle these issues due to insufficient study of archaeological materials, written sources and lacunas in the research on the history of the tribes and nations in peripheral areas of the Eastern Europe.

The issues that are least examined by the researchers relate to the study of mutual relations between nomads and the Roman Empire. One of these specific aspects is the way the products manufactured in Greece, western Rome and the Byzantine Empire as well as Italic goods were spread beyond Italy, in the areas that were not linked with the ancient central regions, with the exception of the Dnieper, the Don and the Kuban regions which have now been studied over one hundred years.

The study we present is devoted to some poorly studied and in some respects disputable aspects in the history of the tribes and nations inhabiting the Volga and Kama Rivers Region.

The main objective of the research is to generalize and systematize the existing written records, archaeological and numismatic materials which reflect trade and economic relations of the region. To do this we set the following tasks:

1. To perform a comprehensive study of the historical sources (written, archeological and numismatic).

2. To determine the reliability degree of the above sources and their information value; to specify if possible the dating, chronologically classifying all kinds of the sources; to compare the results of the analysis conducted for each source type.

3. To determine the ways the imported products were spread in various chronological periods.

The study is also aimed at generalization of the new data and materials on the specified issue, as well as comprehensive study of the products manufactured in Rome and the Byzantine Empire and found in archaeological complexes in the territory of the contemporary Eastern Russia (the Volga and the Kama Rivers Region) within the 6th century BC – 7th century AD.

Our research is mainly focused on the imported products found on the territories along the rivers Ural, Volga and Kama. For comparative analysis we used the archaeological materials both from the neighboring regions and from the territories of the Northern Black Sea Region, the Kuban Region, the Lower Don Region, the Northern Caucasus, Transcaucasia and Middle Asia. These are the territories from which a considerable part of similar imported products came to the territory covered by our research.

The imported products found in the aforementioned regions are of a special interest as these territories to a greater or lesser degree were all the areas where imported goods arrived on their way to the East or North-East. The necessity to hold a complex examination of the findings under study as historical sources of trade and economic relations in the Volga and Kama Rivers Region is also stipulated by the fact that imported products were spread eastward along the Great Silk Road. Therefore, the study is focused on the functioning of the northern branch of the Silk Road that stretched through the Lower Volga region and Southern Cisurals.

It is also important for our research to analyze the written records, the archaeological materials and the numismatic data. All of them will help to identify the main trends of trade communications.

The present work has been consequently incorporated into the general research covering both the area where individual objects and groups of imported items were found and the relationships and commercial links between the barbarian tribes and the ancient centers, on the whole.

The work summarizes data on the imported products found on the territory of the Ural, Volga and Kama regions, as well as the publications and descriptions of the artifacts. The imported products found in the areas under study are regarded in the present paper as the source that characterizes economic, political and cultural relations between the tribes of the Eastern Europe and the ancient states in the West and the East. They also allow us to clarify the historical and economic relations within the regions and the countries that participated in the exchanges. A special consideration is given to the possible equivalents of exchanges and trade relations between the tribes of the barbaric hinterland and ancient civilizations.

Each object is analyzed in terms of its designation, origin and age as well as the contents and symbolism of images, if any. The attribution (chronology and geographical appurtenance) derives from comparison with similar artifacts, i.e., from the place in the group of related objects. The nature of the individual conclusions in respect of place and time of production of imported items is preliminary due to scarcity of reference materials. Undoubtedly, they will be updated depending on accumulation of new archeological data.

Due to certain peculiarities of the present research caused by the nature of the subject it is worth while making the following comments. Firstly, the paper contains numerous terms "Roman" and "Byzantine" imported items which should be construed broadly as the objects related to the entire territory of the Roman empire (including its provinces), and thereafter to Byzantium, unless the place of manufacturing is specified in more detail.

Secondly, certain difficulties arise due to different levels of knowledge about the ancient history of individual areas of this region, especially, when compared to the districts which are adjacent to the Northern Black Sea region. Nevertheless, actually, the archaeological and numismatic sources allow the most profound and comprehensive study of the complex processes of the economic life in the interior territories of the hinterland in the 2nd c. BC – 2nd c. AD.

The novelty of the paper is that for the first time in the national historiography, and as far as we know, this subject was hardly considered by foreign researchers, it compiles and systematizes a significant volume of narrative, archeological and numismatic materials related to studies of ancient imports and trade routes in the peripheral barbarian territories of the Eastern Europe (the Urals, Volga and Kama regions) starting from the time the first imported objects appeared and covering the period until the early Middle Ages.

For every area under review we identified the main categories of imported items typical for various chronological periods and the principal directions of commercial links.

The methods for studies of ancient imported objects allow to compare the archeological and numismatic data with the records of the written sources and were developed by H.J. Eggers, V.V.Kropotkin, V.P. Shilov and other researchers.

The geographical and chronological frames of the study cover a certain cultural and historical region and period and have been determined by the location of the foreign items. The geographical names 'the Ural Region', 'the Volga Region' and 'the Kama Region' are mostly used for convenience of the reader. These names define, respectively, the territories of the Cisurals, the Middle and Southern Ural river region, Trans-Urals, the Kama river region, the Lower and Middle Volga river region. At present the above areas correspond to the following regions: Astrakhan region, Volgograd region, Kurgan region, Orenburg region, Perm region, Samara region, Saratov region, Sverdlovsk region, Chelyabinsk region as well as the republics of Bashkortostan, Mordovia and Tatarstan.

§ 2. HISTORIOGRAPHY OF THE PROBLEM

Initially the imported products (finds of silver vessels) discovered on the territory of the Ural region, the Volga region and the Kama region were mentioned by F.Stralenberg [1730], the founder of the hypothesis about the sameness of the Upper Kama Region and "The Great Perm" of the Russian Chronicles and Biarmia and about the trade route which connected the Northern Europe with the Middle Asia via Biarmia.

An elevated interest for the finds of imported items, and particularly, for the silver vessels of eastern and Byzantine origin discovered in the Kama region was demonstrated by the Archeological Committee which was established in 1859 and was publishing records about the unearthed treasures in its "Reports". Consequently, in 1890 a paper by I.I.Tolstoy and N.P.Kondakov was published. In this paper we can find a full list to date of silver vessels (58) discovered mostly in the Kama Region. The inflow of these articles can be explained by the demand from the local population to possess silver vessels in order to use them for cultic purposes [Tolstoy I.I., Kondakov N.P., 1890: 79-94].

Some of the first publications about the ancient imported articles found beyond the Northern Black Sea region mostly in the rich kurgans of the Scythian and Sarmatian period on the adjacent territories of the Dnieper region, the Kuban region, the Don region and the Northern Caucasus appeared quite late – in the end of the 19th – beginning of the 20th centuries and were related to the prominent Russian archeologists of the 19th century: I.I.Tolstoy and N.P. Kondakov [1854, 1890, 1899], P.S. Uvarova [1899, 1900], B.V. Farmakovskiy (1902), N.I. Veselovskiy (1905), I.I.Tolstoy [1912, 1914] and M.I. Rostovtsev [1918, 1922, 1925].

Classical examples of work with the archeological materials can be the publications by B.V. Farmakovskiy and M.I. Rostovtsev whose papers for the first time in the national study of antiquity include a qualified description of imported objects. In his papers M.I. Rostovtsev mentions numerous complexes where ancient products were found, the age of the items was specified correctly. Focusing on the historical problems of the Roman Empire and the Northern Black Sea region, at the same time, M.I. Rostovtsev expressed a series of general ideas about the nature of economic ties of the Northern Black Sea region with the tribes of the Eastern Europe. In the English publication [Rostovtseff M.I., 1922: 214-217] he noted that in the first centuries AD the tribes of the steppe and forest-steppe areas of the Dnieper region shifted from barter to monetary trade due to the cultural influence of the Teutons; this is evidenced by many hidden hoards with Roman silver coins of the 1st-3rd c. AD, while the Sarmatian tribes practiced only simple swap trade. His paper of 1918 is of our special interest since it describes the finds on the territory of the former Orenburg Province in Prokhorovka and Pokrovka kurgans; the author analyzed the imported items and drew an analogy between the objects, mainly, of the Asian and Iranian origin [Rostovtsev M.I., 1918a: 22-26, 76-79].

Thus, among all the researches of antiquities in the 19th – early 20th centuries only M.I. Rostovtsev provided detailed descriptions of burial complexes and dating of burials based on the objects found in the grave goods, paying a significant attention to the imported items.

Concluding the overview of the studies made by Russian scientists and published in the above period, in our opinion, it makes sense to underline a few distinctive features which shaped the characteristics of a series of subsequent research endeavors.

Firstly, the main drawback was that none of the mentioned scientists aimed at systematizing of the accumulated materials or presenting a general picture of the economic ties between Rome and the Northern Black Sea region and the barbarian lands on the basis of analysis of the imported articles.

Secondly, in their majority they limited themselves by more or less detailed mentioning of the antiquities found in the Eastern Europe, the Northern Caucasus and even in the South Cisurals without considering the immediate analogies for identification of potential production centers or ways of the imported articles inflow.

Probably, this can be mainly explained by the relatively small total quantity and quality of the archeological materials from the region under review which is definitely not sufficient for preparation of reports on various categories of imported articles found in the inland barbarian territories; low level of knowledge both on the regions distant from the Northern Black Sea region and on the various aspects of the Sarmatian history. Another important factor was the scope of the archeological works, since the pre-revolutionary researchers were interested only in the Northern Black Sea region and adjacent areas, and their scientific papers focused mostly on luxury items and jewelry giving little attention to household goods, general structure of sepulchral complexes and intertribal exchange.

In the subsequent period thanks to extensive archeological research in the areas of our interest in the 20–30s of the 20th century new materials were found relating to the imported objects on the peripheral barbarian lands. The archeological research started in the 20-30s of the 20th century in the Volga region and contributed a lot to accumulation of archeological materials on the history of the cultures of the Volga region of the Early Iron Age. This work touched partially upon the problem of the imported articles of the Roman produce found mainly in the Sarmatian burials of the Lower Volga region. This was reflected in the papers by P.S.Rykov [1925, 1927, 1936] dedicated to description of Roman imported articles from Suslovsky burial ground and in the works by P.D.Rau who published the results of her excavations on the territories of the Lower Volga region and the Trans-Volga region making references to imported items of Roman origin [1927a, 1927b].

In 1926 B.V.Zaikovskiy compiled and published his paper "From the monetary chronicles of the Lower Volga region" about the monetary hoards and accidental finds of coins at different times on the territory of the Lower Volga region. Along with coins of Greek cities of the Northern Black Sea region, among these finds were listed Roman and Byzantine coins and even Parthian drachms; he also described the conditions of discovery and topography of the most authentic monetary hoards and individual finds until and including the 13th century.

The paper by L.A.Matsulevich [1940] was one of the first research works laying the foundation for further studies of the imported ancient items found in the Kama region and the Ural region. Based on the analysis of the Byzantine silver vessels (the majority of which originates from the Kama region and the Ural region), the researcher came to the following conclusions: the lower chronological border for the Byzantine finds was the first quarter of the 6th c. (a scoop found at Cherdyn), the upper border corresponds to Irakli's silver platter (629/30–641). A minor chronological interval (max. 20–30 years) between the two Byzantine platters of the Turushevsk hoard, use of the same dies for embossment of stamps on one of Turushevsk platters and Pereshchepinsk platters, a Byzantine silver plate found in Ust-Kishert convinced L.A.Matsulevich that "the time of inflow of the Byzantine silver vessels cannot be much later than the time of their manufacturing, therefore, direct routes existed connecting the Kama region and the Byzantium" [Matsulevich L.A., 1940: 74].

After a profound analysis of the stamps (Byzantine hallmarks) on the silverware of the 4th-7th c. and comparing the stamps with Byzantine coins he could suggest new dating for the silverware. His dating is still considered commonly accepted in the world literature about the Byzantium.

Individual finds of Roman bronze items in the Kama region deserved a close attention of A.M.Volkovich whose article gives a detailed and thorough description of the imported bronze objects; using the reference materials, she attempted to identify the center of their production, possible ways and time of their arrival to the Kama region, while Tanais was especially mentioned as the intermediary [Volkovich A.M., 1941: 226-233].

We should highlight an article by B.N.Grakov [1947] as one of the most important works analyzing Herodotus' passage [Herod., IV, 23, 24] and finds of mirrors of the so-called "Olbian type" discovered in the Volga region and Cisurals. The author concentrated on reconstruction of a proposed route (probably, of commercial nature) which in the 6th–4th c. BC connected the Northern Black Sea region with the Volga region and the South Cisurals. This paper, showing an attempt to verify the data from the written sources using the available archeological materials, initiated an active discussion on the Herodotus' route problem, its directions, origin and destination, itinerary, nature, chronology, potential participants of barter trade and its equivalents.

An important step was the paper by M.G.Moshkova [1956] with the main accent on the problem of ancient imports into the territory of the Volga River Region. This paper compiled both research results of the authors of the past and the conclusions of the contemporary archeological surveys; M.G.Moshkova identified different groups and categories of imported articles, specified the possible production centers, presented evidences of ancient historians and a list of coin finds.

D.B. Shelov made a significant contribution to studies of imported Roman articles [1965, 1969, 1972, 1983]. In his paper of 1965 he analyzed the finds of imported bronze and silver vessels in the burials of the Sarmatian nobles of 1st c. BC – 1st c. AD in the Don region and the Volga region and discussed their origin. Highlighting the leading role of Tanais in the trade with the barbarians, however, D.B.Shelov proposed that there might exist other sources and routes for the Sarmatians of the Volga region and the Cisurals coming to possession of the expensive imported articles, because not all the items found in the rich Sarmatian burials of the region were available in Tanais [Shelov D.B., 1965: 273-274].

In his article of 1983 dedicated to the finds of Roman bronze ware in the Eastern Europe D.B. Shelov used the new materials and adjusted dating for further addressing the problem of attribution and chronology of the Roman bronze items which were also found in the regions under our consideration.

An important contribution to studies of the imported Roman articles was made by V.V.Kropotkin [1967, 1970]. His papers summarize all then known finds of Roman and Byzantine imported articles from the enormous territory of the former USSR. The research materials in the book are grouped by categories (pottery, metal utensils, fibulae, decorations, arms etc.). Such work allows to define the place of this region in the overall distribution map of imported articles and to compare the periods of arrival of imported objects to different districts of the barbarian peripheral lands. The book also contains an overview of the written sources dedicated to this problem. It is also important that the area of distribution of the Roman articles in addition to the conventional regions (Northern Caucasus, the Don region, the Kuban region, the Dnieper region and the Bug region) includes the areas of Cisurals, the Volga region and the Kama region.

In 1961-1962 V.V.Kropotkin published individual collections of all then known individual coin finds and hoards of Roman and Byzantine coins discovered on the territory of the USSR among which there were Roman and Byzantine coins provening from the Volga region and the Kama region [1961, 1962]. These collection books contain all the information about the circumstances in which the items were found, the topography as well as diligent and detailed description of the coins, chronology of the coins penetration into the territory of the Eastern Europe and analysis of the causes of the stronger inflow of the monetary items.

A series of publications by V.P.Shilov in 50-70s of the 20th century were based on the results of the long-time archeological surveys undertaken by the researcher in the Lower Volga region. A significant portion is constituted by the descriptions of the objects belonging to various categories of imported items found in the rich Sarmatian burials (Italic mirrors, silver and bronze utensils, red varnish ceramics, fibulae, beads and decorations). Separately, the researcher studied the issues of their origin, manufacturing centers, routes and means of distribution of the Italic metal utensils [1956, 1959, 1972, 1973, 1974, 1983]. Analysing the imported articles found in the Sarmatian burials of the Don region and the Lower Volga region in comparison to the famous sets of Roman imports from the Greek cities of the Northern Black Sea region, V.P.Shilov was able to conclude that there existed a steppe route which bypassed the Northern Black Sea Region [Shilov V.P., 1974: 60-65].

In his thesis [1971] V.Yu.Leshchenko focused mainly on the finds of silver vessels of the 7th–13th centuries in the Ural region. V.Yu. Leshchenko analyzed 104 hoards of silver vessels among which he named about 30 authentic finds of Byzantine silver vessels, reviewed the chronology, routes and ways of arrival of the oriental silverware. According to the researcher who compared a significant part of the hoards with the burial sites and settlements of Lomovatovo and Rodanovo cultures and also took into account the chronology and attribution of the local articles, in particular, the so-called grivnas of "Glazov" type often encountered in the hoards together with imported silver vessels, a major part of the imports including Byzantine articles arrived to the Kama Region in the 9th–11th c. from the Middle Asia with the aid of Middle Asian, Khazar and Bulgar merchants [Leshchenko V.Yu., 1971: 240-246].

In terms of analysis of the intercontinental trade routes on the basis of archeological materials and written sources, the research works of E.I.Lubo-Lesnichenko [1988, 1994] and L.A.Mamleeva [1999] are of special interest, since in these papers we can find the information about the Northern branch of the Great Silk Road which crossed the Lower Volga region and the South Cisurals and influenced the material culture of the Sarmatian tribes of this area. In the opinion of L.A.Mamleeva, we need to take into account the fact that not all the complexes containing imported articles are examples of purely commercial contacts, sometimes presence of such items in the monuments can be explained by diplomatic interests which, in their turn, determined the priorities in the commerce, that is why analysis of the political relationships in the region is invaluably helpful for the research [Mamleeva L.A., 1999: 53-61].

In the last twenty years there were a few publications about new finds of imported items and trade routes in the Ural and Volga region and the Kama region. For instance, A.G.Mukhamadiev [1984, 1990] addresses the issue of rudimentary commodity-money relations in the Kama region and in Cisurals when bronze ingots and imported silver vessels became means of exchange, i.e., early forms of money. In the author's opinion, the abundant flow of coins (from Sassanid, Byzantium and Khorezm) is related to the development of the commodity-money relations [Mukhamadiev A.G., 1990: 24-

35]. M.Yu.Treister analyzes the imported Italic mirrors found in the burial sites of the Volga region and in Cisurals, their origin and possible manufacturing centers [1991].

Among the latest works based on the analysis of modern topographic maps, hydrological literature and maps of archeological excavations dedicated to the land communications of the Scythian period which crossed the estuary of the Don river and connected the lower reaches of the Hypanis and the Borysthenes with the Volga region and Cisurals, it is worth while mentioning the articles by K.K. Shilik [1989] and V.V. Kopylov [1994].

The archeological research work in the Kama region in the last decade allowed to expand the list of finds of Byzantine coins [Goldobin V., Lepikhin A.N., Melnichuk A.F., 1991; Goldina R.D., Nikitin A.B., 1997].

An article by A.V.Kolobov, A.F.Melnichuk and N.V.Kulyabina [1999] describes the unique find of a Roman phalera in the Kama region which is a clear evidence of cultural contacts in the age of the great transmigration of people.

Individual aspects of the trade and economic relations of the nomads from the South Ural region with the neighboring regions were reviewed in the papers by I.M. Akbulatov [1999] and E.A. Kruglov [2002].

In the foreign research we need to specially mention the great importance of publications of the book by H.J.Eggers "Roman imports in the Free Germany" [Eggers H.J., 1951] and some later articles of the same author which were dedicated to the absolute chronology of the imported Roman articles. The classification of the objects by H.J.Eggers, the suggested chronology which was prepared by him on the basis of the huge volume of the dating materials until now are being used as the foundation for analysis of the imported Roman articles found beyond the Roman empire. After these publications the scientists obtained the first firm dating complexes for their research of the finds of the imported Roman articles.

A great number of sources and factual evidences are presented in the voluminous monograph by M.G.Raschke who actually denied existence of the Great Silk Road as a consistent caravan track, at least, in the ancient period. From his point of view, it was a myth that the land trade between the west and the east was a system of well-trodden roads on which the merchants moved their caravans for long distances. Chinese goods, in particular, silk, arrived to the steppe regions only as gifts, tribute, booty from plundering of the Chinese territories by nomadic raids and by other means which cannot be defined as economic ties [Raschke M., 1978: 606-622]. Unarguably, such forms of goods spreading existed in the very beginning of the contacts between China and the steppe peoples. However, there is no doubt that gradually the normal commerce also developed including the caravan trade.

For the methodological foundation we are using the concept of exchange in early societies initially formulated by K. Polanyi [1963, 1968] and his school at the theoretical level. Polanyi was an active supporter of the position later developed by his follower Finley, according to which the economy in the ancient societies did not represent an independent life field, but was "intertwined", "integrated" into the entire system of relationships typical for such society.

The above overview of the materials and publications available to date shows that at present there is no consolidated generalizing research on the trade and economic ties of the Ural and Volga Rivers region and the Kama region.

Certainly, there is not doubt "that the archaeological material alone cannot provide answers to many questions related to real development of trade relationships; it allows only to determine the general aspects of development of commercial ties; while their analysis is based mainly on studies of ceramics and ancient beads, thus, inevitably, the conclusions will be somewhat one-sided" [Akbulatov I.M., 1999: 68]

Undoubtedly, only a comprehensive analysis of all types of sources will provide for a certain degree of reconstruction authenticity for the trade and economic ties of the region under review with some of the ancient countries and nations. We have three main types of sources at our disposal:

§ 3. RESEARCH SOURCES

3.1. Written records

In their works the ancient authors repeatedly mentioned the trade between Rome and later between Byzantium and the neighboring states including the Greek cities of the Northern Black Sea region, but we do not find any direct references to contacts between the Greeks, the Romans and the barbarians or to any trade routes to the subject regions of the Eastern Europe.

The first individual fragmentary data about the region under review are encountered in the writings by Aristeas of Proconnesus (7th c. BC). In his poem "Arimaspeia" Aristeas of Proconnesus described his alleged journey from the northern coast of the Black Sea to the Ural region to visit the country of the mysterious Issedones. Currently some scientists discuss the timing of this journey. T.M.Kuznetsova believes that the journey was undertaken in the last third of the 7th c. BC. [Kuznetsova T.M., 1991: 29], whilst A.I.Ivanchik and some other researchers assume that the journey took place later – between the second half of the 6th c. BC and the first quarter of the 5th c. BC. [Ivanchik A.I., 1987: 48-55]. Different variants of Aristeas's story about the Issedones and Hyperboreoi rendered by Herodotus were presented by Diodorus of Sicily (90-21 BC) in his "Historical Library", by Roman authors – Pliny the Elder (23-79 AD), Pomponius Mela, the author of "Description of the world" (c. 44 AD), some other historians, geographers and even poets.

Important data about the regions of our interest and trade routes connecting the Ural region, the Volga region and the Kama region with the Greek cities of the Northern Black Sea region are contained in the so-called "Scythian logos" by Herodotus (484-425 BC) in Book IV of his "History".

Later some valuable information about the contacts between the Greeks and the barbarians in the Northern Black Sea region was given by Polybius (200-120 BC), the author of "The Histories", as he underlined the important role of Tanais as one of the major intermediaries in the Greek-Barbarian trade.

In relation to the various aspects of life of the tribes inhabiting the peripheral lands of the world known to the ancients, it is essential to pay attention to the data from "Geography" by Strabo (64 BC.–20 AD). Only in Strabo's writings [Strabo, XI, V, 8] we can find the life description of nomadic tribes which was much different from the traditional interpretations of ancient authors by Greek and Roman historians.

The information about the trade routes connecting the West and the East, geography and population of the steppes to the north of the Northern Black Sea Region is contained in "Natural history" by Pliny the Elder (23-79 AD) [Plin., IV, 88-91].

The trade routes on the periphery of the ancient world, the main itineraries and destinations are described in "Geographia" by Claudius Ptolemaeus, a Roman geographer who lived in the 2nd c. AD (1st-2nd c. AD). Judging by the highly informative contents, many of his data were obviously obtained from Roman military reports, maps and itinerarii. This ancient author is famous for giving more complete and accurate information than his predecessors.

Ammianus Marcellinus, the author of "Roman history" (4th c. AD) confirms the existence of the Northern branch of the Great Silk Road, a significant part of which was controlled by the Alans.

Ancient writers, historians and geographers wrote about various goods which were delivered by Greco-Roman merchants to the Pontian cities, described the trade routes connecting the Empire with the remote countries and mentioned the cities and trade emporia located on the Roman borders from the Black Sea region to Britain.

Greek and Roman authors highlighted the growth of exchange and establishment of money trade between Rome and the neighboring barbarian tribes, indicated the directions of the trade routes which linked the most distant areas of the West and the East, presented valuable information about the nature of this trade.

3.2. Archeological and numismatic materials

However, the valuable information from the Greek and Roman authors about the international commerce and the trade routes in the north-eastern direction in the last centuries BC – the first half of the 1st millennium AD does not allow to shape a full picture of development of the economic links between the ancient states and the peripheral areas of the barbarian world. Moreover, the ancient authors did not pay much attention to the above problem, and the available written evidences are scarce and contain significant gaps in relation to this issue.

Thus, researchers can source a plenty of concrete material mainly from the archeological data which include, first of all, ancient imported products and coins found in the Ural and Volga rivers region and the Kama region in the course of archeological works or discovered occasionally.

The archeological materials are the priority source for studies of the problem of the trade and economic ties between various countries and exchange between different tribes and peoples, but one needs to give objective and real assessment of the informative value of archaeological sources, because we were able to obtain only those evidences of exchange and trade which could be preserved for long time, while the majority of the exchanged products (food, textile, wooden and leather articles, salt etc.) is hardly represented in the archaeological materials [Akbulatov I.M., 1999: 64]. They can be conventionally divided in two large categories:

a) Bulk import items – various glass, stone and metallic beads, cowrie shells, fibulae of diverse types. This category of imported items is of premium importance for studies of the economic links because these items spread usually as a result of trade, that is they were goods, and the area of their distribution reflects both foreign trade contacts and daily internal exchange as an indicator of economic development of the region. Obviously, the bulk imports had a broad sales market in all social classes, and we can quite authentically reconstruct the probable directions of the links as well as define the degree of their busyness in various chronological periods.

b) Luxury items: these are mainly silver and bronze vessels, gold and silver coins. Due to their high value compared to their weight, it was especially profitable to trade these items to distant regions, although the transportation of pricey imported articles to the barbarian hinterland was very cumbersome and expensive.

Certainly, we need to note that objects of this category were gained during the military campaigns or as payment for services, much more often than the "bulk import items", and thus, in the studies of economic links we naturally have to consider such objects individually in every specific case.

Therefore, the precious items can be predominantly used to characterize the international trade which was obviously carried out by the tribal elite of the local barbarian peoples.

Identification of potential centers of production of high-value items allows to determine the countries which participated in the trade. The trade could be carried out in transit or via the intermediary cities and states situated directly on the main commercial routes. Changing owners, the imported items often travelled great distances. Their chronology marks the periods of emergence, prosperity and gradual decline of the relations with certain regions of the ancient oecumene. The chronology of the complexes in which the imported items were found will also allow to identify the time of their use by the local tribes, and in our opinion, it reflected a certain level of their importance both in the material and spiritual culture of the population of that region.

Numismatic materials represent an independent category: copper, bronze, silver and golden coins. For us coins are especially valuable because they constitute a source of information about the history of the trade and economic links and for reconstruction of the trade routes. In this regard, we are especially interested in the proposed place of coin minting and the location where the specific coin was found, since the numismatic topography, i.e., mapping of findings of coins and hoards gives us a possibility to outline the area of their distribution in certain chronological periods.

Since the role of commercial centers and routes changed with the time depending on socioeconomic and political situation, the chronology of the unearthed objects helps to define the role of each of them in a given period. The topography of such finds allows to reconstruct the communication routes and to assess their busyness, and the concentration of imported items helps to identify the main directions of the communications, their possible itineraries and merchant points. Finally, the conditions of their discoveries, most likely, reflect the social status of the exchange participants.

Chapter I. DATA FROM WRITTEN RECORDS ABOUT THE POPULATION AND TRADE COMMUNICATIONS IN THE URAL, THE VOLGA AND THE KAMA RIVERS REGION

This section presents all currently available written sources and references of the ancient authors about the nature of interrelationships between the tribes which populated the remote periphery of the ancient oecumene and the ancient cities and states.

We do not aim at solving the problems of the ethnical history of the regions or the issues of geographical localization of various tribes and objects; bringing in such information would make sense only depending on its relevance to the solution of the set tasks. We are mainly interested in the aspects related to the nature of the trade and economic relations which were reflected in the evidences of the ancient historians and geographers.

In this regard, it will be necessary to involve the data about the economic history of the adjacent areas and neighboring regions, especially, the Northern Black Sea region as it is largely connected with the major part of data which shed light on the above problem.

§ 1. DATA FROM THE WRITTEN RECORDS DESCRIBING THE POPULATION AND THE TRADE COMMUNICATIONS IN THE URAL, THE VOLGA AND THE KAMA RIVERS REGION IN THE 6TH–4TH C. BC

According to the traditional ancient writings, the eastern neighbors of the Scythians were nomadic tribes with the way of living similar to that of the Scythians. These tribes were known to the Greeks as "Sauromatians" which were already mentioned in Herodotus' *History*. The reference to Herodotus is not occasional, since all the ancient successor historiographers, Greek and Roman authors in certain ways refer to Herodotus' information about the tribes and peoples populating the steppes and forests of Eastern Europe from the Dnieper to the Urals.

These data are of special interest because they contain references of the names of individual tribes localized presumably in the steppe and forest-steppe zone of Cisurals, the Kama region and the Volga region. One should not forget that the relation of geographical perceptions of Herodotus and his "indigenous informers" to the modern map, as mentioned a few times before, was always one of the most difficult and controversial sides in the interpretation of his writings [Moshkova M.G., 1989: 153].

Herodotus relies mainly on the narration of Aristeas of Proconessus about his journey to the Issedones:

> Έφη δέ Άριστεης ό Και)' στ ροβίου άνηρ ΐΐροκοννήσιος ποιέων επεα, άπικεσθαι ες Ύσση – δόνας φοιβόλαμπτος γενόμενος, Ίσσηδόνων δέ ύπεροικέειν ' Χριμασπούς άνδρας μουνοφθάλμονςι ύπερ δε τούτων τούς χρυσοφύλακας γρΰπας, τούτων δε τούς Ύπερβορέους κατήκοντας επί θάλασσαν. τούτους ων πάντας πλην [Herod., IV, 13].

Beyond the Issedones dwell the one-eyed Arimaspians, beyond whom are the griffins that guard gold, and beyond these again the Hyperboreans, whose territory reaches to the sea.

The analysis of the sources and etymology of the Hyperboreans' name allows to identify, to a greater extent, the cultural and mythological origins of the conceptualization about this nation rather than ethnographic; probably, this is a purely Greek interpretation rooted in the local Scythian legends [Kuklina I.V., 1971: 17-19; Selivanova L.L., 1998: 102-106].

Nevertheless, in the writings by many ancient authors of later periods we can find numerous evidences about the Hyperboreans who were mainly worshipping Apollo and had a tradition to send him gifts to Delos. This was clearly mentioned by Diodorus of Sicily [Diod., II, 47, 2] and Gaius Plinius Secundus who wrote that: "nec licet dubitare de gente ea: tot auctores produnt frugum primitias solitos Delum mittere Apollini, quem praecipue colunt. virgines ferebant eas, hospitiis gentium per annos aliquot venerabiles, donec violata fide in proximis accolarum finibus deponere sacra ea instituere iique ad conterminos deferre atque ita Delum usque." [Plin., IV, 91].

Nor is it possible to doubt about this race, as so many authors state that the Hyperboreans regularly send the first fruits of their harvests to Delos as offerings to Apollo, whom they specially worship... instituted the custom of depositing their offerings at the nearest frontiers of the neighbouring people, and these of passing them on to their neighbours, and so still they finally reached Delos.

According to I.V.Kuklina, the further development of the legend is linked to the cultic tradition of worshipping Apollo in Delos and Delphi, and it was the Delphic version that created the conception of the Hyperboreans as a happy and holy nation chosen by Apollo to whom all the Hyperboreans were votaries [Kuklina I.V., 1971: 20].

The level of the Greeks' interest to the remote countries and peoples is seen in the ancient art objects which reflect the myths and legends with the main scenes developed beyond the territory of Greece or even the Mediterranean. We know about a Bosporan red-figure vase depicting an Arimaspi on horse fighting against a griffin [Blavatskiy V.D., 1953: 271].

Scarce data and absence of reliable information about the peripheral districts of Scythia are explained by Herodotus that:

"τῆς δὲ γῆς, τῆς πέρι ὅδε ὁ λόγος ὅρμηται λέγεσθαι, οὐδεὶς οἶδε ἀτρεκέως ὅ τι τὸ κατύπερθε ἐστί: οὐδενὸς γὰρ δὴ αὐτόπτεω εἰδέναι φαμένου δύναμαι πυθέσθαι: οὐδὲ γὰρ οὐδὲ Ἀριστέης, τοῦ περ ὀλίγῳ πρότερον τούτων μνήμην ἐποιεύμην, οὐδὲ οὗτος προσωτέρω Ἰσσηδόνων ἐν αὐτοῖσι τοῖσι ἔπεσι ποιέων ἔφησε ἀπικέσθαι, ἀλλὰ τὰ κατύπερθε ἔλεγε ἀκοῇ, φασ᾽ Ἰσσηδόνας εἶναι τοὺς ταῦτα λέγοντας." [Herod., IV, 16]

With regard to the regions which lie above the country whereof this portion of my history treats, there is no one who possesses any exact knowledge... Even Aristeas does not claim to have reached any farther than the Issedonians. What he relates concerning the regions beyond is, he confesses, mere hearsay, being the account which the Issedonians gave him of those countries..." But, unlike the mythical Hyperboreans for whom the Greeks were searching later in various geographically defined locations, not only in the North [Kuklina I.V., 1971: 17], the Issedones can be realistically localized either in the forest-steppe Trans-Urals [Smirnov K.F., 1964: 197; Salnikov K.V., 1966: 118–124], or in the steppes of the South Ural region (at present this idea is prevailing) [Machinskiy D.A., 1971: 30-37; Shilov V.P., 1975: 139].

There is an active discussion about the ethnical identification of the Issedones: they are either related to the Dahaes-Massagetean family or to the tribes of the Ugric origin [Desyatchikov Yu.M., 1972: 68-77; Machinskiy D.A., 1971: 30-37; Pyankov I.V., 1975: 67-68; Vasiliev V.N., Saveliev N.S., 1983: 3-5]. It might be that in the 6th-5th c. BC the steppes of the South Ural region were occupied by the Dahaes and the Massageteans, and the ethnonym "Sarmatians" cannot be applied to them [*ibidem:* 4].

Their location may be the base for a belief that there existed a trade route to the Issedones' country, as from the very ancient times the South Cisurals was attractive for the surrounding tribes and remoter nations as the land of rich ore deposits and valuable furs.

At the same time, there is a hypothesis that the Scythian legend about the griffin-like creatures has local features linking it with the regions at the borders of Bactria and India. These regions are identified as the places of origin of the ethnonyms and toponyms related to the legendary tribe of Arimaspi who were depriving the griffins of gold. The struggle between the Arimaspi and the griffins for gold links this legend with the Indian and Iranian tales about the Ants' Gold of the Dards [Elnitskiy L.A., 1970: 73], but at this moment we have no serious grounds for placing them far in the south.

The ancient authors were confident that the above mentioned and known to them peoples and countries further of Scythia were situated in the north (South Ural), but not in Kazakhstan (Argippeans), in Altai (Issedones) or in China (Hyperboreans) [Bongard-Levin G.M., Grantovskiy E.A., 1983: 32-34].

In addition to the above tribes, there are references to the Thyssagetes who were "living by the chase", the Argippeans – "the bald men" and the Iyrcae inhabiting the periphery of the world known to the Greeks, and Herodotus stressed that:

"μέχρι μὲν δὴ τούτων γινώσκεται, τὸ δὲ τῶν φαλακρῶν κατύπερθε οὐδεὶς ἀτρεκέως οἶδε φράσαι. ὄρεα γὰρ ὑψηλὰ ἀποτάμνει ἄβατα καὶ οὐδεὶς σφεα ὑπερβαίνει. οἱ δὲ φαλακροὶ οὗτοι λέγουσι, ἐμοὶ μὲν οὐ πιστὰ λέγοντες, οἰκέειν τὰ ὄρεα αἰγίποδας ἄνδρας, ὑπερβάντι δὲ τούτους ἀνθρώπους ἄλλους οἳ τὴν ἑξάμηνον κατεύδουσι. τοῦτο δὲ οὐκ ἐνδέκομαι τὴν ἀρχήν..." [Herod., IV, 25].

Thus far, therefore, the land is known; but beyond the bald-headed men lies a region of which no one can give any exact account. Lofty and precipitous mountains, which are never crossed, bar further progress

He also made one of the first mentions of the trade route which connected the Greek colonies of the Northern Black Sea region and the South Cisurals:

"μέχρι μὲν νυν τῶν φαλακρῶν τούτων πολλὴ περιφανείη τῆς χώρης ἐστὶ καὶ τῶν ἔμπροσθε ἐθνέων: καὶ γὰρ Σκυθέωντινὲς ἀπικνέονται ἐς αὐτούς, τῶν οὐ χαλεπόν ἐστι πυθέσθαι καὶ Ἑλλήνων τῶν ἐκ Βορυσθένεος τε ἐμπορίου καὶ τῶν ἄλλων Ποντικῶν ἐμπορίων" [Herod., IV, 24]

Now as far as the land of these bald men we have full knowledge of the country and the nations on the hither side of them; for some of the Scythians make their way to them, from whom it is easy to get knowledge, and from some too of the Greeks from the Borysthenes port and the other ports of Pontus. It is probable that along with Olbia the trade also involved other Greek colonies of the Northern Black Sea region, since the exchange with the barbarians played an important role in the economic life of the ancient cities. Lack of sufficient archeological materials does not allow us to make certain conclusions about the composition of the Herodotus' "the other marts" which were obviously familiar with this commercial route [Bezrukov A.V., 2003: 231]. It is notable that when naming the biggest rivers of Scythia and other countries: the Ister, the Tyras [Herod., IV, 51], the Hypanis [Herod., IV, 53] and the Tanais [Herod., IV, 57], Herodotus did not even mention the Volga which was already at that time an important commercial river route connecting the northern forest regions with the southern steppe areas.

The above data from the traditional ancient writings evidence the extreme scarcity of information about the north-eastern regions of the world known to the Greeks. Strabo mentioned that the "ancient Hellenic historians" including Herodotus were not able to give any definite information about the north-eastern part of the oecumene when narrating about the war of Cyrus against the Massageteans [Pyankov I.V., 1975: 23]. A similar situation occurred in respect of the regions of the Ural, the Kama and the Volga rivers.

However, it is exhibitive that the ancient authors extended their attention and interests to the regions of the present Eastern Russia which in the ancient times were deemed as peripheral regions, thus, we can see the general trend of broadening geographical perceptions of the ancient Greeks.

§ 2. TRADE COMMUNICATIONS IN THE URAL, THE VOLGA AND THE KAMA REGIONS FROM THE 3RD C. BC TILL THE 4TH C. AD (ACCORDING TO WRITTEN RECORDS)

This period is mainly characterized by emergence of the Sarmatian tribal unions and alliances in the historical stage of the Northern Black Sea region and their dominance in the huge territory of the Eurasian steppes from the Danube in the west to the Ural in the east. For this purpose, the name "Sarmatians" is used exclusively as the collective name for the Iranian-speaking nomads of the Eastern European steppes, regardless of their specific provenance [Skripkin A.S., 1988: 125].

After the Scythians were defeated by the Sarmatians, there was a change of political dominance in the steppes of the Northern Black Sea region where the Sarmatian tribes penetrated from the interfluve area between the Volga and the Don rivers. Continuous invasions and sporadic movements of individual tribes from the Lower Don region and the north-eastern coast of Moeotis ended up in a massive migration after which the steppes of the Northern Black Sea region between the Don and the Dnieper turned into a territory subordinate to the Sarmatians "where their nomadic routes stretched" [Moshkova M.G., 1989: 154)].

The political history of the Sarmatian tribes and the nature of their relationships with Rome are generally presented in the writings by Roman authors. As the Sarmatian tribes were approaching the Greek cities of the Northern Black Sea region and the borders of the Roman Empire, the Greek authors became much more informed about them. However, these data remain quite controversial and less informative when covering the areas further east of Rome.

It was a special epoch for the Iranian-speaking nomads of the Eurasian steppes, but it left virtually no traces in written records where it is incredibly difficult to find either an overview of the nations inhabiting the steppes or a clear story about commercial or cultural contacts. F.Bozi explains this incompleteness by "loss of the major part of the historical and geographical literature" and also by the idea that "the new intellectual environment of the Hellenistic period had to give less attention to the nations known since the ancient times, such as the Scythians and the Sarmatians" [Bozi F., 1997: 34].

But, as we see it, to a greater extent it relates to the peoples which were in direct contact with the Greeks, and the tribes who lived in the steppe areas on the periphery of the Eastern Europe enter into the focus of attention of the ancient historians, geographers and politicians actually during the Hellenistic epoch.

Important political and socioeconomic changes occurred within the bounds of the entire steppe belt of Eurasia, so we can say correctly, maybe, with a few reservations, that actually, there was being formed "the Eurasian nomadic civilization as a society with a producing economy, developed ideology capable of stimulating its continuous improvement, efficient functioning and reproduction of the socio-cultural system able to maintain the high level of mobility, sociability and adaptability of the community, a certain extent of the urbanization culture development. The main phases of the Eurasian nomadic civilization development take place within the Eurasian steppes and the adjacent foothills, highlands, forest-steppes and semi-desert oases, while the 1st phase (VII-VI c. BC to I-III c. AD) rolls out in the primary nomadic civilizations when its main features and structure as the continental system were established in the ancient nomadic stage" [S.G. Botalov, 2009b: 207-208].

Important information about the commercial ties of the Eastern European nomads in the Hellenistic period is contained in Polybius' *The Histories*:

"πρὸς μὲν γὰρ τὰς ἀναγκαίας τοῦ βίου χρείας τά τε θρέμματα καὶ τὸ τῶν εἰς τὰς δουλείας ἀγομένων σωμάτων πλῆθος οἱ κατὰ τὸν Πόντον ἡμῖν τόποι παρασκευάζουσι δαψιλέστατον καὶ χρησιμώτατον ὁμολογουμένως: πρὸς δὲ περιουσίαν μέλι, κηρόν, τάριχος ἀφθόνως ἡμῖν χορηγοῦσι.

δέχονται γε μὴν τῶν ἐν τοῖς παρ᾽ ἡμῖν τόποις περιττευόντων ἔλαιον καὶ πᾶν οἴνου γένος: σίτῳ δ᾽ ἀμείβονται, ποτὲ μὲν εὐκαίρως διδόντες, ποτὲ δὲ λαμβάνοντες." [Polyb., IV, 38].

For as regards necessities, it is an undisputed fact that the most plentiful supplies and best qualities of cattle and slaves reach us from the countries lying round the Pontus, while among luxuries the same countries furnish us with abundance of honey, wax, and preserved fish, while of the superfluous produce of our countries they take olive-oil and every kind of wine. As for corn, there is a give-and-take, they sometimes supplying us when we require it and sometimes importing it from us.

Not going into details, it is difficult to speak with certainty about some specific areas of the Pontus, but most probably, this indication by Polybius can be related to the entire Bosporus which is famous, in particular, for the significant scope of the fishing industry and for the large slave market in Tanais.

Later in his description of the trade between Tanais and the neighboring Meoto-Sarmatian tribes Strabo gives interesting information about the nature of these relations:

"νεωστὶ μὲν οὖν ἐξεπόρθησεν αὐτὴν Πολέμων ὁ βασιλεὺς ἀπειθοῦσαν, ἦν δ᾽ ἐμπόριον κοινὸν τῶν τε Ἀσιανῶν καὶ τῶν Εὐρωπαίων νομάδων καὶ τῶν ἐκ τοῦ Βοσπόρου τὴν λίμνην πλεόντων, τῶν μὲν ἀνδράποδα ἀγόντων καὶ δέρματα καὶ εἴ τι ἄλλο τῶν νομαδικῶν, τῶν δ᾽ ἐσθῆτα καὶ οἶνον καὶ τἆλλα ὅσα [p. 693] τῆς ἡμέρου διαίτης οἰκεῖα ἀντιφορτιζομένων" [Strabo, XI, II, 3].

Recently, however, it was sacked by King Polemon because it would not obey him. It was a common emporium, partly of the Asiatic and the European nomads, and partly of those who navigated the lake from the Bosporus, the former bringing slaves, hides, and such other things as nomads possess, and the latter giving in exchange clothing, wine, and the other things that belong to civilized life". Camel bones found in Tanais can represent a proof of the assumption that these enduring animals were used for transportation of goods along the caravan routes from Europe to Asia already in the ancient times [Tsalkin V.I., 1966: 89].

Broadening of the geographical view of the Greeks and the Romans, penetration of ancient imported articles to the peripheral lands could depend not only on the military successes of the Greeks and then of the Parthians and the Romans in the eastern direction, but in a major part also on the merchants' private initiative. In this regard, Strabo wrote that:

"...καὶ γὰρ δὴ πολύ τι τοῖς νῦν ἡ τῶν Ῥωμαίων ἐπικράτεια καὶ τῶν Παρθυαίων τῆς τοιαύτης ἐμπειρίας προσδέδωκε, καθάπερ τοῖς μετὰ τὴν Ἀλεξάνδρου στρατείαν, ὥς φησιν Ἐρατοσθένης..." [Strabo, I, II, 1].

... the spread of the empires of the Romans and of the Parthians has presented to geographers of to-day a considerable addition to our empirical knowledge of geography, just as did the campaign of Alexander to geographers of earlier times, as Eratosthenes points out. Probably, this observation is also valid for the Sarmatians who got into the focus of the ancient historiography, basically, from the years of Mitridate's wars.

The agile and belligerent, strong and numerous Sarmatian tribes appear at the empire's borders and at the same time draw the interest of the Roman politicians, historians and geographers. On the official map created by Agrippa, associate of Augustus, among the 24 regions of the Roman world number IX was assigned to Sarmatia with the western border on the Danube [Rostovtsev M.I. 1925: 43-44]. Almost in the same period the ancient geography and history demonstrates a clearer division into the European and Asian Sarmatias with the separating border on Moeotis and Tanais.

Strabo's *Geography* contains the first mentions of the Siraces and the Aorsi as the largest tribal alliances of the Asian Sarmatia [Strabo, XI, II, 1]. The majority of the researchers agree that Strabo's map of distribution of the tribes reflects the actual situation correctly [Machinskiy D.A., 1974: 122-124].

Special attention should be paid to Strabo's indication about the trade of the "upper Aorsi" which were mentioned only in Strabo's writings and, probably, occupied the areas of the western Caspian Sea region:

"ὁ τῶν Ἀόρσων καὶ εἴκοσιν, οἱ δὲ ἄνω Ἄορσοι καὶ πλείονας: καὶ γὰρ ἐπεκράτουν πλείονος γῆς καὶ σχεδόν τι τῆς Κασπίων παραλίας τῆς πλείστης ἦρχον, ὥστε καὶ ἐνεπορεύοντο καμήλοις τὸν Ἰνδικὸν φόρτον καὶ τὸν Βαβυλώνιον παρά τε Ἀρμενίων καὶ Μήδων διαδεχόμενοι: ἐχρυσοφόρουν δὲ διὰ τὴν εὐπορίαν." [Strabo, XI,V,8]

...the Aorsi... could import on camels the Indian and Babylonian mechandise, receiving it in their turn from the Armenians and the Medes, and also, owing to their wealth, could wear golden ornaments. The researchers were not able to find a common understanding with regard to this episode. Traditionally, it is assumed that the Aorsi carried out an independent intermediary trade [Lukyashko S.I., 1984: 164]. It sounds more convincing that the Aorsi did not practice intermediary trade because such interpretation contradicts to Strabo who wrote about the nomads' primitive natural barter [Bezrukov A.V., 2008: 129]. The tribe became wealthy because it occupied the old trade route from India and Babylonia via Media and Armenia to Tanais; the merchants' payments gave them significant funds and ability to generously pay to the Bosporan Greeks for wine, clothes and precious items [Rostovtsev M.I., 1918b: 130; Vinogradov Yu.G., 1994: 163].

In the initial development state the commercial relationships were apparently of barter nature, especially, in the inter-tribal trade; this concept is supported by Strabo's statement and evidenced by the numismatic material from Tanais where the coins found were dated to not earlier than I c. AD. [Shelov D.B., 1993: 44-45]

Ptolemy's "Geographia" for the first time ever shows the Volga, Ural and Kama rivers on the geographic maps [Ptol., V, 8, 1-13], although earlier the Volga (then unnamed) was included into the Greeks' geographical horizon (through Diodiorus' story about Jason and the return journey of the Argonauts) [Shramm G., 1997: 80].

This part of Ptolemy's map is especially interesting in relation to the trade route because the map gives a detailed and, most important, accurate description of the Northern Caspian Sea region, Trans-Caspian countries, the flow of the Volga and the Ural.

The precise data about the upstreams of the Volga and Ural rivers and the mountains of the South Ural are even more surprising because in the later maps (from Idrisi's map of the 12th c. to Herberstein's map of the 16th c.) the Ural River was either not shown or its flow was indicated schematically; Idrisi knew Ptolemy's map perfectly, but the part of his map where the Volga and the Ural rivers are shown is much less accurate than Ptolemy's map, so the knowledge of the ancients about the South Ural were forgotten [Chlenova N.L., 1983: 63].

Based on the available data, one can infer that there existed an itinerarium (road map) prepared for commercial and military purposes which included data about the route crossing the steppes of the Lower Volga region and the South Cisurals as the main source for Ptolemy. Remarkable is that despite the available relatively accurate information about the regions to the north of the Caspian Sea the data about the Caspian Sea itself, the estuaries of the inflowing rivers and local settlements contain gross discrepancies [Elnitskiy L.A., 1961: 200-203]. Although Ptolemy knew nothing about the delta of the Volga, he gave exact data about the direction of the river bed, inflow of the Kama, as well about the Rhipaean (Ural) mountains [Ptol., III, 5, 5].

Later the above trade route was registered by Ammianus Marcellinus (Amm. Marc., XXXI, 2, 15). Besides, he laid out interesting data about a medicinal plant bearing the same name as the Ra river on which banks it grew and was widely used in medicine [Amm. Marc., XXXIII, 8, 28). In the opinion of G.Shramm, the homonymy between the name of the medicinal plant exported partly from the lands close to Pontus and partly from India along the "barbarian coast" and the modern term "rhubarb" has a certain sense. Probably, if the rhubarb root was not produced in the Volga region, then, anyway, it was traded there [Shramm G., 1997: 75].

Thus, the presented data from the ancient writings evidence that there existed steady river ways and land trade roads which tied the regions of the Ural, the Volga and the Kama with the ancient cities and states during various chronological periods starting from the 6th c. BC till the Early Middle Ages.

In terms of the topics related to interpretation of the data from the written sources, the archeological data may sometimes act as a reliable verification criterion. Therefore, due to insufficient direct indications and fragmented nature of the data by the ancient authors the archeological and numismatic materials play a more important role.

Chapter II. TRANSIT TRADE IN THE VOLGA AND THE KAMA REGION IN THE SECOND HALF OF THE 1ST MILLENNIUM BC – FIRST HALF OF THE 1ST MILLENNIUM AD (ACCORDING TO ARCHAEOLOGICAL SOURCES)

As noted above, archeological materials are a primary source of information about the transit trade and intertribal exchange between various states, tribes and nations. Identification of possible centers of manufacturing of imported articles allows us to define the trading countries. The trade could be carried out in transit or via the cities and intermediary states located immediately on the main trade roads. Changing hands, the imported articles were often transported for great distances. Their chronology consists of the periods of emergence, prosperity and gradual decline of the ties with certain regions of the ancient oecumene. Since the importance of commercial centers and routes changed with time, depending on the socioeconomic and political situations, the chronology of the found objects will help to define the role of each item in a specific period.

§ 1. IMPORTED CERAMIC UTENSILS

The earliest known finds in this category of imported objects were discovered in Astrakhan region (Krivaya Luka, Chernoyarskiy district) in a rich woman's burial of the 3rd c. BC, where there were found a black varnish vessel and an amphora of Greek origin with a Herakleia hallmark, both vessels dated to the 1st half of the above century [Bulatova N.M.. Dvornichenko V.V., Zilivinskaia I.D., Fedorov-Davydov G.A., 1989: 5]. Besides, in kurgan 1 (burial 10) at Nikolskoe village (Enotaevskiy district, Astrakhan region) a foot of a black-varnish vessel was found, the burial is dated to the end of the Early Sarmatian – beginning of the Middle Sarmatian period [*ibidem*: 69, fig. 48, 3].

Also known are the finds of a few red-clay oval-section handles of amphoras of the Hellenistic age (4th-3rd c. BC) which were discovered in kurgan 8 of Kalinovka cemetery (Bykovskiy district, Volgograd region) [Shilov V.P., 1959a: 452; table I, 4].

The above single finds point at the most remote eastern points of the modern Russia where the Greek objects were found. From the quality and quantity sides, the fragments of Greek ceramic ware discovered in the Lower Volga region, are much inferior to the samples of valuable Greek black-varnish utensils from the rich burials of the nomadic nobles in the Kuban region, the Don region and the Dnieper region.

One of the causes of such situation should be seen in the fact that distribution of expensive and fragile utensils using steppe roads for distances over one thousand kilometers was not economically viable neither for the Greeks, nor for the local merchants. Consequently, there were hardly any imported ceramic ware of the Greek origin.

The subsequent period (1st c. BC – early centuries AD) saw some changes when the imported ceramic ware became more frequent [table I, 1,2,3,6]. Currently we know about some ten different imported vessels found mainly in the Trans-Volga and in the South Ural regions [Rykov P.S., 1925: 34; Smirnov K.F., 1964: 186, fig. 6, 13; Sinitsin I.V., 1960: 33].

Typically, these are red-varnish pots, jugs, cups. The closest analogies to the majority of them are seen among the products of various Asia Minor centers and Bosporan ceramic workshops. In many Greek cities and necropola of the Northern Black Sea region there are often found samples of such utensils [Gushchina I.I., 1971: 127; Zubar V.M., 1982: 70; Mordvintseva V.I., Sergatskov I.V., 1995: 122]. In Tanais, ancient settlements of the Lower Don region and the Kuban region similar vessels, both intact and fragmented, were encountered in large numbers.

Chronologically, virtually all the found vessels relate to the period between the 1st c. BC – 2nd c. AD, i.e., the period of the most active trade relations between the ancient cities and states and the nomads of the surrounding steppe peripheral lands. Moreover, these articles were encountered not only in rich Middle Sarmatian burials, but also in ordinary graves.

Thus, the major part of the imported ceramics found in the area under review is represented by mainly inferior quality products from the artisan centers of Asia Minor and Bosporan ceramic workshops. These are distinguished by reddish-brick colour varnish of poor quality which was usually applied only to the upper part of the vessel; most of the vessels relate to the Middle Sarmatian period [Shelov D.B., 1972: 138]. In the majority of the cases it is not possible to give a more precise indication of the center or place of production of this category of imported items.

No ceramic utensils of proper Italic production were unearthed. Quite possibly, this can be explained by the fact that in Bosporus itself the Italic ceramics were found in much smaller quantities [Knipovich T.N., 1955: 373] than, for instance, in Olbia or Chersonesos, although most of the imported ceramics reached the Sarmatians of the Volga region and Cisurals via Bosporus and Tanais.

Almost no amphorae were encountered among the artifacts. The only finding was a light-clay narrow-necked amphora [table I, 7] discovered in the Late Sarmatian burial of Lebedevka burial site (Shyngyrlau district, West-Kazakhstan region) [Kropotkin V.V., 1970: 132]. Besides, ring-fence 1 – group V from the cultic complex of the same burial site contained light-clay sherds of walls, a few fragments of the neck, complexly profiled handles and a small narrow foot as an annular tray; according to D.B.Shelov, they belong to light-clay narrow-necked amphorae of type C dated to the 2nd c. AD and pertaining to the products of Sinope workshops [Shelov D.B., 1978: 20; Moshkova M.G., 1984: 197].

Possibly, absence of amphorae can be explained by the fact that liquid or bulk goods (oil, wine, bread etc.) from the ancient cities and states were delivered to the steppe areas in leather bottles or other vessels convenient for transportation on baggage animals. However, there are no real evidences in support of this hypothesis [Shelov D.B., 1972: 216]. The above list of imported ceramic items should also include quite a significant group of vessels provening from various Bosporan, Don and Kuban ceramic centers; it will allow answering the questions about the distribution routes of ceramic articles in the Volga and Ural regions. Some of similar vessels originate from the territory of Astrakhan and Volgograd regions including mostly big black-glazed and grey-glazed jars on annular trays and red-clay jars on annular trays which are said to have been produced in the Don region, the Kuban region and in Bosporus [Zasetskaya I.P., 1979: 104; Sinitsin I.V., 1960: 38, fig. 13, 10; Skripkin A.S., 1974: 60, fig. 3, 3; Gushchina I.I., Moshkova M.G., 1990: 30]. Ceramic ware of other types is encountered less often, for instance, red-clay balsamarias and censers [Ivanov A.Yu., Myshkin V.N., 1991: 109-111; Myskov E.P., 1992: 126, fig. 6, 2].

A unique find of its kind occurred in 1975 during the excavations conducted by V.I. Mamontov at Tsarevo (Leninskiy district, Volgograd region) – a flask of Mesopotamia self-glazing faience with slightly convex sides discovered in kurgan 23 of the Bronze Age in the entry chamber of a Sarmatian grave of the 1st c. AD [Sergatskov I.V., 1989: 236]. This find acts as a direct evidence of more intense contacts between the Sarmatians and the Middle Asia and Transcaucasia, because in that period, on the one hand, the quantity of imported items of western origins in the Sarmatian burials of Cisurals grows, on the other hand, in the Sarmatian burials of the Volga region more objects of eastern origins are found.

Such a trend is also typical for the Sarmatian graves in Cisurals in the 1st c. BC – 3rd c. AD which contained both red-clay pottery originally associated with the Middle Asian civilizations [Pshenichnyuk A.H., 1983: 131], and grey-glazed jars with cylindrical necks which belong to the products of the ceramic centers of the Kuban region and the Northern Caucasus, judging by the nature of clay and its burning [Gushchina I.I., Moshkova M.G., 1990: 29].

In the South Ural region, in a nomad's burial of the Sarmatian epoch near Ishtuganovo water reservoir at the Belaya River, Ishtuganovo village, in kurgan 5, burial chamber 4 dated to the turn of BC and AD eras, among other imported objects there was found a grey-clay jug with a handle, a spout and a ball-shaped body [Akbulatov I.M., Obydennov M.F., 1984: 51]. Similar vessels were widely used by the Meoto-Sarmatian population of the Lower Don region and the Kuban region [Kropotkin V.V., Obydennov M.F., 1985: 243-244].

Close analogies to this vessel come from the Lower Volga region [Sinitsin I.V., 1953: 89, fig. 1, 4], the Northern Black Sea region [Pogrebova I.N., 1951, p. 271] and the Crimea [Gushchina I.I., 1971: 46, fig. 2, 1], but mainly, they are known in the Lower Don region and in the Kuban region [Shilov V.P., 1959b: fig. 54, 1]. According to I.N.Pogrebova, the grey-clay jars with wide elevated spouts and ornamentation in form of double circles connected by parallel lines are related to the Olbian production which was imitating the ornamentation of the Sarmatian ceramics [Pogrebova I.N., 1951: 271].

The grey-glazed ceramic jug with a rounde biconical body, quite a high neck and a spout found in the Sarmatian burial (woman's) of kurgan 6 of the 1st Sorochinsky burial site (Orenburg region) dated to the beginning of the 1st c. AD is similar to the objects discovered in the Caucasus [Zhelezchikov B.F., Pyatykh G.G., 1981: 271-275].

In Group Lebedevka V kurgan 23 stand out where a black-glazed ceramic jug dated to the 2nd c. – 1st half of the 3rd c. AD was found. Among other objects, the finds included pitchers, a double-handled large pot, obviously, of Middle Asian origin. First of all, it is interesting that in the burials there were found moulded vessels imitating the shapes of the Northern Black Sea region, grey – and black-glazed ceramic ware, in the neighboring graves the archeologists discovered nine red-clay pottery jugs of Middle Asian production [Moshkova M.G., 1982: 82-84, fig. 1, 7; 1, 6].

Red-clay pottery of Middle Asian production is being regularly found in the burials of South Cisurals, starting from Prokhorovka period and during the entire Late Sarmatian period confirming the existence of close commercial and cultural relations between the nomads of the South Ural steppes and their neighbors – herdsmen of the Middle Asia and Kazakhstan [Lopatin V.A., 1997: 199].

On the whole, for Late-Sarmatian burials of the South Ural region more typical is the red-clay pottery originating mainly from pottery workshops of Khorezm, like a red-clay vessel from a kurgan near Miloradovka (Krasnopartizansky district, Saratov region) dated to the 2nd – early 3rd c. AD. [*ibidem*: 204].

Summing up, we should note that the comparatively small quantity of proper imported items and the limited area of their distribution (virtually no red-varnish ceramics were found in the Ural region and the Kama region, and their finds are concentrated mainly on the limited territory of Volgograd Transvolga) can be explained by the fact that the local artisans and the large ceramic centers of the Don and the Kuban regions managed to fully satisfy the demand for such products from the nomads and the nations of the forest areas.

Product-wise, the most frequently encountered are simple red-clay vessels of ancient shapes which, in the opinion of D.B.Shelov, were mainly produced in the Bosporan or Asia Minor workshops in the 1st c. BC – 2-3rd c. AD [Shelov D.B., 1972: 216].

In the same period, the Sarmatian ceramic complex is characterized by round ceramic ware originating from the Lower Don region, probably, from the Kuban region and other production centers, mainly, in the Northern Black Sea region [Skripkin A.S., 1988: 124]. Imported ceramics come from the Bosporan centers, primarily, to the Volga region, while ceramic pottery from Middle Asian workshops, possibly, from Khorezm prevails in Cisurals. Such a division apparently shows the spheres of influence and potential economic interests of large national unions in the ancient times in the regions under review.

At the same time, such division is quite conventional because in Lebedevka and in individual burials of the Southern Cisurals there were found ceramics of both oriental and occidental origins. A small part of imported items could penetrate to the west due to movement of certain nomadic groups, not only due to barter trade.

Mapping of the found imported ceramics including single fragments of black-varnish vessels and the found amphorae allows to trace with a high degree of probability the possible way of spreading of imported articles from the Northern Black Sea region via the interfluve area between the Volga and the Don to the territory of Volgograd Transvolga (Kalinovka, Bykovo) and then to the north to the rivers Eruslan and Torgun (Berezhnovka, Staraya Ivantsovka), to the valley of the Bolshoy Karaman river (Susly) and further to the Cisurals [see the map I].

Thus, the products from Bosporan, Don, Kuban and various Middle Asian centers prevail among the imported ceramics found in the region under review. Such products seem to have been brought there (along with ancient imported ceramics) in the Prokhorovka period (4th c. BC) until the middle of the 3rd c. AD (the conventional upper border of this chronological period is obviously the defeat of Tanais by the Goths in the middle of the third centenary), thereafter the inflow of imported pottery basically ceases.

§ 2. IMPORTED BRONZE UTENSILS

Bronze vessels of diverse shapes, types and functional applications represent a significant share among various categories of imported products found in rich burials. These items were produced in the artisan workshops of Italy and also in other regions of the empire – in Gaul, the Rhine region, Frakia and Pannonia.

In the literature these products are conventionally named "Roman bronze utensils", although a major part originates not from Rome itself, but from other Italic centers, primarily, from Capua and workshops of North Italy, while many vessels were manufactured by craftsmen in provinces and various regions of the vast Roman empire [Shelov D.B., 1983: 55].

The value of the Roman bronze utensils for a modern researcher lays not in the number of found objects, for example, D.B.Shelov indicated a bit more than two hundred (200) finds for the entire Eastern Europe [*ibidem*: 57], or in their artistic merit which is not so high, as we will see by the finds of bronze vessels; important is the information which these objects carry.

This section is dedicated to the finds of the Roman bronze vessels discovered in the Ural, the Volga and the Kama regions in the burial complexes of 1st c. BC-4th c. AD. The analysis of sample bronze utensils and mapping of their locations allows to express ideas about the way and itineraries of such items coming to possession of the barbarians of the peripheral lands [see the map II].

The earliest finds of imported bronze vessels occurred in the rich burials of the Lower and Middle Volga region and the Kama region [table II, 1]. During the excavations led by V.P.Shilov in 1954 in the famous burial 55/8 of Kalinovsky burial site a bronze vessel was found which turned out to be a product of Italic, namely, Campanian craftsmen and has numerous analogies among vessels which originate from South Italy [Shilov V.P., 1956: 45]. Two similar vessels were discovered in one of the graves of Kobansky cemetery [Uvarova P.S., 1900: 85, fig. 81] and among the grave goods at Dakhovskaya village in the Northern Caucasus [Lunin B.V., 1940: 33-39]. They are dated, respectively, to the 2nd c. BC and 1st c. AD. [Shelov D.B., 1983: 64].

The vessel with a ball-shaped body from the same complex, undefined by V.P. Shilov, is compared by D.B.Shelov in relation to the shape details with bronze vessels of South Italic production found in the excavations in Pompeii, Boscoreale and Hildesheim hoard in the 1st c. BC – 1st c. AD [Shelov D.B., 1972: 207].

Judging by the nature and method of burial, as well as the grave goods, burial 55/8 is accurately dated to the turn of 1st c. BC – 1st c. AD [Shilov V.P., 1973a: 35].

Among quite diffused types of bronze vessels of Italic origin there are ladles and bowls found mainly in the burials of the 1st c. BC – 1st c. AD along with other imported objects. An Italic bronze ladle was discovered in 1887 by I.A.Volkov during excavations in one of the kurgans of Bolshaya Dmitrievka [table II, 2] (Shirokokaramyshskiy district, Astrakhan region) in a burial of the 1st c. AD. [Maksimov E.K., 1957: 158; Kropotkin V.V., 1970: 93]. The only similar object was the bronze ladle with a ring handle and a Latin hallmark dated to the Flavian period, the second half of the 1st c. AD found during the dig by V.P.Shilov in 1961 at Staritsa village (Astrakhan region) in kurgan 11 (burial 1) [Shilov V.P, 1968: 300–310; Shelov D.B., 1965: 267].

Similar vessels were very popular in Dacia and are dated to the end of the 1st c. AD or beginning of the 2nd c. AD. According to D.B. Shelov, the most similar objects to the ladle from Bolshaya Dmitrievka are seen among the products of the South Italic manufacturer Lucius Cipius Polibius who produced them in the second half of the 1st c. AD. [*ibidem*: 265-267].

In 1913 in Susly, before P.S. Rykov started diggings in the Sarmatian burial of the 2nd–3rd c. AD, a bronze bowl was found; similar objects are present among the products from the Western Europe of the 1st c. BC. [Shelov D.B., 1972: 208]. We should note that the bowl from the Suslovsky burial site comes from a sepulcher of a later period which was dated to the 2nd-3rd c. AD. [Rau P., 1927: 11; Kropotkin V.V., 1970: 93]. A forged bronze bowl similar to the one from Susly was found in the Middle Volga region (Ichalkovskiy district, Mordovia) in Andreevskiy kurgan in a burial of the 1st–2nd c. AD. [Stepanov P.D., 1964: 219-221, fig. 2; Kropotkin V.V., 1969: 34].

In terms of depth of penetration of Roman bronze articles special attention should be given to the finds of bronze vessels in the Kama region [table II, 5-7]. In 1898 a ladle was found near Nyrgynda village (Karakulinskiy district, the Kama river, Udmurtia) [Volkovich A.M., 1941: 231-233, table VI, 2-3; Kropotkin V.V., 1970: 95]. The ladle shape and body ornamentation are similar to the bronze ladles of Hedacker type with a flat handle; such items were produced in South Gaul, Lugdunum area (Lyon) and are dated to the 3rd c. AD. [Shelov D.B., 1972: 210]. Such dating is the most likely, because at the same location there was found a single-segment fibula of the 2nd-3rd c. AD which might be produced in Tanais [*ibidem*: 205]. Obviously, this is an evidence of the route and time of distribution of bronze imported vessels in the Kama region.

Another sample of the Italic bronze casting art is a bronze semi-spherical bowl found in the Kama region (former Elabuga county, Akhtial village), on a ring tray with a Latin hallmark on the inner side AFRICANSVF; there survived twelve fragments of the bowl [Volkovich A.M., 1941: 230-233; Shelov D.B., 1965: 268, fig. 10, 3, 4]. In the paper by V.V.Kropotkin this bowl is considered a silver one, although we do not know the reasons for that [Kropotkin V.V., 1970: 93].

The closest analogies exist among the bowls from Pompei, therefore, it is likely that these bowls have Italic or, probably, Capuan origin [Melyukova A.I., 1962: 199]. In Russia a similar vessel was discovered during excavations at Tiflisskaya village [Veselovskiy N.I., 1902: 70] and is dated to the 1st – 2nd c. AD. [Eggers H.J., 102].

Furthermore, similar bowls were popular in the 1st-2nd c. AD in Germany, Skandinavia, then in Pannonia in the 3rd-4th c. AD [Shelov D.B., 1972: 269], therefore, these items were in use for quite a long time. Individual imported vessels dating to the turn of the first centuries AD were found in sepulchral complexes of the 3rd–4th c. AD.

In the subsequent period, starting from about the middle of the 2nd c. AD, among this category of imported articles a trend was observed to substitute the products of Italic workshops with the items made by provincial Roman craftsmen, especially, in Gaul and the Rhine region, that is evident in the grave goods of the rich burials of Cisurals, the Volga region and the Kama region [Bezrukov A.V., 1999: 57-58]. Articles from Italic workshops were still present among the finds of bronze vessels, but the time of their manufacturing relates mainly to the preceding period of the 1st c. BC – 1st c. AD.

It is worth while mentioning the set of Italic bronze vessels from a rich Late Sarmatian complex found at Lebedevka settlement [table II, 8-11] which along with a bronze calix with a cylindrical tray included a bronze jug with a high cylindrical neck and a horizontal crown, thus, belonging to the so-called "dissected jugs". At present we know two more similar jugs, one of which was purchased by E.R.Shtern in Olbia in unknown circumstances, the other provenes from the 3rd Sokolovskiy kurgan in the Lower Don region [Shelov D.B., 1983: 62]. According to B.A.Raev, dissected jugs were produced in South Italy as early as in the end of the 1st c. BC – beginning of the 1st c. AD and were distributed beyond the Roman empire in the second half of the 1st c. AD – beginning of the 2nd c. AD. [Raev B.A., 1976: 131].

In one of Late Sarmatian burials of Lebedevka cemetery a bronze oenochoe was discovered [Bagrikov G.I., Senigova T.M., 1968: 73–86]. Bronze oenochoes similar to the one from Lebedevka are usually found in rich burials along with other bronze vessels. This type of oenochoes is characterized by a ball-shaped body and overall more stumpy proportions [Eggers H.J., 125]. The ornamental handle of the oenochoe from Lebedevka below has a raised shield with an image of Dionysos's bearded head which is typical for oenochoes of Capuan origin of the 1st c. AD. Two similar vessels provene from Kertch burials, two more were found in rich kurgan graves in the Kuban region and one in Gorgippia [Shkorpil V.V., 1910: 69; Kruglikova I.T., Tsvetaeva G.A., 1963: 71, fig. 25, 4].

In addition to the oenochoe, in kurgan 2 (woman's grave) of Lebedevka burial site there were found a bronze cauldron belted with an iron band on which two ring-shaped handles were fixed, and a bronze pot with a rounded bottom and a bronze handle with a raised shield decorated with Dionysos's bearded head [Kropotkin V.V., 1970: 132].

Identical bronze vessels similar to the ones from Lebedevka, obviously, of Gaul-Roman production were also encountered in other areas of the Ural and Volga rivers region. At Krasnogorsky settlement (Burtinsky district, Orenburg region) in 1935 I.A.Zaretsky found a bronze pot in a Sarmatian sepulcher of the 2nd-3rd c. AD [Berkhin I.P., 1961: 150]; in the same region in 1955 (Akbulaksky district) during earth works in a destroyed sepulcher a similar object of Gaul-Roman production was discovered [Sinitsin I.V., 1966: 18].

In Saratov region in a Sarmatian sepulcher of the 1st-3rd c. AD of Rovnensky kurgan cemetery (Rovnoe village, Rovnensky district) there was found a cauldron with straight walls and a rounded bottom [Sinitsin I.V., 1961: 101]; a bronze cauldron of Gaul-Roman production was discovered in a destroyed sepulcher of one of Novolipovsky kurgans on the bank of the Bolshoy Karaman river) [Maksimov E.K., 1969: 115].

In the Kama region (Akhtial village, former Elabuga county), in 1913 a well-preserved bronze ladle was found near the village, obviously, in a sepulcher of Pyanoborsk culture of the 3rd c. AD: the ladle had a ring-shaped handle ornamented with a triangle of six rounds [Volkovich A.M., 1941: 255]. In literature there is a large number of similar ladles originating both from the territory of the Roman state itself and from the lands which were quite distant from the Roman frontiers. Since the majority of the ladles come from the southern and middle parts of Apennine Peninsula, we are obviously dealing with the products of the Capuan bronze industry of the 2nd c. BC – 1st c. AD, this is evidenced by the proportions, material, treatment type and ornamentation of the ladle [ibidem: 228].

In contrast to A.M. Volkovich, D.B. Shelov states that the ladle has not Capuan, but Gallic origin and was made in Karat workshops, so he relates the ladle from Akhtial to the type of ladles from Nizhnegnilovsky necropolis and the burial at Staritsa village (Chernoyarsky district, Astrakhan region) dating all these vessels to the 2nd c. AD; they resemble by details, ornamentation and a sort of a hallmark of a few small rounds on the handle [Shelov D.B., 1972: 209].

The datings and argumentation proposed by D.B. Shelov for the bronze ladles of Akhtial and Nyrgynda seem the most preferable for us in terms of determination of the place and time of production of such articles.

Among the recent finds we believe it is worth mentioning the bronze ladles from the burial dated to the late 2nd c. – the first third of the 3rd c. AD discovered in the summer of 2010 in Agapovka district, Chelyabinsk region, in kurgan 21 of Magnitny burial site where "the largest part of the grave goods consisted of metallic items which could be considered as the Roman "wine set" (jug, ladle, strainer, scoop, cup):

Bronze ladles with horizontal handles were one of the most widely spread categories of Roman imports in the Eastern Europe, and the bronze ladle found in the burial is definitely similar to the bronze amphora from burial 1 of kurgan 9 of Valovy I burial site. The authors of the publication of the materials about this burial site point out that this rare find was not typical for Roman imports. Probably, the object was made in the Danube region provinces of the Roman Empire" [Botalov S.G., Ivanov A.A., 2012: 269, 276-277].

Therefore, it is obvious that unlike the preceding period when the most diffused were the products of Italic workshops, mainly, closed-shape vessels (oenochoes, jugs), in the 2nd-3rd c. AD another category of Roman bronze utensils prevailed: cauldrons and pots of various shapes and kinds.

As for the most probable routes and ways of arrival of the imported bronze vessels to the Ural, Volga and Kama regions, the researchers do not have a clear answer. The largest part of the grave goods consisted of metallic items which could be considered as the Roman "wine set" (jug, ladle, strainer, scoop, cup).

Presence of imported glass, silver and bronze articles of Italic or Northern Black Sea region production is typical for rich burials of Sarmatian nobles in the 1st c. BC – 1st c. AD. To a certain extent, probably, it can be associated with the overall process of movement of the Sarmatian tribes to the west and intensification of their activities in the Northern Black Sea region and at the Danubian borders of the Roman Empire.

Various imported articles could be brought to the Sarmatian lands by barter trade, as gifts or a fee for service or as war trophies, but war trophies obviously represent the least part of imported products. The finds of oenochoes of Italic origin in places very remote from the Roman empire borders clearly evidence the wide area of distribution of Roman imports in that period when the Roman empire had the greatest territory and the international trade was flourishing.

A large share of bronze vessels found in the region under review arrived there by normal barter trade via Bosporan cities.

Speaking about Bosporus, it is necessary to stress the special role of Tanais as the largest supplier in the Greek-Roman-Barbarian trade. A large part of the articles was brought to the Lower Volga region and then to Cisurals and the Kama region via the Lower Don region, the Kuban region and Tanais. In particular, this hypothesis is supported by regular finds of metallic utensils being scattered in many kurgans and by presence of other imported archaic items in such kurgans [Shelov D.B., 1965: 262]. In rich graves of Sarmatian nobles in the interfluve steppe area sometimes are found light-clay amphorae, bronze swivel fibulae like AVCISSA (except the Volga region and Cisurals), bronze rounded and rhomboid fibulae with multi-coloured enamel for which Tanais was one of the main centers of distribution.

The geographical route can be tracked by the finds in kurgans of the Don region, the Lower and Middle Volga region and Cisurals.

It is fair to admit the fact that we cannot define accurately how the items were brought to the interfluve steppe areas: via Tanais and the Don region or via the Kuban region, since the ties of the Sarmatians of the Volga region with the Kuban region have quite reliable evidences; thus, the researchers believe they need to name the Kuban and Don rivers region [Shelov D.B., 1972: 217].

At the same time, absence of South Italic imported articles of the Late Latin period among the finds in Tanais suggests that there was another route – via the steppes. Occupation of the Northern Black Sea steppes by the Sarmatians and their further movement to the borders of the Roman provinces on the Danube provided for distribution of metalware made by Campanian craftsmen via the steppes to the Volga region and to Cisurals bypassing the ancient cities of the Northern Black Sea region, probably, from Pannonia via the Danube trade route [Shelov D.B., 1965: 251-254; Shilov V.P., 1973: 35].

According to B.A. Raev, the imported utensils were spread in the Asian Sarmatia from Transcaucasia, since there are no such findings in the North Black Sea Region. Thus, the bronze vessels "mark the routes of imports penetration from Northern Italy to Sarmatia via Asia Minor; the goods were delivered not only via Daryal pass, but also via mountain passes of the Western Caucasus. In any case, one can make a conclusion that the Celtic articles produced in Northern Italy were distributed not through the Danube provinces, but via Asia Minor and the Caucasus" [Raev B.A., 1993: 174-175].

While Italic and Gallic-Roman bronze single-handled ladles were found in Moesia, lower Danube provinces, Olbia and in the inland regions of the barbarian peripheral lands, we need to note that they were never encountered in the Northern Black Sea region, except Olbia, whence the imported vessels arrived from Olbia via the steppes to the Lower Don region and then via "the ancient caravan route which ran through the Dnieper region and the steppes of the Azov Sea region" [Shelov D.B., 1965: 274].

Individual imported bronze vessels were present in the burials of the 4th–5th c. AD, i.e., after the destruction of Tanais by the Goths in the middle of the 3rd c. AD; thus, it proves the existence of another trade route which could be used for bringing imported bronze ware to the steppes of Cisurals and the Volga region bypassing Tanais and the Greek cities of the Northern Black Sea region. The trade route from the Northern Black Sea region to the Volga region and Cisurals was known even earlier, and one of the reasons why the steppe route appeared was probably the massive movement of the Sarmatian tribes westwards in the first half of the 1st c. AD. [Shchukin M.B., 1989: 70-83] and, consequently, reaching the borders of the Danubian provinces of the Roman empire.

Thus, in various chronological periods, depending on the political and socioeconomic situation both in the Northern Black Sea region and in the Roman empire as well as in the barbarian community, preference was given either to the Northern Black Sea route with active participation of the cities of Bosporus and Tanais or to the steppe trade communications.

The insufficient quantity of archeological materials does not allow us to give a clear answer to this question. It may be also that some imported items, in particular, the inexpensive bronze utensils arrived to the Sarmatians of Cisurals and the Volga region by the Northern Branch of the Great Silk Road which stretched through the South Cisurals and Lower Volga region. On the return route in the Roman Syria it was possible to purchase glassware, silver articles and Italic bronze ware. In this case the Sarmatians received a major part of imported bronze articles as payment for caravan crossing their territory and for escorting along the route. Further accumulation of archeological materials will give us an opportunity to formulate our answers to these questions more accurately and definitively.

§ 3. IMPORTED SILVER ARTICLES

Silver ware is represented by a significant quantity of imported objects found during archeological research work or by occasion.

This section is based on the products of artistic crafts of Rome and Byzantium discovered in Cisurals, the Kama region and the Volga region. Among the imported articles of this category a major part is constituted by daily-usage goods of mundane nobles produced by diverse techniques (casting, embossing, engraving, incrustation, gilding, blacking), various precious ware (platters and saucers, bowls and ladles).

These items are a valuable source for studies of economic ties of the tribes and peoples of the region with ancient city-states, the Roman and Byzantine empires. Especially informative are the products of Constantinople craftsmen whose hallmarks allow to clearly identify the time and place of production of this category of imported articles.

3.1. Roman silver articles

The proper Roman products are represented by individual finds in rich Sarmatian burials in the Volga region and the Ural region [see the map III]. In 1953 during the dig led by V.P. Shilov at Verkhnee Pogromnoe village (Bykovsky district, Volgograd region) in a Sarmatian burial (kurgan 1) there were found two silver semi-spherical bowls of Syrian production dated to the 1st c. BC [V.P. Shilov, 1959: 78; Kropotkin V.V., 1970: 89], and a silver jug discovered in grave 8 of kurgan 55 of Kalinovsky burial site [Shilov V.P., 1956: 45; Shilov V.P., 1975: 143].

Besides, in Sarmatian burials of the Volga region and the Ural region two silver strainers of Roman production were found [Eggers H.J., 160]. A silver gilded strainer was discovered in a kurgan at Bolshaya Dmitrievka village [Shilov V.P., 1973b: 39]; the end of the strainer handle had a rectangular spatula shape. According to A. Radnoti, such strainers were produced in South Italy in the 1st c. AD. [Radnoti A., 1938: 76]. The majority of such articles is dated to the BII period (50-150 AD), V.P. Shilov suggests to date the strainer to the second half of the 1st c. AD relying on the datings of other South Italic vessels from this complex. [Shilov V.P., 1973a: 255]. D.B. Shelov believes the strainer is of Gallic origin, since the holes of this strainer are arranged similarly to the strainer from Siscia which bears a hallmark of Gallic craftsman Gasatus [Shelov D.B., 1965: 266]. That is why the question about the place of production of such items remains open. A silver strainer of semi-spherical shape with a flat rounded handle was found in a woman's grave (kurgan 2) of the Late Sarmatian period at Lebedevka burial site [Bagrikov G.I., Senigova T.M., 1968: 71 sl.].

The researchers have no fundamental disagreements regarding the routes of penetration of imported silver articles into the territory of the Lower Volga region.

Tanais is indicated as the most probable source of precious imported items of Roman origin. These goods were brought to Tanais from the largest cities of Bosporus – Panticapaeum and Phanagoria by barter trade; this is evidenced by the composition and quantity of imported articles of this category compared to the finds in other regions which lay beyond the frontiers of the Roman empire but maintained close relationships with it – in Germany, Scandinavia and Poland [Shelov D.B., 1965: 251-255].

It is obvious that distribution of Roman silver ware occurred mainly via the cities of Bosporus, but we need to make a few remarks. In Tanais before the turn of the eras there were no imported metallic articles, although imported bronze and silver vessels start to appear in Sarmatian burials of the Don region and the Lower Volga region from the 1st c. BC to and including the 4th-5th c. AD [Shilov V.P., 1974: 61]. Such imported goods could not have been obtained directly in military combats of the Sarmatian tribes with the Roman squads and during occupation of the Greek cities of the Northern Black Sea region; the silver vessels were obviously presented to the Sarmatian elite as gifts from the Bosporan rulers or as tribute.

The quantitative and qualitative change of composition and assortment of the imported goods at the turn of eras – in the first centuries AD towards more high-worth objects in the international trade was, according to A.A. Iessen, "the consequence of further development of the trend of strengthening the role of the tribal nobles among the local population and further social differentiation which was a typical characteristic of the highest level of barbarity" [Iessen A.A., 1952: 228]. In the age of "the great migration of people" strong political alliances emerged having no captive production base, so to demonstrate their mightiness and wealth the leaders of these alliances often collected quite diverse treasure gained in different ways [Lvova Z.A., Marshak B.I., 1998: 490].

The objects from the burials of nomadic nobles in South Trans-Urals hold a special place in this category of imported items which, in the opinion of the authors, "represent a certain reflection of the reciprocal western vector, the movement from the Danube region to the steppes of the Urals and Kazakhstan. The specific origin of the imported items from Magnitny suggests that, apparently, they could have been received as gifts, remuneration, donations somewhere far away in the west (most likely, in the immediate vicinity of the Pannonian Limes) and then brought for more than three thousand kilometers to the steppes of Trans-Urals where then they were used as ritual goods for a long time" [Botalov S.G., Ivanov A.A., 2012: 287].

Thus, silver articles of Roman production penetrated in Trans-Volga and in the Ural region as a result of normal barter trade contacts via an intermediation of the Bosporan cities and through an intertribal exchange with the related Sarmatian tribes of the Don region and the Kuban region.

3.2. Byzantine silver articles

A large group of Byzantine silver vessels found in the Kama region and in Cisurals contains a great number of items of various types, shapes and themes of images. We mentioned a few times that imported objects of Byzantine origin were present in these regions, but we do not have concrete data about direct ties of the Kama region and Cisurals with Byzantium or about direct exports from Constantinople workshops or other Byzantine crafts centers to those regions, nor about manufacturing of such goods for the purpose of exports to Cisurals and the Kama region [table III, 1-23].

At that, existence of such a significant number of Byzantine articles (at present we know about some thirty finds which represent over two-thirds of the total number of similar Byzantine products found in Russia), as L.A. Matsulevich fairly observed "… cannot be considered an occasional phenomenon which is not worth our attention, instead, it requires a special analysis" [Matsulevich L.A., 1940: 139].

In this regard, among the most important are the issues related to identification of the chronology of Byzantine imports, analysis of routes and ways of distribution of the Byzantine imported items taking into account that there is almost no relatively cheap bronze ware of Byzantine origin, while silver vessels were numerous [Darkevich V.P. 1976: 149].

The chronology of penetration of the Byzantine silver vessels found in the Kama region and in Cisurals is now one of the most complicated and debatable problems of the Byzantine imports studies. Uncertainty of determinations is largely dependent on the conditions and circumstances of discovery of the imported silver vessels.

None of the Byzantine vessels were found in the course of archeological activities on the ancient settlements or cemeteries. The majority was encountered in quite similar specific circumstances: tilling of wild land, extraction of stumps, forest clearing, and just a few objects were found in gullies eroded by spring torrents. According to I.A. Orbeli and K.V. Trever, "plowed-out" is the most appropriate term to define the conditions of finding of silver articles in the Kama region and Cisurals [Orbeli I.A., Trever K.V., 1935: 11]. O.N. Bader and A.P. Smirnov stress the fact that out of the twenty archaic oriental silver articles found, seventeen were plowed-out and only two Arabic medieval vessels were discovered in the burial site [Bader O.N., Smirnov A.P., 1954: 20]. Underlining the existing sameness of conditions of the finds, V.Yu.Leshchenko suggested explaining this phenomenon most authentically as "concealment" when silver goods were hidden in taiga bush using makeshift means – branches of coniferous trees or forest moss [Leshchenko V.Yu., 1971: 25].

Based on the analysis of Byzantine vessels from Constantinople workshops, L.A. Matsulevich proposed to fix the lower chronological border to the finding of a silver ladle dated to the first quarter of the 6th c. (Anastasios' time – 498-518) at Cherdyn (Cherdynsky district, Perm region) [table III, 17], and the upper border to the finding of a silver saucer at Turusheva village (Omutninsky district, Kirov region) [table III, 19-20] with an image typical for Heraclius' coins of 629–641. [Matsulevich L.A., 1940: 139, 140]. In terms of the manufacturing times, the found vessels constitute a continuous chronological row from the first quarter of the 6th c. to the middle of the 7th c. when they were interred, "thus we cannot state can their inflow was irregular or occasional" [. *ibidem*: 147].

V.Yu.Leshchenko pointed out that in the Kama region there were no hoards of Sassanidian coins of only the 5th or 6th c., but there were hoards of the 7th c. containing coins of the 5th and 6th c. meaning that these coins got into these hoards in the Kama region only with coins of Khosrau II, i.e., in the end of the 7th c. Besides, in the burial sites of Lomovatovo period in the Upper and Middle Kama region the Sassanidian coins were found along with objects of the 8th-9th c., this trend was noted everywhere. [Leshchenko V.Yu., 1971: 231]. Thus, V.Yu.Leshchenko defines the beginning of the 6th c. as the lower chronological border for inflow of Byzantine silver ware, and its major part was brought in the 9th-11th c.

Using the archeological research results, V.Yu.Leshchenko attempted to identify an interlink between the finds of silver vessels and the ancient settlements. In the total number of silver vessels found (104 hoards), he managed to do it with various extents of credibility for just a little bit more than twenty hoards which contained only two Byzantine vessels found at 500-600 m from the ancient settlements of the 8th-9th c. [*ibidem*: 111-112].

Sometimes there are no sufficient grounds for uniting silver vessels, coins and local decorations into the same complex while such items differ in origin and time of their discovery. In order to define the time of bringing the Byzantine ladle of Anastasios' period and the Sassanidian vessels of the 5th-7th c. from Anikovsky complex as one of the most important dating elements, V.Yu. Leshchenko uses hryvnas of "Glazov" type without determination of the finding location [*ibidem*: 235].

Besides, V.Yu.Leshchenko unites all the Bartym finds (three Khorezmian bowls, a Byzantine platter, a Sassanidian bowl, a goblet and a bowl of Bactria) into one complex dated to the end of the 8th c. [Leshchenko V.Yu., 1976: 187]. More credible is an assumption that the Bartym hoard and other seven vessels found at Bartym do not constitute a unique complex since they were all found in different years [Morozov V.Yu., 1996: 157]. Finally, even if these items originate from the same complex, it does not mean that it was not assembled on site. Should the Bartym complex really belong to the tribal nobles, such valuable objects could be kept in use for centuries, and the tribal treasury could be replenished from time to time.

Following V.Yu.Leshchenko, V.P. Darkevich believes that the start of trade with the northern lands coincides with the first centenary of Abbasides' dominance (second half of the 8th c. – first half of the 9th c.), and the majority of the oriental silver ware, including the Byzantine products, arrived in the Ural region not earlier than in the 9th century. Such process is directly linked with the growing demand for sable, marten, ermine, squirrel and beaver furs in the world market in the 7th c. which were exchanged for silver ware [Darkevich V.P., 1976: 147-148].

V.Yu. Morozov believes that, most credibly, the Byzantine vessels were brought in the 7th c.; there are no vessels in the Kama region and in Cisurals dating to later than Heraclius' period; this is explained by the fact that right in the middle of that century the trade routes from Iran to Middle Asia were shut off [Morozov V.Yu., 1996: 158]. Besides, we can mention a series of studies by national and foreign researchers; based on the archeological (finds of Sassanidian and Byzantine bronze and silver vessels) and numismatic data (hoards and single finds of Sassanidian, Byzantine and Cufic coins) the period of the 5th-7th c. is indicated as the most likely for penetration of oriental silver ware and coins [Teploukhov F.A., 1895: 247-295; Fasmer R.R., 1931: 20; Bader O.N., 1951: 75; Yanin V.L., 1956: 85; Ghirchman R., 1962: 203].

Moreover, the authors highlight the circumstance that the main inflow of imported Byzantine silver ware is related to the events of 626-629, the military campaign of Emperor Heraclius in the Northern Iran and his Khazar allies who gained a huge quantity of precious items in military raids and as gifts of Byzantium to the Khazar army elite for the armed support [Goldina R.D., Nikitin A.B., 1997: 111-125].

At present this position seems the most valid, we have no serious reasons for a later dating of the inflow of imported Byzantine silver ware.

Another essential and natural phase in researching of the problems related to the Byzantine imports is how the silver utensils of Byzantine origin were brought to Cisurals and the Kama region, because, obviously, Byzantine silver coins and imported Byzantine artistic objects arrived there in different ways.

Regarding the potential route for Byzantine silver ware, it is more likely that the items came via Middle Asia which route was used for the major part of imported silver articles, obviously, together with Middle Asian goods. Indirectly the above can be evidenced by Sogdian, Khorezmian, Middle Persian and Turkic runic inscriptions of the 7th c. on the Byzantine vessels found in the Kama region and Cisurals [Matsulevich L.A., 1940: 146; Livshits V.A., Lukonin V.G., 1964: 173-176]. Probably, the Byzantine vessels could be brought to the Middle Asia both from Byzantium on the route laid to the north of the Caspian Sea which was used in the late 6th c. – early 7th c. and through the Iranian territory due to participation of Iran as a trade intermediary [Levchenko M.V., 1940: 69; Masson M.E., 1951: 98].

Very important is the issue whether imported articles arrived in the Kama region by direct trade or via intermediaries. I.S. Noonan believes that direct trade was impossible, and the Khazars who controlled the route from the Volga estuary to the Kama estuary acted as middlemen. One of the factors causing participation of intermediaries and hindering the direct trade for the merchants who brought Byzantine and Sassanidian coins and vessels was the circumstance that the merchants moving from Byzantium and Transcaucasia could not use the steppe route, since it was occupied by the Khazars [Noonan Ih. S., 1982: 271-275, 281].

Analysing the ways of spreading of Sassanidian coins in the Kama region, V.Yu. Morozov makes a justified remark that it was not necessary to cross the steppes, and Sassanidian coins were found either on the river bank or in a few kilometers from the bank. The merchants did not travel by land routes, but used water ways – the Caspian Sea, the Volga and the Kama rivers. Therefore, in the 5th–7th c. the Khazars could not be intermediaries for Iran and Byzantium in the trade with the Kama region and Cisurals. Any other tribes or nomadic peoples were not ready to play such role on the Volga route [Morozov V.Yu., 1996: 158-159].

In the opinion of R.D. Goldina and A.B. Nikitin, there are no direct proofs of existence of the straight route which could connect the people of the Kama Region with Iran and the Byzantine Empire. The silver articles of Byzantine and Iranian production were exchanged for furs and delivered to the above region via the steppes of the Volga region where Khazars acted as the main intermediaries [Goldina R.D., Nikitin A.B., 1997: 123-125]. Besides, the inflow of imported Byzantine and oriental silver ware, on the whole, is linked either to the advancement of Turkic tribes into the Kama region in the 6th-7th c. [Khalikov A.H., 1971: 34], or with intermediation of the Sarmatian tribes [Noonan Ih. S., 1982: 290].

At the same time, according to the studies by S.A. Pletneva, in the 5th-7th c. the peoples of the Eastern European steppes were in the first nomadic stage [Pletneva S.A., 1982: 28]. This stage was characterized by the interest of the nomads in possession of lands when the entire population with all its property took part in a military campaign. The destroyed and burnt-down settlements and small towns could not provide them with abundant trophies. It is not occasional that "nomadic graves of that period contain quite modest goods, very seldom there are found expensive imperial objects", it can largely be explained by the social relationships in the period of military democracy [Pletneva S.A., 1991: 99].

Consequently, none of the peoples could not act separately as an intermediary, for this purpose a chain of nations would be required, thus, the time for passing the coins to the Kama region would be much longer, but this does not correspond to the conditions in which the coins were found in this region. Therefore, in that period the trade represented a direct commerce of the Iranian, Byzantine and Middle Asian merchants with the Kama region and Cisurals.

G.A. Mukhamadiev underlined the important role of Sogdian merchants and pointed out that there existed commercial ties between the tribes of the Volga region, on the one hand, and the nomads, on the other hand; in the 6th-7th c. merchants could reach the Kama region travelling with the khagan's staff or his attendants across the dunes of the Volga, the Ural and the Don rivers. The lower courses of the rivers acted as intermediate points where the commercial routes crossed. The final destinations in the north were the certain districts of the Kama region where the khagan and his staff reached in the mid-summer; probably, there he also conducted assemblies of the subordinates and the auctions. Leaders of the Turkic or Khazar army received silver utensils as war trophies or gifts from the tsars of Turan, the Iranian shah or the Byzantine emperor to the nomadic tribe leaders [Mukhamadiev A. G, 1990: 28].

In his solution of the above problem V.Yu.Leshchenko assigns a significant role to the Transcaucasia-Volga steppe route and considers the Khazars as intermediaries; they got into possession of a large quantity of silver ware after their raids to Caucasus in 626 and 628, therefrom the silver ware could be brought in the Kama region. In the 7th-8th c. it was quite difficult for the Middle Asian merchants to move to the northern lands which were controlled by the khagan, unless they had the khagan's support [Leshchenko V.Yu., 1971: 242-243].

However, in the 5th-7th c. the Khazars being in the phase of establishing their state could control the Volga river and the Volga route only from the turn of the 7th-8th c., since before they were based in the Northern Caucasus whence they were pushed out by the Arabs to the Volga region [Magomedov M.G., 1983: 59, 188-193]. Obviously, the Khazars could not play any significant role of trade intermediaries.

The imported silver articles of oriental origin cannot be dated, in general, to the 6th-7th c., this period should be extended to the 12th c. inclusive [Darkevich V.P., 1976: 143] as an evidence of centuries-long traditions of the trade between those areas and Middle Asia. Consequently, the Byzantine as well as Middle Asian silver vessels were brought into this land mainly through trade intermediation of the Middle Asian and Transcaucasian merchants.

Thus, the majority of Byzantine silver vessels penetrated to the territory of the Kama region and Cisurals from the Middle Asia together with other Middle Asian coins and artistic goods from various centers. The route from the Middle Asia obviously ran via the Ustyurt plateau to the Caspian Lowland and the Lower Volga region and then downstream the Volga, the Kama and the Chusovaya rivers to the north of the Kama region or to the south – to the Sylva river basin.

The statement that the most probable communication routes ran on the Volga and the Kama rivers is supported by the places where the majority of the Byzantine vessels were found: in the basins of the Kama, Vyatka, Cheptsa, Belaya and Ural rivers, i.e. in the Middle, Upper and Lower Kama region and in South Cisurals[see the map III].. Only a small part, for example, two Byzantine vessels of the Bartym complex, could arrive via the Volga route from Transcaucasia or from the Northern Black Sea region, from the Byzantine Chersonesos.

The trade exchange between the regions was carried out mostly with direct participation of Middle Asian and Transcaucasian merchants and minor intermediation of the nomads who stayed at different sections of the international trade routes. At the same time, we cannot deny that a minor part of Byzantine silver ware could be brought into the region under review either by exchange between the nomads and cultivators at the border of the steppe and forest-steppe lands or as a result of movement of some Turkic tribes to the Kama region. In their turn, the nomads could obtain those items as war trophies or gifts to the leaders of Khazar or Turkic army from Middle Asian, Iranian or Byzantine rulers.

The discovery of a significant quantity of silver vessels of Byzantine, Sassanidian and Middle Asian origin of diverse shapes, functionality, themes and images within a relatively small area of Cisurals and the Kama region has raised questions for the researchers about the ways and forms of use of the silver utensils by the local tribes.

Commonly accepted is the opinion about the prevailing cultic use of the silver utensils. Such statements are largely supported by the results of ethnographic research carried out in the late 19th – early 20th c. among the Khanty and Mansi people which confirmed that they used silver vessels in their sanctuaries and during various local religious rites.

Based on the above, F.A. Teploukhov suggested that the metallic plates were not a mere decoration, but a significant part of an idol [Teploukhov F.A., 1895: 1]. Later researchers also wrote about the dominance of cultic use of silver platters by the population of the Ural region in the function of disks of holy luminaries or idols' faces [Orbeli I.A., Trever K.V., 1935: 21]. According to O.N. Bader and A.P. Smirnov, ancient oriental metallic utensils were diffused in those societies which maintained traces of ancient cults related to worshipping of eternal luminaries [Bader O.N., Smirnov A.P., 1954: 21].

Probably, the one-sided approach to the solution of this problem did not provide for obtaining objective answers to the existing questions. L.A. Matsulevich used a more careful and weighted way to address this issue and suggested to identify "really mass products, products for a limited circle of tribal nobles, special products for cultic use tied with shamanism" from the general volume of objects of Byzantine origin [Matsulevich L.A., 1940: 156]. This trend was later naturally developed by the domestic researchers.

Making another reference to the ethnographic research materials, V.Yu.Leshchenko notes that from the ethnographic sources of the 19th-20th c. we do not have any authentic data about use of silver vessels of undoubtedly oriental origin by the Khanty and the Mansi in the local sanctuaries [Leshchenko V.Yu, 1976: 20]. According to his observations, the vessels of proper cultic function represent 23% of the total quantity of silver utensils. Obviously, the cultic use of metallic utensils in the Ural region helped partly to prevent its destruction, but besides, such objects could be used in households or for manufacturing of decorations [Darkevich V.P., 1976: 148].

Thus, a large part of silver vessels of Byzantine origin was used by the ancient population of the Ural region as luxury items. A much smaller quantity of silver articles could be used for cultic purposes, and a minor part was probably utilized for production of local decorations and cultic objects.

§ 4. IMPORTED GLASS ARTICLES

The majority of the glass vessels found in the Eastern Europe were produced by Syrian and provincial Roman workshops, and today the number of such vessels is not large, despite the finds of the recent years. The question about local production of glass vessels remains open, that is why it is very complicated to define whether the glassware was made locally or imported. Tanais had proper glass production, the products of its workshops of the 2nd c. – the first half of the 3rd c. AD has numerous analogies among the Western European glassware; probably, some vessels were brought to Tanais from Western Roman provinces and were used as templates for local vessels [Alekseeva E.M., Arsenieva T.M., 1966: 188]. Development of the local production began in the late 2nd – early 3rd c. AD and is possibly linked with the Roman occupation of the Black Sea region, movement of the Roman military squads, their bases in Bosporus, Olbia, Chersonesos and Tyre.

The earliest find is a cast semi-spherical bowl of the 1st c. AD made of opaque greenish-yellow glass, possibly, produced in Syrian workshops and found by V.P.Shilov in 1954 in kurgan 55 (entry chamber) of Kalinovsky burial site (Bykovsky district, Volgograd region) [Shilov V.P., 1959a: 488, fig. 57]. Similar objects of Roman production were found mainly in rich Sarmatian burials in the Don region and the Kuban region dated to the turn of the first centuries AD.

A few glass vessels were encountered in the Late Sarmatian graves of Lebedevka burial site which included a glass painted tumbler from the entry chamber of kurgan 23; similar objects were found in the territories of eastern Roman provinces made probably in Asia Minor [Moshkova M.G., 1982: 82-84]; "Glass vessels whose fragments were found in kurgan 9 at Pokrovka and in four kurgans at Lebedevka were identified by N.P. Sorokina as a pot of Bosporan production dated to the second half of the 2nd c. – first half of the 3rd c. AD, in the first case; in the second case, presumably, the fragments belong to a glass tumbler; the most interesting find was the painted wineglass, allegedly, of Bagram or Antioch production dated to the 2nd-3rd c. AD." [Moshkova M.G., 2004: 36].

Besides, the grave goods of kurgan 1 (2nd-3rd c. AD) of the Lebedevka VI group contained a glass pitcher of Bosporan origin [ibidem: 83]. In 1953 in Ufa in a destroyed burial of the 5th-8th c. there was found a thick-walled bowl of opaque glass with the external surface ornamented with numerous oval incisions of irregular shape [Akhmerov R.B., 1958: 218]. Similar vessels are not known in the Ural region [Zasetskaia I.P., 1994: 103], but quite close analogies originate from the Caucasus [Arakelyan B.N., 1953: 155, 156, fig. 6; Akhmerov R.B., 1958: 219-220], as close analogies in shape, ornamentation and glass colour, we need to mention the glass goblet found at Kara-Agach (Northern Kazakhstan) dated to the 5th c. AD. [Zasetskaia I.P., 1994: 103].

In the South Ural region in the burial of the already mentioned Magnitny burial site there was found a glass tumbler; the author of the publications finds its analogies "among Roman glassware (The Metropolitan Museum); similar glasses with outlined ribs appeared in collections dated not earlier than to the 2nd c. AD and existed till the 4th c. AD" [Botalov S.G., Ivanov A.A., 2012: 270-272].

Virtually in all other cases known to us we deal with individual fragments of glass vessels. The parts of the nonextant glass vessels from the kurgans of Volgograd region have similar items among the glassware from Panticapaeum and Tanais [Sorokina N.P., 1961: 226, fig. 7, 2; Sorokina N.P.., 1965: 204-205, fig. 1, 1-8]. Besides, the fragments of walls and handles of blue, yellow and greenish colours were found in the Middle Sarmatian burials in the Volga region [Sinitsin I.V., 1960: 164; Shilov V.P., 1974: 6; Dvornichenko V.V., Fedorov-Davydov G.A., 1989: 17; Mordvintseva V.I., 1993: 129] and in Cisurals [Yablonskiy L.T., 1999: 332].

The total number of finds of glass vessels and their fragments should be complemented with the two clay vessels from the Lower river region with glass inserts in the bottoms; in the German literature they were named "Fensterglassgefasse". In 1951 during the excavations led by I.V. Sinitsin in a Sarmatian burial of the 2nd-3rd c. AD (kurgan 15) there was found a grey-gloss jug with a non-transparent glass insert in the bottom [Sinitsin I.V., 1959: 91, fig. 36, 1; Kropotkin V.V., 1970: 20]. During the dig by V.P.Shilov in Kalinovka (Bykovsky district, Volgograd region) in a Sarmatian burial (kurgan 4) a molded vessel was found; it had a flattened bottom with a light glass insert [Shilov V.P., 1959a: 480]. The functionality of such vessels is not quite clear.

The political dependence of Bosporus on Rome in the period of Kotys I provided Italic merchants with the road to the Northern Black Sea region. The connections of the cities of the Northern Black Sea region with the Northern Pontus regions were fixed in a quite short chronological period which for Bosporus coincides with the period of the closest ties with Rome; this is especially clearly seen in the imported Roman glass vessels the number of which is relatively small even in general for the Greek cities of the Northern Black Sea region [Sorokina N.P., 1969: 221], without mentioning their penetration in the remote barbarian territories.

We need to admit that due to objective reasons the glassware did not become widely popular among the people of the Ural, Volga and Kama regions; although individual glass vessels were encountered, in our opinion, this was occasional and irregular [see the map IV].

Firstly, trade of such fragile items in the regions distant from the Northern Pontus region does not look profitable, since it was quite risky that the glassware would not reach the customer.

Secondly, for the Sarmatians leading a nomadic life it looks impossible that glassware could be in use for a long period as essential household items.

Therefore, the eastern regions inhabited by the Sarmatian tribes apparently received the products of Tanais and Bosporan glass-making workshops, although it may be possible that individual Mediterranean items arrived from Panticapaeum and Tanais. Evidently, the painted glass vessel from Lebedevka burial site belongs to this range of products [Moshkova M.G., 1989: 195].

Regarding the most likely routes for bringing the Roman glassware to the Ukrainian territory, E.A. Symonovich noted that the volumes of glassware imports became significant only when glassware turned to a popular market commodity in the Roman Empire. The barbarians' invasion and disruption of production put an end to the import of all glass articles [Symonovich E.A., 1964: 11]. A similar situation can be suggested for the regions under review because the earliest finds of glass vessels are dated to not earlier than the 1st c. AD.

§ 5. DECORATIONS

The most popular and numerous category of imported goods in the entire Eastern Europe were, obviously, beads of diverse shapes, types and materials. The scope of this paper does not allow considering this issue in more details, since it requires a special study, but we will specify the main types and materials, as well as the distribution area and chronology illustrated by the most characteristic and typical finds of imported decorations of this category.

Glass beads, either transparent or made of opaque glassy paste, were always the most popular. Beads and pendants of jet or gagate are encountered in smaller quantities, but also often and everywhere, a bit less frequent are cornelian items, the most numerous group included decorations made of topaz, calcedony, crystal, amber and agate. Many ancient peoples including the tribes of Cisurals, the Volga region and the Kama region used beads and pendants in connection with various beliefs and superstitions. Special magical properties were ascribed not only to images or shapes, but also to the material – the stone used for making beads and pendants.

It is extremely difficult to define where the beads were brought from and where they were produced because they were extraordinarily widely distributed in the entire ancient world, and their production centers were located in the Mediterranean, the Black Sea region, in the Middle East, in the ancient cities of Fore-Asia, Central Asia and Transcaucasia. Egypt was one of the top suppliers, that is why we should speak about the production place of certain types and groups of beads with some reservations.

5.1. Decorations made of amber, semi-precious stones and minerals

As we see it in the archaeological materials, the earliest types of stone decorations were the items made of amber and various semi-precious stones popular in the ancient times: cornelian, crystal, agate, chalcedony and other minerals [see the map V]..

In the Lower Volga region there is known a large number of sets which included amber pendants, 14-facet beads of cornelian, agate and amber [Gushchina I.I., Moshkova M.G., 1999: 51-53]. In Saratov Trans-Volga (Usatovo village, Saratov region) in 1928 in kurgan F16 [Sinitsin I.V., 1947: 51-54, fig. 26] P.D. Rau found beads made of amber, mother-of-pearl and gold; the burial itself is dated to the first half of the 3rd c. AD. [Yatsenko S.A., 1986: 17].

In South Cisurals in the burials of Temyasovo kurgans there were found big 14-facet flat cornelian beads (4 pc.) [Pshenichnyuk A.H., Ryazapov M.Sh., 1976: 143]. In a woman's grave (kurgan 2) of Lebedevka burial site there were discovered massive amber beads (49 pc.) and 14-facet cornelian beads (19 pc.), close analogies to which were encountered in the Sarmatian burials of the Lower Volga region [Sinitsin I.V., 1947: fig. 18, 5; Bagrikov G.I., Senigova T.M., 1968: 74]. Sets of cornelian and amber beads discovered in the Late Sarmatian burials of Ilek kurgan group evidence that there were close cultural ties of the nomads of South Cisurals with the herdsmen inhabiting the Middle Asia and Kazakhstan [Yablonsky L.T., 1999: 326].

Cornelian and amber decorations were extraordinarily popular not only among the nomadic peoples of the Volga region and Cisurals, but also in the Kama region in the early medieval period. Calcedony decorations and beads were found in the Kama River Region mainly in graves of the 5th-8th c., and large disk-shaped amber beads were discovered in graves of Kharinoi period of Lomovatovo culture dated to the 5th-6th c. [Goldina R.D., Kananin V.A., 1993: 71-75]

Cornelian and amber beads were found in the dug-out part of the Verkh-Sainskoe settlement dated to the 6th c. AD. [Goldina R.D., Vodolago N.V., Volkov S.R., 1994: 41]. Crystal and cornelian beads (200 pc.) made a part of the complex of objects of Glyadenovo culture of the early medieval period in the Ust-Sylvenskoe settlement on the bank of the Sylva river (Permsky district, Perm region.) [Goldobin A.V, Lepikhin A.N., Melnichuk A.F., 1991: 39-40]. Amber bead were found at Kargort village of Ibsky local council in a destroyed kurgan of Kharino type; similar decorations were spread in the Kama River Region mainly in the 5th-6th c. AD. [Vasqul I.O., 1987: 79]

In the ancient times cornelian had a special role among diverse stones since it was used in magic rites. It was believed that it can protect the owner not only from diseases, but also from poverty [Markovin V.I., 1965: 270-273].

Thus, the cornelian beads found in the burials of Cisurals, the Volga region and the Kama region belong to the broad range of jewelry items known in the Middle East, Transcaucasia and Northern Black Sea region. It is quite possible that the decorations from the Volga region were put in the Sarmatian graves together with gagate decorations from Transcaucasia and Northern Black Sea region while a large part of cornelian decorations discovered in the burial complexes of Cisurals and the Kama region had Middle Asian origin. In this case we need to take into account the traditionally close commercial ties of Cisurals and Khorezm which played an important role as a trade intermediary.

Besides, we know about relatively early finds of disk-shaped and cylindrical gagate beads in the archaeological complexes, for instance, in some burials of Kalinovsky burial site of the Prokhorovka period [Shilov V.P., 1959a: 440].

Sets of gagate beads originate from some Early Sarmatian burials of the Pokrovka 8 cemetery in the south of Orenburg region [Yablonsky L.T., 1999: 327]. In South Cisurals during the archeological activities in 1970-1972 in Temyasovo kurgans located on the high right bank of the Sakmara river (Baymak district, Bashkortostan) among other imported objects there were found 538 beads made of gagate and lignite. [Pshenichnyuk A.H., Ryazapov M.Sh., 1976: 132-143].

The beads and pendants made of gagate or jet, an amiable black mineral, were found in large quantities on the burial sites of Transcaucasia and Middle Asia [Obelchenko O.V., 1992: 202]. A.V. Fersman called this mineral "the favorite stone of antiquity" [Fersman A.V., 1954: 316].

Thus, the majority of jet decorations could arrive from Transcaucasia via the Kuban river region by the ancient trade route to Tanais which ran along the eastern coasts of Pontus and Moeotis and then to the Volga region [Manandyan Ya.A., 1954: 13-15], although some of gagate decorations could have been produced from local raw materials in the South Cisurals.

In this case Dioscuriada could play an important role of a trade intermediary which is indirectly confirmed by Strabo:

> "...Διοσκουριάς ἐστι καὶ ἀρχὴ τοῦ ἰσθμοῦ τοῦ μεταξὺ τῆς Κασπίας καὶ τοῦ Πόντου καὶ ἐμπόριον τῶν ὑπερκειμένων καὶ σύνεγγυς ἐθνῶν κοινόν· συνέρχεσθαι γοῦν εἰς αὐτὴν ἑβδομήκοντα, οἱ δὲ καὶ τριακόσια ἔθνη φασίν, οἷς οὐδὲν τῶν ὄντων μέλει, πάντα δὲ ἑτερόγλωττα διὰ τὸ σποράδην καὶ ἀμίκτως οἰκεῖν ὑπὸ αὐθαδείας καὶ ἀγριότητος· Σαρμάται δ᾿ εἰσὶν οἱ πλείους, πάντες δὲ Καυκάσιοι. ταῦτα μὲν δὴ τὰ περὶ τὴν Διοσκουριάδα." [Strabo, XI, II, 16].

This same Dioscurias is the commencement of the isthmus lying between the Caspian Sea and the Euxine. It is a common mart of the nations situated above it, and in its neighbourhood ... All speak different languages, from living dispersed in various places and without intercourse, in consequence of their fierce and savage manners. They are chiefly Sarmatians, but all of them Caucasian tribes. The above is supported by the fact that from the 3rd c. BC the Sarmatians established close ties with the Northern Caucasus and Asian Bosporus, and jet articles become very popular among the Sarmatians in that period [Skripkin A.S., 1990: 115]. V.P. Shilov attributed the distribution of gagate to Transcaucasia [Shilov V.P., 1959a: 440], where well-known are not only numerous finds of gagate items, but also its mining locations [Kuftin B.A., 1949: 53-54].

It is possible that a part of these decorations was brought via Middle Asia where in the burials of Sogd kurgan cemeteries many beads and bugles made of gagate or jet were found [Obelchenko O.V., 1992: 203]. It is also possible that the tribes of the Volga river region and Cisurals obtained some decorations of this type via the Northern branch of the Great Silk Road. According to E.B. Vadetskaya, the burials of the Minusinsk hollow contained all types of beads which were especially widely diffused in the Northern Black Sea region in the 1st-2nd c. AD. The affinity of the types of Siberian and Black Sea beads obviously confirms their Northern Black Sea region origin, and distribution of the beads is explained by the activities of the Chinese merchants on the Northern Road which intensified after the defeat of the Hunnu [Vadetskaya E.B., 1992: 80-81].

5.2. Scarabaei and Egyptian faience decorations

In the first centuries AD very popular were Egyptian faience articles in form of scarabaei and plates depicting lying lions [Alekseeva E.M., 1982: 28-30; Skripkin A.S., 1990: 115]. In the Sarmatian burials of the Volga region and Cisurals the faience scarabaei and beads are found starting from the 4th c. BC till the 3rd-4th c. AD.

They were discovered in significant quantities in Tanais where Egyptian paste decorations are found in whole complexes, similarly to the Volga region and the Kama region. Egyptian faience scarabaei were found in the Sarmatian burials of Suslovsky burial site [Rykov P.S., 1925: 12], twice – in kurgan 20 of the 2nd Berezhnovsky cemetery [Sinitsin I.V., 1960: 12, 162, fig. 10, 11, 12], and in kurgan 35 of the same period in Kalinovsky kurgan cemetery [Shilov V.P., 1959a: 390; Shelov D.B., 1972: 214]. On the reverse side of the scarabaei from Berezhnovka there were hieroglyphs, so we may suggest that they originated from Alexandria [Moshkova M.G., 1956: 237].

In Zuevsky burial site of the Ananino period in the Kama region during the excavations by P.A. Ponomarev in two women's burials there were found in total 354 (three hundred fifty four) beads of Egyptian faience [Smirnov A.P., 1938: 143].

In the 2nd group of Kharkovsky kurgan cemetery located on the szyrt of the Ostrozhenka river in the interfluve area of the Solenaya and the Bolshaya Kuba rivers – tributaries of the Eruslan river (Saratov region) in a burial of the 1st c. AD among the beads of a necklace there was a scarab of bright-blue Egyptian paste [Gushchina I.I., Moshkova M.G., 1990: 30-33].

A set of 6 (six) blue Egyptian faience scarabaei was found among stone and glass beads in a woman's grave of the Middle Sarmatian period (kurgan 6) of the 1st Sorochinsky burial site (Sorochinsky settlement, Orenburg region) located on the left bank of the Sakmara river [Zhelezchikov B.F., Pyatykh G.G., 1981: 274]. In the researchers' opinion, kurgan 6 is dated to the 1st c. BC – 1st c. AD [ibidem: 275]. This finding of scarabaei is unique for the South Cisurals area. We should highlight one of the latest finds of Egyptian paste beads during the excavations of the kurgan cemetery at Privolnoe village in Ileksky district on the bank of the Ilek river in Orenburg region. In burial 6 (central) of kurgan 2 there was found a flat heart-shaped bead of blue Egyptian faience, another quite similar bead was discovered in burial 10 of the same kurgan. Both burials, according to D.V. Meshcheryakov, are dated to the 3rd-2nd c. BC. [Meshcheryakov D.V., 1997: 45-47].

Egyptian faience beads and scarabaei were encountered in diverse regions of the ancient world which were sometimes quite distant from each other [Vasqul I.O., 1987: 76-78]. In the burials of Rechkino II (Western Siberia) in kurgan 3 (grave 3), there were found figures of Harpokrates together with imported beads made of spinel and cornelian [Matveev A.V., Matveeva N.P., 1985: 69-75].

Inclusion of Egypt into the Roman Empire in the 1st c. AD was one of the most probable causes of such a broad distribution of Egyptian faience articles and appearance of these items in Eastern European steppes in the Sarmatian period.

Findings of Egyptian scarabaei in the kurgans in the interfluve area between the Volga and the Don rivers, in particular, in the burials of the Zhutovo kurgan, evidently, point to the barbarian settlements of the Lower Don region through which the Egyptian faience articles were brought to the Lower and Middle Volga region, the Kama region and the South Cisurals.

5.3. Coral and seashell decorations

This group of imported decorations of organic origin is quite significant both quantitatively and chronologically and is represented by the finds from the burial complexes of Cisurals, the Volga region and the Kama region.

Coral beads and pendants were already known in the Early Sarmatian burials of South Cisurals in Orenburg region. Bright-red coral pendants were discovered in the graves of Pokrovka 8 cemetery [Yablonsky L.T., 1999: 327], as well as in grave 1 of kurgan 2 near Privolnoe village [Meshcheryakov D.V., 1997: 45, fig. 1, 4]. In South Cisurals a coral pendant was found in a Sarmatian kurgan in the estuary of the Baza river, the left-side tributary of the Belaya river at Atasovo village (Ilishevsky district) in Bashkortostan [Vasiliev I.B., 1973: 89-90, fig. 3.6].

Seashells, in particular, cowrie shells from the Indian ocean used as decorations (pendants, galloons), just from the end of the Neolithic age were circulating among the tribes of the Ural region and the Volga region as a means of exchange. Cowrie and gryphea shells were found along with other imported objects in Prokhorovka and Pokrovka kurgans (former Orenburg province) [Rostovtsev M.I., 1918a: 18, 22]. According to L.T. Yablonsky, gryphea shells become a ritual part for women's burial in the Sauromates and Prokhorovka period [Yablonsky L.T., 1999: 329], this is evidenced by the finds in the burials of the South Cisurals.

Pendants, white or rose coral beads were found in large quantities in the Sarmatian burials of Saratov and Volgograd Trans-Volga: at the 2nd Berezhnovsky, Suslovsky, Usatovsky and Novo-Molchanovsky burial sites on the Eruslan river [Rykov P.S., 1925: 12, fig. 21; Sinitsin I.V., 1947: 21, 52, 53; Sinitsin I.V., 1960: 90, 137].

Most likely, the pendants and beads of this type have Mediterranean origin, although V.P.Shilov points to the Caspian Sea area as a potential source of coral beads and pendants [Shilov V.P., 1959a: 439-441].

The nomadic peoples of the Volga region and Cisurals received such decorations, in general, in the same ways as the imported glass and stone beads originating from the ancient centers of the Mediterranean, Black Sea region and Trans-caucasia.

In the burials of Ananino period in the Kama region there were found 3 (three) cypraea moneta shells [Smirnov A.P., 1938: 143]. The cypraea shells were brought to Eastern Europe, most probably, from the Mediterranean and Asia Minor which, in their turn, maintained close commercial ties with the ancient cities and states located on the coasts of the Indian Ocean and the Persian Gulf [Kropotkin V.V., 1970: 37].

5.4. Metallic decorations

We hardly know any bronze, silver or gold decorations with precious and semi-precious stones produced in Rome or Roman provinces.

Probably, Bosporan jewelers and local craftsmen fully satisfied the demand of the local nobles for such goods. Medallions in golden settings, golden pendants, golden cast earrings and bronze earrings with oval shields found in the Volga region have their analogies, first of all, in Bosporus [Sinitsin I.V., 1947, p. 53, table 2, 1; Shilov V.P., 1959a: 463-466]. According to M.G. Moshkova, the images on two bronze rings from the Sarmatian burials of Kalinovka (on the first ring there is an embossed palmette, on the other one – a running Cupid), were very popular on Greek and Roman golden and silver rings in the 4th-3rd c. BC-2nd c. AD. [Moshkova M.G., 1956: 235]. The idea about their Bosporan origin is the most credible, but we should not deny that they may have Western European origin, since there is no precise indication of the production place of such decorations [ibidem].

The bronze signet rings with images of "some birds or animals" found in Temyasovo kurgans [Pshenichnyuk A.H., Ryazapov M.Sh., 1976: 145, fig. 4, 6-11] have obviously Middle Asian origin. The nearest analogies of these rings are known from Fergana where such type was characteristic for decorations of the 3rd-5th c. AD. [Zadneprovsky Yu.A., 1960: fig. 59, 8; Litvinsky B.A., 1973: 15, 18, 26, table 3, 3-7].

Single finds of jewelry decorations made of precious metals with stone inserts provene from Perm region (former Perm province, Krasnoufimsky county) where in 1858 there was found a round insert of a ring with silver setting depicting a deer's profile [Zakharov A.A., 1928: 132]. This piece was presumably made of glass paste or aquamarine and was brought, most likely, from Tanais [Kropotkin V.V., 1967: 97]. In the territory of Ust-Sylvensky settlement (Permsky district, Perm region) in the complex of Glyadenovo culture of the 7th c. AD there were found a fragment of a silver ring with a golden insert for stone decorated with granulation and a large amethyst insert for a ring [Goldobin A.V, Lepikhin A.N, Melnichuk A.F., 1991: 39-40].

An example of wide distribution of imported articles made in polychromatic style is a set of jewelry from the often-mentioned woman's grave of kurgan 2 of Lebedevka burial site where the following objects were discovered: a golden pendant decorated with small granulation and ruby inserts; a ring decorated with granulation and cornelian inserts, as well as an insert of a ring with an inscription [Bagrikov G.I., Senigova T.M., 1968: 71, fig. 1-15; Kropotkin V.V., 1970: 132]. Whole complexes of such polychromatic decorations from the Northern Black Sea region were brought in the 3rd-5th c. in large quantities to the north up to the Kama region, South Cisurals and the Caspian Sea region.

As an exception, we can mention a unique finding of a chalcedony head of Cupid found in 1991 during the excavations in the Mokinsky burial site (close to Perm) in a warrior's grave which shows traces of nomadic, possibly, Sarmatian influence [Soboleva N.V., 1991: 73].

According to the researchers, in the first case we are dealing with a phalera – a medal of Roman legionaries dated to the early Empire period and manufactured during Caligula's reigning (37-41 AD.) [Kolobov A.V., 2000: 129-135].

Regarding the way the Roman phalera got to the Kama region, possibly, it was brought by the Sarmatian nomads who took part in wars on the Danubian borders where a calcedony phalera could be a valuable trophy. The unique finding of a Roman phalera is an indirect evidence of the trend of intensification of trade and cultural contacts between the various tribes of the steppe and forest-steppe lands during the period of the Great Transmigration of the peoples of Eurasian steppes [Bezrukov A.V., 2008: 132].

This series of unique objects undoubtedly includes one finding in an early medieval grave in Ufa – a bronze plate medallion bearing an image with the figures of two fully-armed officers. According to G.N. Garustovich, in this case "the words "shield" and "medallion" are used in this paper for convenience only. Probably, it was attached as a shield to a parade fibula; the steppe people could use the trophy for a different purpose than its manufacturers – the craftsmen of the Mediterranean empire. One of the Late Sarmatian groups influenced by the Hunnic ethno-cultural environment moves to the east as a new ethnos – to Cisurals where they left the monuments known as Turbaslin. The newcomers brought lots of ancient decorations looted in the Balkans and in Crimea or received from the Romans as tribute". [Garustovich G.N., Ivanov G.A., 2010: 88-89].

Thus, we can definitely say that the decorations of proper Western European origin were not much distributed among the peoples of Cisurals, the Volga region and the Kama region in the chronological periods under review. This occurred not only because of relatively high prices of the Roman imported jewelry decorations, but also due to developed production of jewelry in Bosporan workshops which were quite able to satisfy the demand of the barbarian nobles for such products.

5.5. Fibulae

In addition to beads, diverse fibulae which varied in shape, material, production method, ornamentation origin, including the imported ones were one of the most popular decorations and an essential part of outerwear for numerous nomadic tribes which inhabited the vast steppe areas from the Danube river in the west to the Ural river in the east.

This is evidenced by numerous finds of this category of imported objects in the archeological complexes related to various chronological periods in the vast area. In the north they are known from the territory of today's Lithuania, Latvia, Estonia and Moscow region, on the east – in Western Siberia (Novosibirsk region). Based on the material below and in the light of the broad distribution and relatively large number of such items, we can more precisely define the directions of the trade routes which connected the ancient centers and the barbarian hinterland area in different periods.

Among the earliest finds there are Gallic swivel fibulae of AVCISSA type of the 1st c. BC – 1st c. AD which were broadly spread in the Danubian provinces of the Roman empire and in Eastern Europe [Ambroz A.K., 1966: 26]. One Gallic fibula was found in kurgan 5 of Arkharinsky burial site in Kalmykia in a Late Sarmatian burial [Skripkin A.S., 1977: 12] which exemplifies the later utilization of imported articles, although the time of their wide use had already gone.

In this regard, it looks paradoxical that no fibula of this type was found in the interfluve area of the Ural and Volga rivers and in the Kama region. In Trans-Volga where the majority of Middle Sarmatians burials are concentrated, only one fibula with a clamp dating to the Middle Latin period was found in Kalinovka [Moshkova M.G., 1989: 190].

As for the finds of much-profiled fibulae which were very rare in the South Cisurals, M.G.Moshkova thinks that those items arrived in the region «quite definitely from the west, most probably, from Tanais workshops; moreover, the South Ural fibulae are almost identical to Tanais products" [Moshkova M.G., 2000: 192].

D.B. Shelov uses the finds of highly-profiled fibulae and bow shaped garters typical for the Black Sea region and mostly popular with the nomads of the steppes of the Ural and the Volga regions to track the possible route of their distribution via Tanais to the remote areas of the barbarian periphery: across the interfluve area of the Volga and the Don rivers (finds at Abganerovo and Zhutovo). Then the distribution route ran to the south-east (Astrakhan region, Staritsa village) or up north to the area of Saratov Volga region and Trans-Volga (Kotovo, Novaya Norka, Staraya Ivantsovka, Usatovo, Kalinovka, Verkhnee Pogromnoe etc.), as well as to Volgograd Trans-Volga (Politotdelskoe, Borodaevka, Berezhnovka, Rovnoe, Susly etc.). In the north they reached Nizhniy Novgorod and Udmurtia [Shelov D.B., 1972: 204-205].

In the second half of the 2nd c. AD the Gallic fibulae were substituted for imported plate-type and swivel fibulae with colourful enamels which were also found in the Sarmatian burials of the Volga region and the Ural region. In 1934 in kurgan 6 of Suslovsky burial site in a Sarmatian burial of the 2nd–3rd c. AD P.S.Rykov discovered a swivel fibula with a convex hexagonal shield, the upper part of the shield was enameled, the shield edges had traces of gilding [Rykov P.S., 1925: 12].

In the Lower Volga region there were also found several provincial brooch fibulae which are believed to have been mainly produced and distributed in Pannonia and the Rhine region [Ambroz A.K., 1966: 26]. During the dig led by P.S. Rykov in 1926–1927 at Kano village (Saratov region) in kurgan B7 there was found a swivel rhomboid fibula with gilding and an engraved pattern [Rykov P.S., 1927: 117; Skripkin A.S., 1977: 117; Gushchina I.I., Moshkova M.G., 1999: 51]. Similar swivel rhomboid fibulae with gilding and enamel are known from Volgograd region [Shelov D.B., 1965: 270] and north-western Kazakhstan [Bagrikov G.I., Senigova T.M., 1968: 71 sl.).

Three more fibulae (Temyasovo, Lebedevka, Tselinny I, kurgan 25) obviously belong to the type of provincial swivel fibulae with enamel and apparently originate from Gaul-Roman workshops [Moshkova M.G., 2000: 187]

In South Cisurals a swivel rhomboid fibula decorated with dark-blue and red enamel was found in kurgan 3 of Temyasovo group [Pshenichnyuk A.H., Ryazapov M.Sh., 1976: 145, fig. 4, 2].

In a burial of kurgan 21 of Magnitny burial site in Chelyabinsk region there was found a similar "fibula with a rhomboid shield and an anthropomorphic image on enamel (blue, rose, greenish hues) which were also encountered among the Roman materials dating not earlier than to the 2nd c. AD as well as found in Sarmatian complexes of the 2nd–3rd. c. AD in the Carpathian hollow" [Botalov S.G., Ivanov A.A., 2012: 277-281].

They are dated to the second half of the 2nd c. AD, in this period they were exported to the eastern regions, but the export volumes were sharply reduced in the early 3rd c. AD due to the change of the military and political situation in the Northern Black Sea region [Skripkin A.S., 1977: 117]. Analogies are found among the fibulae of the 2nd-3rd c. AD in the Black Sea region and in Western Europe; these items are said to have Greek or Roman origin.

We know a large number of similar fibulae from the archeological complexes of the Black Sea region, the Kuban region, the Don region, the Dnieper region, North Ossetia, Moldova, Belorussia, Lithuania, Latvia, Estonia as well as many regions of Ukraine, and distribution thereof is directly linked with the Northern Black Sea trade.

"Quite unique for the eastern regions is the find of the so-called tong-type swivel fibula at the Lipovka cemetery (the Buzuluk basin). Fibulae of this type are very rare for Eastern Europe, and for Sarmatian graves the fibula from Lipovka is the only one. They were most frequently found in Eastern Alps and in Northern Italy". The Lipovka grave is dated to about the 2nd c. – first half oa the 3rd c. AD. [Moshkova M.G., 2000: 188]

Thus, the main suppliers of imported fibulae for the peoples of the Ural, Volga and Kama regions were the Greek colonies of the Northern Black Sea region, and Tanais acted as the main intermediary from where the fibulae penetrated to the territory of the Middle Volga region, Trans-Volga, Cisurals and the Kama region by the traditional trade routes which ran along the ridges and tributaries of the Volga, the Ural and the Kama rivers.

5.6. Toiletries and household items

This category of imported articles should include the finds of mirrors, marble and alabaster spindle whorls, small toilet vessels, as well as seashells with remnants of chalk or powder.

Among the above listed imported articles the mirrors of proper Italic origin are an important information source for the studies of ancient communications. Mirrors also played an important role in the spiritual culture of Sarmatian tribes and performed diverse magic functions [Kuznetsova T.M., 2001: 129-134].

First of all, the category of imported items should include the mirrors from Alt-Weimar (now Staraya Ivantsovka village, Volgograd region) and Berezhnovka [Treister M.Yu., 1991: 93] found in Sarmatian burials. The mirror unearthed in 1954 in Berezhnovka II burial site in kurgan 36 (9×7,5 cm) belongs to the small rectangular mirror type which was the most common for Italy. The origin of this type is not clear, but by the 1st c. AD it became one of the most popular forms diffused almost in all provinces of the Roman Empire. There were a few centers for production of such mirrors, an especially large number of mirrors was found in the Lower Rhine region, in Nijmegen and in North Italy, Emona [*ibidem*: 98–100].

Among perforated mirrors there was a mirror found on the Torgun river at Alt-Weimar in kurgan B7 during the excavations by P.D. Rau and T.M. Minaeva in 1924 (diameter 4 cm) [Shilov V.P., 1972: 274]. A similar mirror provenes from the Don region, for which V.P. Shilov suggests it was produced in South Italy [*ibidem*: 276]. This type of mirrors was extraordinarily popular in the 1st c. AD, and an extremely large number of such mirrors is concentrated in Cisalpine historical sites of the Po river valley, probably, those mirrors were produced in several Roman provincial centers [Treister M.Yu., 1991: 94].

Due to the finds of mirrors in the Volga region and in Cisurals a question arises regarding the ways of their penetration to these regions. Distribution of mirrors of Italic origin, finds of mirrors of the Han type in Hakasso-Minusinsk Lowland, in three sepulchers of Tillya-Tepe in the Northern Afghanistan where they were found together with Roman articles and coins, as well as in the Sarmatian burials of Kazakhstan, the Volga region, Cisurals and the Don region are within the itineraries of the steppe trade route. Probably, their large part got into the Sarmatian burials as a result of normal trade exchange with intermediation of Bosporan cities, because they were quite sellable and inexpensive, and only a small part could be owned as military trophies of the Rhoxolani [*ibidem*: 99-100].

For the perforated mirrors V.P. Shilov suggested that they were acquired without participation of the ancient Bosporan cities, during the Rhoxolani movement to the Danube where they were immediate neighbors of the Romans. This can be confirmed by the fact that perforated mirrors appeared in Bosporus a bit later than rectangular ones, and judging by the finds in the Volga region, both types of mirrors coexisted originally. [Shilov V.P., 1972: 264].

Thus, the distribution of finds of provincial Roman and Italic mirrors in the Volga River region and in Cisurals is in a way similar to distribution of cheap bronze and glass vessels and fibulae and is different from distribution of expensive highly-artistic silver and bronze utensils which were hardly found in the cities of the Northern Black Sea region, but are widely present in the rich Sarmatian burial complexes.

Various spindle whorls, small vessels and seashells were found in the classical Sarmatian cemeteries at Susly, Berezhnovka and Rovnoe [Rykov P.S., 1925: 14, 15; Sinitsin I.V., 1959: 98,143-144, 151-152, 202; Sinitsin I.V., 1960: 34, 54, 105, 161; Gushchina I.I., Moshkova M.G., 1999: 51] and at Kalmykovo village on the Ural river [Shelov D.B., 1972: 216]. A swivel whorl made of ivory similar to the articles from Syria and Egypt of the first centuries AD was discovered among the finds of the Sarmatian period from the graves of the Pokrovka I burial site [Yablonsky L.T., 1999: 330].

Undoubtedly, these items are imported, probably, of Bosporan origin, although in those ancient centers they were not widely diffused.

Chapter III. ROLE OF COINS IN INTERTRIBAL TRADE IN THE VOLGA AND KAMA RIVERS REGION

In comparison to Krasnodar Krai, Rostov region, Ukraine, Caucasus and Transcaucasia, in the Ural and the Volga rivers region and in the Kama region a relatively low number of authentic finds of Roman and Byzantine coins was discovered. Probably, one of the reasons was that, unlike the agricultural tribes, the nomads of the steppe and forest-steppe belt of the Eastern Europe did not bury their treasures in the ground [Kropotkin V.V., 1967: 26]. Besides, throughout the period of dominance of the Iranian-speaking tribes in the Eurasian steppes the nomadic tribes carried out basically barter trade, so the monetary relationships were poorly developed.

§ 1. COINS FROM GREEK CITIES OF THE BLACK SEA REGION

The coins from Olbia and other cities of the Black Sea region were the earliest finds of ancient coins in the territory of the Ural, the Volga and the Kama rivers region [table IV, 1-2].

At present we know 5 (five) coins found on two sites on the left bank of the Volga river: three Olbian coins, one coin from Chersonesos and one coin from Panticapaeum [Shelov D.B., 1970: 176].

With respect to the chronology of the found Olbian coins D.B. Shelov posits that they should not be dated to later than the 3rd c. BC, therefore, we can say that "the Boristhenes" were brought there in the late 4th-early 3rd c. BC [ibidem: 296].

Penetration of Olbian coins into the Lower Volga region is not linked with the functioning of Herodotus' trade route, because the ancient road ran more to the north, to Samarskaya Luka, but Olbian coins were also found in Astrakhan region. Besides, nowhere in the Black Sea region steppes along the entire route from Olbia to the Volga region no Olbian coins were found, and the trade route from Olbia to the Lower Volga region ceased to exist by the 3rd c. BC. [ibidem: 297–299; Mielczarek M., 1989: 88 – 104]. Finding of Olbian coins in the Lower Don region proves that the most probable route in which coins from Olbia could be brought to the Volga region ran from the North-Western Black Sea region via the Cimmerian Bosporus and then across the lower reaches of the Don and the Kuban rivers, but not on the steppe roads [see the map VI].

Studies of Bosporan coins involve some intrinsic difficulties. In the majority of the cases we know only about the fact of coin finding, but we are not familiar with either types or dating of such coins; as for the known cases, most of the coins date to the second half of the 3rd c. – early 4th c. AD. Obviously, distribution of late-Bosporan coins in the Volga region, as well as distribution of Roman coins in the Eastern European steppe and forest-steppe lands occurred not via the ancient cities of the Northern Black Sea region, but by other ways. Certainly, we cannot say that such diverse, mainly, copper coins were in circulation [Shelov D.B., 1972: 216].

Penetration of the Olbian and Panticapaean copper coins found in the Lower Don and Lower Volga regions could be much facilitated by the Bosporan "trading-posts" established on the Kuban river [Mielczarek M., 1997: 132]. Their activities as intermediaries in the trade between the Greeks and the barbarians could finally provide for distribution of individual coins. At the same time, the composition of the coin finds and the conditions of their discovery do not give us sufficient grounds to make final conclusions on this issue.

In South Cisurals ancient coins [see the map VI] were discovered during archeological studies. In the excavations of a kurgan cemetery near Ishtuganovo (Meleuzovsky district, Bashkortostan) coins were found in a nomad's grave (kurgan 4, grave 4) [Akbulatov I.M., Obydennov M.F., 1984: 46-54; Kropotkin V.V., Obydennov M.F., 1985: 242].

One coin was a tetrahalk minted during the reigning of Mitridate VI Eupatore (120-63 BC) in Amastria in Asia Minor and is dated to 105 – 90 BC. [*ibidem*: 243-244].

The second coin was an obol belonging to the period of reigning of Mitridate VI Eupatore or of his son Farnakes (63–47 BC), it is dated to 73-63 BC. [Zograf A.N., 1951: 187; Kropotkin V.V., Obydennov M.F., 1985: 245].

Thus, the composition of the coin finds, on the whole, shows the occasional and irregular nature of their bringing to the Volga region and to Cisurals [Shelov D.B., 1969: 296 – 299] . The practical value of the finds of inexpensive Greek coins lies in the fact that they point to the cities – main players and intermediaries in the trade between the ancient centers of the Northern Black Sea region and in the regions under review in various chronological periods.

The routes which could be used for delivery of coins to the Volga region were changing with time depending on the political situation both in the steppes and in the ancient cities of the Northern Black Sea region, and therefore, could not remain constant.

In the initial phase of establishing of the trade contacts a significant role belonged to the steppe road which began in the North-Western Black Sea region (Olbia), and later, when Panticapaeum and the Bosporan kingdom strengthened their positions in the trade with the barbarians, the main trade communications linking the Northern Black Sea region with the Lower Volga region and the South Cisurals ran through the Kuban region and the Lower Don region.

§ 2. ROMAN COINS

The earliest finds of Roman copper, bronze and silver coins are dated to the second half – late 2nd c. BC-1st c. AD when the Roman republican denarius was in active circulation and widely used in the international trade [table V, 8-9]. The circulation of the Roman republican denarius in the East was limited by the borders of the Roman expansion, preemptively, by the territory of Transcaucasia. Penetration of those coins into the Middle and Lower Volga region was occasional and irregular, then they were found only in later hoards together with Roman imperial denarii. The majority of the hoards containing Roman republican denarii were probably buried only in late 2nd – early 3rd c. AD. [Kropotkin V.V., 1967: 17]. Such a long-time functioning is explained by the fact that silver denarii were used not only as a payment means, but symbolized a definite social status of the owner of such coins.

Finds of coins and hoards of the 3rd c. AD in Eastern Europe are rare and probably show that the barbarians did not accept the depreciated Antonian coins and switched mainly to barter trade [Kropotkin V.V., 1961: 101]. The overall level of socioeconomic development of the barbarian tribes of Eastern Europe in that period did not allow using a standard equivalent for trade exchange, and relatively rare finds of Roman coins cannot illustrate any special preferences of the barbarian nobles with regard to Roman coins.

As a result, the extended circulation of Roman coins did not lead to establishment of a local monetary-weight system, thus, treasures were intensively accumulated, and the Roman coins fell out of circulation promptly [*ibidem*: 36]. The process is quite clearly supported by written and numismatic data. We can only say that the Roman coins being, first of all, a consequence of contacts between the barbarians and the Roman world, performed diverse functions in their distribution areas depending on the socioeconomic development of the regional population.

The largest number of finds of Roman coins and the only hoard of Roman coins are dated to the 3rd–4th c., although the ancient cities of the Northern Black Sea region suffered from a general decline. It is quite possible that a significant quantity of Roman coins could be brought into the barbarian territories after the Gothic campaigns [*ibidem*: 42].

The bronze coins from Rozhdestvensky (Laishevsky district, Tatarstan) and Izhevsk (Udmurtia) burial sites are dated to the first half of the 3rd c. AD [table V, 12,13]. It is quite likely that Roman coins and articles reached the Northern Black Sea region in that period not only through trade contacts, but mainly as a result of successful plundering raids of the Black Sea region tribes [Budanova V.P., 1982: 155-175]. However, copper coins could not represent a valuable trophy for the nomads. Judging by the holes, the coins from Tatarstan and Udmurtia were used as pendants.

The hoard of Roman silver coins found at Krasny Kut [see the map VII] is the only hoard of Roman coins discovered in the regions under review [table V, 7]. The hoards of Roman coins similar to the one from Krasny Kut which contained both Antonian coins and coins of the Thirty Tyrants' period (3rd c. AD) are not typical for Eastern Europe [Kropotkin V.V., 1961: 41].

The economic and political crisis of the Roman Empire of the 3rd c., the Goths' invasion in alliance with a number of Black Sea region tribes, undoubtedly, did not promote development of the international economic ties. It is natural that due to the overall socioeconomic and political crisis in the Roman Empire resulted in degradation of the Roman silver coins, prompt exclusion of the Antonian coins from circulation and, consequently, strengthening of the naturalization process in the international trade contact.

Only single Roman golden coins were found in the Volga region and in Cisurals. In Astrakhan region on the right bank of the Volga river at Zamyany village (Enotaevsky district) there was found a golden coin of Eudocia (408–414), wife of Theodosius II (408-450), and a well-preserved golden coin of Theodosius I (379-395) provenes from a burial discovered in Ufa [ibidem: 48; table V, 15].

Golden Roman coins arrived in the Volga region and in the South Cisurals through a complex exchange to that territory in the period when the golden Roman coins were brought from the Danube and the Dnieper regions to the Crimea and Bosporus [Abramzon M.G., Maslennikov A.A., 1999:79-83].

These coins do not represent a valuable historical evidence of the economic relations between the ancient cities and the barbarians because golden coins could not play a serious role in the international commerce and money circulation in the adjacent territories, and certainly, not in the peripheral lands [Bezrukov A.V., 2011: 80]. A major part of such coins usually has lugs for appending or holes, i.e., they were basically used as decorations [Kropotkin V.V., 1961: 36]. These regions had no socioeconomic conditions for development of golden coins circulation, nor any demand for that.

Golden and other "outlandish" coins were not obligatory used as payment means, but they could "fulfill an important symbolic functions along with other treasures" [Gurevich A.Ya., 1984: 230-233].

Possibly, the barbarian nobles of the nomadic tribes of Cisurals and the Volga region exchanged the excess of livestock, furs and metal for expensive imported articles which they did not have, so that to strengthen and reconfirm their high social status. A minor part of the coins could return as a result of trade, the other part could be melted to ingots; graves often contain coins with holes which were thus converted to decorations. The main quantity of coins, especially, golden ones, was accumulated by the tribal nobles and was subject to "intense demonetization" [Kropotkin V.V., 1967: 117].

Finding of a Vespasianus' aureus (69-79) in Saratov Trans-Volga (Dergachi village, Dergachevsky district) [table V, 4] is obviously a reminiscence of a powerful impulse, as since the period of this emperor's reigning the major part of Roman coins including golden ones start to arrive in Europe [Lebedeva E.Yu., 1990: 121]. They probably reached Eastern Europe via the Lower Don region.

After Nero's reform of 64 AD which resulted in a poorer coin composition and its reduced weight, for a certain time only pre-reform coins were exported outside the empire because they were heavier and had a better composition. Analysis of the hoards found beyond the Roman Empire show that export of coins minted after the reform of 64 AD started only during Hadrian's reignship (117-138) [Zeimal E.V., 1962: 146].

E.Yu. Lebedeva compared the dynamics of Roman coins imports in the eastern (Indian) and northern (European) directions and obtained evidences that the Nero's period was the final phase of the coins export to the East, but for Europe it meant the start of active imports of Roman coins. In Vespasian's period the majority of coins were directed to Europe and only a few coins went to India. A huge number of coins was brought to Hindustan during the Nero-Augustus' period, and mass imports to Europe began since Nero's time and lasted till the reigning of Commodus. Therefore, in the 1st–2nd c. AD the consolidated monetary model of the Roman foreign trade experiences a very significant shift to coins exports [Lebedeva E.Yu., 1990: 119-122].

Thus, the earliest finds of copper coins from Olbia and Panticapaeum, as well as coins of other ancient centers relating to the 4th–3rd c. BC cannot be used as an evidence of early establishment of money circulation among the barbarian tribes of the Volga region. More complicated is the issue about the inception of goods-money exchange due to the massive inflow of silver Roman coins which started in the 1st c. AD.

The coin finds from the territory of the present Ukraine demonstrate the abrupt growth in volumes of Roman silver coins starting from the 1st c. AD. The peak quantities of the Roman silver coins were brought during the reigning of Antoninus Pius and Marcus Aurelius, then, in early 3rd c. AD the inflow slowed down and virtually faded out. The intensity of the ties which promoted imports of Roman denarii from the Lower Danube region to those territories was so great that the South Russian steppe lands once focused exclusively on Bosporus seem a sort of fringe of "the Roman-Danubian trade" [Rostovtzeff M., 1922: 216]. The close contacts broke almost simultaneously with the Goths' invasion into the Roman dominions on the Lower Danube river when a sturdy protective line was created along the northern and north-western borders of Dacia as per the order of Septimius Severus for prevention of the Gothic threat [Kropotkin V.V., 1961: 243-245].

According to M.G. Moshkova, the major part of the imported goods were certainly exchanged directly for the nomadic herdsmen' products, but since there already existed a significant material differentiation which is evidenced by existence of poor and very rich burials, we have to assume that the nobles accumulated large riches, and therefore, they could also possess money [Moshkova M.G., 1956: 188].

Establishment of goods circulation can be proven by the similar trends in the inflow of coins to the Volga region which were typical, on the whole, for the entire Eastern Europe, as well as the identical proportions in distribution of silver and copper coins confirming that they were used as money. Finally, the fact that in the Volga region there was found a large quantity of exclusive Roman coins, but not of those from Bosporus, although it might be expected, is an indirect proof of the hypothesis about existence of money circulation [*ibidem*: 187-189].

Thus, the general trends in distribution of Roman coins are typical also for distribution of Roman coins in the peripheral land, but with a certain time lag which means that the remote barbarian territories were involved in the general economic processes which are also characteristic for more developed regions of the Eastern Europe.

Relying on statistical data, N.A. Frolova made a conclusion that from the second half of the 2nd c. AD Bosporan tsars received regular subsidies from Rome not for establishment of defense barriers to protect the borders of the Roman Empire. These subsidies were spent either for paying the barbarian mercenaries or for bribing the elites of the tribes which represented the highest danger for Bosporus. These facts explain the relatively small number of finds of Roman denarii in the territory of the Bosporan kingdom, and thus, mass penetration of Roman silver coins into the steppes of the European Sarmatia [Frolova N.A., 1982: 58-63].

Therefore, the mass inflow of Roman silver coins was mainly caused by political reasons rather than by economic needs of the barbarian societies and, consequently, we have no sufficient grounds to speak about any significant distribution of money circulation among the barbarian tribes of the Volga region, Cisurals and the Kama region, nor about active use of Roman silver coins by the barbarian elite in the intertribal exchange and in international trade.

Moreover, the mass inflow of Roman silver coins during a relatively long chronological period did not result in creation of a local monetary-weighting system.

So, money circulation in the barbarian environment was in its initial phase when the functions of the money did not gain all the necessary conditions for growth and expansion of the area of its influence onto the economy and daily life of the respective tribes [Nudelman A.A., 1982: 125]. However, we should admit that in their majority, the Roman coins had no serious influence on the trade between the representatives of the barbarian nobles of the tribes from the Ural region, the Volga region and the Kama region.

§ 3. BYZANTINE AND SASSANIDIAN COINS

Finds of Byzantine copper, silver and golden coins with prevalence of silver hexagrams of Heraclius of the 7th c. discovered on the outskirts of the barbarian world evidence the ambiguity of socioeconomic and political processes which took place on the outskirts of the ancient world in the late ancient period and in the early medieval years. Creation of the Eastern Roman Empire or Byzantium with a capital in Constantinople was one of the most important events which modified the overall political map of the ancient world and had a large impact on the change of directions of the main trade routes in the international trade.

Byzantine copper coins known in large numbers in Chersonesos are represented by single, often doubtful, finds in the Lower Volga region [table VI, 1-3].

Most probably, copper coins were minted only for internal circulation, because they could not compete with silver and golden Byzantine coins for payments in international trade operations, so it explains that such finds were rare beyond the Empire and the regions controlled by the Byzantine emperors. As noted above, a large number of Byzantine copper coins were found in Chersonesos which acted as a stronghold of the Empire in the Crimea [Kropotkin V.V., 1962: 9]. The majority of the coins related to the period of Justinian I (527–565 гг.) and his successors when the Byzantine territory had its maximum area.

Byzantine golden solidi of the 6th c. were present in the finds from the territory of the Lower Volga region and the South Cisurals [*ibidem*: 26]. As for the ways of penetration of golden coins to the Volga region and South Cisurals, we cannot give preference to any single route. It is quite possible that the coin found near Orsk was brought by the steppe road from the Middle Asia which was used to transport almost all artistic imported goods from Khorezm and basically the entire Orient, including Byzantium. This hypothesis is backed by the fact that in the Middle Asia there are known finds of mainly golden solidi, but no Byzantine silver coins [Masson M.E., 1951: 94; Shtatman I.L., 1972: 32-34]. Due to the insufficient quantity of numismatic materials at present we are not in position to provide a clearer answer to this question.

In the Eastern Europe golden solidi of the 7th c. were found mainly in rich nomadic burials which also contained other precious golden and silver articles of Byzantine production as well as glass vessels and fragments of glass vessels; the majority of coins from Pereshchepino have drilled holes, side loops, hooks and seats for stone inserts [Kropotkin V.V., 1962: 10].

Thus, the absolute majority of golden Byzantine coins of the 6th–7th c. were brought to the steppes of Eastern Europe not as a result of trade, but either due to frequent military raids and rampages of the Eastern European nomadic tribes against the Byzantine Empire or as tribute which was regularly paid by Byzantium to the leaders of the nomadic tribal alliances.

The order of 374 AD published in Byzantium prohibited to pay "the barbarians" for their goods with gold which was draining from the Empire and aggravated its financial situation: "Not only shall no gold be furnished to barbarians in payment for slaves or other merchandise. If, however, gold should hereafter be given to barbarians by traders, in, they shall not be fined, but shall suffer death" [Cod. Justin., 4, 63, 2; Pigulevskaya N., 1951: 67-68]. An indirect proof of gold leakage can be the finds of Byzantine solidi discovered in the Volga region and Cisurals which were exported to the barbarian lands as ingots and coins despite the prohibition. Individual coins could thus reach the Volga region and Cisurals through multi-staged intertribal exchange.

A large part of Byzantine silver coins of the 7th c. was found in the Kama region area limited by the basin of the Sylva river. We do not know any hoards of Byzantine silver coins of the 5th-6th c.; in the international trade silver coins were gradually substituted with golden ones, and only in the 7th c. the hoards containing silver Byzantine coins were found in Transcaucasia and the Kama region.

Mapping of the finds of Byzantine silver coins from the Volga region shows that silver and copper coins of Byzantine origin reached the Volga region on the same routes [see the map VIII]. Probably, the major part of the coins was brought to this region via the old trade road from the Byzantine Chersonesos which stretched from the Northern Black Sea region via the Lower Don region and the Kuban region to the Volga region.

Along with golden coin minting, during Heraclius' period in 615 the production of silver coins started – so-called double miliarisia or hexagrams [Kropotkin V.V., 1962: 10]. According to N.L. Kazamanova, due to the regular tribute payment to the Avars which could amount to 80-100 thousand solidi, issue of a new heavier coin was expected to substitute the golden solidus to a certain extent in large trade operations in the external market [Kazamanova N.L., 1957: 71].

In the Kama region we know about three hoards of Byzantine silver coins [table VI, 5, 7-8].

In Perm region at Bartym village (Berezovsky district) in 1950 a Sassanidian silver vessel with two hundred sixty Byzantine silver coins was found; in an exploratory shaft nearby there were found twelve more Heraclius' hexagrams of the same type which were minted in Constantinople in 615-629. [Bader O.N., Smirnov A.P., 1954: 19].

A few similar hoards in which Heraclius' coins are put together with the coins of Heraclius Constantine (610-641) were found in Transcaucasia [Kazamanova N.L., 1957: 74; Kropotkin V.V., 1962: 43-46].

The hoard consists of 272 Byzantine double miliarisia of the same ruler – Heraclius, all the coins relate to the same earlier variant, and a few dozens of those coins are minted with one pair of dies [Kazamanova N.L., 1957: 71-72]. All those coins were put in a Byzantine vessel [Bader O.N., 1951: 19]. The Bartym coinage hoard was made in the Kama region no later than in the middle of the 7th c. [Morozov V.Yu., 1996: 157]. Taking into account its unique contents, his owner was not a Transcaucasian, but a Byzantine merchant. It is very likely that all the Byzantine coins arrived in the Kama region together with the same caravan from the Byzantine Chersonesos in the 630-s which went up the Don, the Volga and the Kama regions. A part of it could be dispersed in small lots, but the major part was deposited in the Bartym hoard. In Ust-Sylvensky settlement (on the bank of the Sylva river) in the complex of objects of Glyadenovo and Ananino cultures, presumably, on an early medieval sacrificial site with an area about 1000 m, seven Heraclius' and

Constantine's hexagrams were found among other silver coins [Goldobin A.V., Lepikhin A.N., Melnichuk A.F., 1991: 40]. Quite possible that these coins are directly related to the Bartym coinage hoard.

At Shestakovo village (Suksunsky district) in 1851 at the Irgen river there was found a hoard of silver articles and coins which contained Sassanidian drams and eleven Byzantine silver coins of Heraclius and Heraclius Constantine [Kropotkin V.V., 1962: 26]. The hoards of similar contents found in Transcaucasia and the Kama region are characterized by co-existence of two different currencies: Byzantine hexagrams and Sassanidian drams of the 5th-7th c., when similar Byzantine coins are put together with Sassanidian drams, such hoards are well known in Transcaucasia.

Explaining the combination of Byzantine and Sassanidian coins in Shestakovo hoard, F.A. Teploukhov suggested that the Byzantine coins were brought from the Middle Asia [Teploukhov F.A., 1895: 227], but in the Middle Asia no silver Byzantine coins were found. A more convincing idea is that the Byzantine coins arrived via the Transcaucasia-Volga route. It is also important that since the 5th c. in the Caucasus and in the Kama region the finds of Sassanidian coins were quite similar [Kropotkin V.V., 1967: 117].

Here we have to note that in the steppe and forest-steppe zones of Eurasia in the ancient and medieval times the preference was given to the land trade roads, as evidenced by the relationships of the Caucusus and the Kama region, starting from the Ananino period [Bezrukov A.V., 2003: 234].

Thus, penetration of Byzantine coins on the territory of the regions under review, as we can see, was generally insignificant and irregular, did not lead to creation of a local monetary-weight system or establishment of money circulation among the nations of Cisurals, the Kama and the Volga regions.

This was mainly caused by the general level of socioeconomic development of the local peoples, when the social relations both among the forest tribes of Cisurals, the Volga region and the Kama regions and in the vast steppes of Eurasia almost everywhere depended on the continuous patrimonial order. Consequently, at present it is not possible to mention any tribes with developed social relationships, high level of economic development and intensive money circulation.

It was often mentioned in numismatic literature that the striking affinity of the money hoards found in Transcaucasia and in the Kama region is a valid proof of the hypothesis about existence of quite close ties between Transcaucasia and the Kama region which took place through direct contacts via the Volga and the Kama rivers.

Nevertheless, the results of the archaeological studies of the last two or three decades in the Volga and the Kama Rivers Regions allow us to hope, in our opinion, that in the future a more clear picture will be shaped with regard to the consequences and results on the inflow of a significant quantity of coins and metals, in general, into the above mentioned territories, in the light of emergence of early money forms such as bronze [Muhamadiev A.G., 1984: 219-221] and silver ingots. The finds of similar silver, money (?) ingots originate from the set of items found in Ust-Sylvensky settlement in the Kama River Region [Goldobin A.V., Lepihin A.N., Melnichuk A.F., 1991: 40].

Therefore, the majority of Byzantine golden and silver coins reached the Volga region, the Kama region and Cisurals via both the land and the river trade routes from Transcaucasia along the Volga and the Kama rivers during a relatively short time span (second half of the 5th – middle of the 7th c.).

Chapter IV. TRADE AND ECONOMIC RELATIONSHIPS IN THE VOLGA AND THE KAMA RIVERS REGION

In Chapter I we already noted that in the ancient literature there are virtually no direct references of the ancient authors about the economic history of the tribes inhabiting the steppe and forest-steppe areas of the Eastern Europe.

The most important feature of this problem is the possibility to reconstruct the ancient trade routes on the basis of a comprehensive approach using the data of archeology, numismatics and written records. In order to rebuild a full image fairly reflecting the process of establishment and development of the main directions of trade and cultural ties of the regions, it is appropriate to consider archeological materials of the earlier period starting from the Bronze Age.

The conditions for formation of the main trade routes in the regions under review which developed in the later chronological periods were noted from the Bronze Age to the Early Iron Age [Chernykh E.I., 1988: 42-43]. The Middle Asia, the steppe regions of the Western Siberia, the Northern Caucasus, the Middle and Lower Volga region and Cisurals belong to one vast domain of steppe cultures which bore the conditions providing for migrations of individual ethnical groups, development of cultural links, barter trade and nomadic farming [Zbrueva A.V., 1946: 185-190; Krivtsova-Grakova O.A., 1955: 51;. Khalikov A.H., 1971: 181, 227-228; Chlenova N.L., 1983: 53; Kuzminykh S.V., 1983: 175; Rudenko K.A., Chizhevsky A.A., 1994: 121; Dudarev S.L., Fomenko V.A., 1996: 4].

Obviously, in that period the fundamental role in establishing the main directions of trade, cultural and interethnical communications between the neighboring regions was played by the factor of geographic, cultural and economic affinity of the numerous tribes of Srubna-Andronovo period which populated the steppe areas of the Western Siberia, the Middle Asia and the Eastern Europe.

Thus, already in that period the regions distant from each other start to establish strong commercial and cultural contacts, successfully overcoming the natural barriers such as the Volga, the Ural and other large rivers of the Eastern Europe; foundations are created for further establishment of transcontinental trade roads spanning for thousands of kilometers in the Eurasian steppes.

§ 1. TRADE AND ECONOMIC RELATIONSHIPS IN THE VOLGA AND THE KAMA RIVERS REGION IN THE 6TH–3RD C. BC

In that period the Sauromatian culture is shaped in South Cisurals in its Ural variant. It was already noted quite a few times that unlike the proper Herodotus' Sauromatians, the Sauromatian-Sarmatian groups of South Cisurals already in the 6th–5th c. BC established close cultural and economic relationships with the cognate regions of the Middle Asia and the civilized countries of the Middle East, especially, with the Achaemenidian Persia [Savelieva T.V., Smirnov K.F., 1972: 117].

Analysing Herodotus' message and the finds of Olbian mirrors of the 6th-4th c. BC in the Volga region and in Cisurals, B.N. Grakov concluded that there might really exist a route which began in Olbia, crossed the Don river, then up north along the Volga reached the southern spurs of the Urals and ended there [Grakov B.N., 1947: 28-36]. After publication of this paper, discussions started about the possible itinerary and nature of the described route and about the actual places from where these objects were brought to Cisurals and the Volga region.

The researchers do not agree on the place of production of so-called "Olbian" mirrors: they either state their "Scythian" or "Olbian" origin [Knipovich T.N., 1941: 112]. It is quite possible that in that period we apparently cannot name a single center of production of the mirrors with animal figures. It could have been Olbia or another Greek city of the Northern, or maybe, Western Black Sea region [Olgovsky S.Ya., 1982: 68; Skrzhinskaia M.V., 1984: 119-123]. Probably, the fundamental idea is that those objects arrived in the Volga region and in Cisurals from the ancient or related centers of the Black Sea – Karpaty basin [Skudnova V.M., 1962: 7-25], and for convenience we will apply the commonly accepted terminology.

A large number of "Olbian type" mirrors were found in the Northern Caucasus, and maybe, the route along the Volga ran from there. According to N.L.Chlenova, since all the mirrors were found only in the western part of the Northern Caucasus which had close ties with the Middle Volga region and the Volga and the Kama rivers region, and since no finds of Caucasian origin were made to the east of the Belaya river and in South Cisurals, it means that the eastern part of this route was not known, and the mirrors were brought to Cisurals in that way bypassing the Northern Caucasus [Chlenova N.L., 1983: 52]. Probably, in addition to the main road, this trade route could have several branches, and a part of imports from the Northern Black Sea region could be brought via the Caucasus. We need to note that the objective and the tasks of this paper do not allow us to analyse this category of imported articles in more detail; moreover, it is hardly possible that any significant number of the aove mirrors could have been produced in the regions of our interest, beyond the Greek cities of the Northern Black Sea region.

In the Volga region in 1919-1921 during the excavations led by F. Ballod it was discovered that the peasants of that area (Vodianskoe settlement, Volgograd region) possessed a few intact commercial leaden seals of the 5th c. BC with Greek inscriptions, Panticapaean and Olbian coins, painted clayware (ancient vases) and clay statuettes (ancient terracotta) [Moshkova M.G., 1956: 189]. These finds evidence that on the right bank of the Volga river there were "strongholds" of "trading post type" where few "merchants" stayed [ibidem: 190]. It is quite possible that similar posts could be located along the main road, not only at river crossing stations.

Narrative sources do not contain any direct indications about participation of Greek merchants in any activities on that route. At the same time, these materials and analysis of Herodotus' text point at direct contacts of the Olbian merchants with the Sauromates, probably, other Greeks joined the Olbiopolitans, therefore, this was the reason why Herodotus mentioned other Greek cities too [Skrzhinskaya M.V., 1998: 92].

Obviously, we should not fully deny the version about participation of the Greek merchants in the trade, but the Scythians seem more relevant as the barter trade intermediaries which is indirectly confirmed by the finds of Scythian psalia of the 6th–5th c. BC at Rtishchev (Saratov region) and Buguruslan (Orenburg region): moreover, the last corneous three-hole psalium has an inscription on its back in Aramaic writing of the 6th-5th c. BC. Their direct analogies are found among the Scythian archaic psalia from the forest-steppe Dnieper region [Chezhina E.F., 1989: 261-263]. K.F. Smirnov suggested that the Scythians could cross the river somewhere near Saratov and then proceed to the Cisurals along the river beds in the Trans-Volga region [Smirnov K.F., 1964: 259].

The scope of the watershed system of the rivers in the Black Sea region is quite large to connect any areas of the Black Sea region, also with Greek cities and the remote peripheral lands; this network includes the navigable sections of the rivers. In the ancient times the land roads in the steppe and forest-steppe areas played a greater role then it is believed. The large rivers which Herodotus names navigable have extremely stepped beds and, thus, are navigable only until the rapids are reached. But the watershed area of these rivers offers quite convenient routes for land roads [Shilik K.K., 1989: 175-176], so Greek and Scythian merchants could take advantage of it.

We should give special attention to the linguistic data about the names of the Volga river used by various tribes at the various sections of the river. It is noted that the coincidence of the Greek, Iranian, Mordovian and Gothic names of the Volga proved that already in the 4th c. AD when the Goths met the Mordovians of the forest-steppe area, the latter were using the same name of the Volga river as their southern Iranian neighbors from the steppe lands; this circumstance illustrates the active integration processes along the Volga route when the difficult natural obstacles were overcome many centuries earlier than in the basins of the other rivers of the Eastern Europe [Shramm G., 1997: 79].

The nature of these contacts needs a special discussion. The traditional opinion highlights the prevalence of commerce in these contacts which were more or less regular [Iessen A.A., 1952: 221; Bondar N.N., 1955: 88; Smirnov K.F., 1964: 259; Stepanov P.D., 1969: 221; Skrzhinskaya M.V., 1984: 119].

T.M. Kuznetsova expresses a contrary position. The presence of "mirrors-phials-pateras" in Cisurals since the 6th c. BC reflects the activities of two religious centers related to worshipping of Apollo-Didyma and Apollo-Dionysos, and it makes sense to talk about existence of the routes linked with the "sacred objects", therefore, such routes nature was different from commercial [Kuznetsova T.M., 1990: 86].

The opinion of the authors referring to the mainly trade nature of Herodotus' route looks more justified. A Greek craftsman produced mirrors with animal-shaped handles, in so called "animal" style as per the taste of the Scythians, and the mirror itself was valuable not only as an object of artistic work, but also as an ingot of expensive bronze weighing 700-800 g. Merchants took mirrors from Olbia as one of convenient and popular goods for barter trade [Skrzhinskaya M.V., 1998: 90].

Cessation of activities on this route is explained by several possible reasons. Decline of Olbia due to the struggle with commander Alexander Zopirion, transfer of control over the trade with eastern nomads to Panticapaeum and Bosporus in the whole, as well as the process of establishment and shaping of the early Sarmatian culture in Cisurals and in the Volga region, and the associated migrations of large ethnical groups destroyed the ancient communications[Tairov A.D., 2004: 4].

In parallel to the described route, in the same period a proper steppe road was created which circumvented the Caspian Sea from the north and led to the Northern Black Sea region; this road was further developed later. Obviously, it emerged on the nomadic migration roads of the Central and Middle Asian herdsmen tribes in Cisurals, the Volga region and further to the west and south-west [Staviskii B.Ya., 1992: 17-18].

For reconstruction of the cultural and commercial ties of the Urals population with the southern regions of the Middle Asia it is important to consider the conclusion about the Middle Asian (Kyzylkum or Kuramen) origin of the turquoise from the graves of Pokrovka 2 burial site. The lazurite used for manufacturing of the beads found on the Early Sarmatian sites of the region has Iranian or Pamir origin [Yablonsky L.T., 1999: 328-329].

Among all the objects of Middle Eastern origin discovered in the kurgan cemeteries of South Cisurals of the 6th-4th c. BC we should highlight the remarkable finds of Egyptian and Iranian origin of Achaemenid period [Rostovtsev M.I., 1918a: 12-22; Iessen A.A., 1952: 206-220; Savelieva T.V., Smirnov K.F., 1972: 106-121; Moshkova M.G., 1981: 175-183].

Besides, we should pay attention to the impressive Achaemenidian imports known in the Sarmatian kurgans of the Cisurals. The items include primarily golden and silver articles (grivnas, rhytons, platters, bowl, goblet), an alabaster flask of Artaxerxes I. The accompanying materials of all these burials are typical for the early Prokhorovo complex of the 4th-3rd c. BC.

In the opinion of N.E. Berlizov: "the Sarmatians gained the Achaemenidian imported items in the early and the late 4th c. BC, and the composition of the items does not prove the "trade" hypothesis of A.A.Iessen: these are mostly socially prestigious goods. The inflow of Iranian articles to the Sarmatian steppes in the early 4th c. BC can be linked with the results of the feud between Cyrus Jr. and Artaxerxes II, in which the nomads of the Cisurals could participate with certain benefits for themselves. Probably, some of the complexes under review really belonged to the Dahaes – allies of the Persians. Therefore, the Sarmatians of the Cisurals could gain the Achaemenidian imports participating in the feud of 400 BC and in the wars of Alexander the Great in 331-324 BC". [Berlizov N.E., 1996: 9]

Considering the difficulty and ambiguity of the problem with regard to the interrelations between the South Ural nomadic peoples with the Achaemenid Persia, we need to pay attention, first of all, to the close ties of the Sauromates of South Cisurals with the Sakes and the Dahaes-Massagetean tribes of the Middle Asia when the military and political ties closely intertwined with the economic links.

It is known that certain "Dahaes" and "Massagetians" supported Darius III in the war, performing greatly at Arbela, and then joined the Spitamana's movement. Probably, some of the complexes under review really belonged to the Dahaes – allies of the Persians [*ibidem*]. Probably, the Sauromates reached the northern borders of Khorezm, this is evidenced by the sets of arrows from Persepolis which were not in use in Iran, but well-known in Khorezm and with the Sauromates in the 6th-5th c. BC. [Smirnov K.F., 1964: 280].

The nearest analogies to the South Ural finds are encountered, primarily, in the Caucasus and in the Middle Asia, thus, we can deduce that the Caucasus (via the Volga and the Kama regions) and the Middle Asia were the most probable routes for penetration of the Iranian imports in the 6th-4th c. BC (the contacts took place via the Middle Asian satrapies).

It is not occasional that writing about the Upper Aorsi, Strabo (XI, V, 8) states that their direct ancestors lived in the steppes of the Aral Sea region and the South Cisurals, therefore, "the Protoaorsi" practiced caravan trade a few centuries earlier, during the Achaemenid times (6th-4th c. BC) when caravan routes from the Orenburg steppes ran on the banks of the Emba, Uzboy, Amudarya and Syrdarya rivers [Savelieva T.V., Smirnov K.F., 1972: 119-120].

Thus, it is obvious that during the Sautomatian-Sarmatian period three kinds of exchange existed in the South Ural River Region: the intra-communal exchange, the exchange between units of different cultural and economic types and the exchange with other economic regions.

Probably, already by the 4th c. BC there was a permanent trade route from the steppes of Cisurals to Khorezm and other countries, and the western section of this route connected the lands of the Aorsi of the Caspian Sea region with Transcaucasia and Media [Smirnov K.F., 1964: 281]. It was noted many times that the relationships with nomadic tribes were always an important factor in the history of Khorezm which was surrounded by deserts. In particular, there is no doubt about the great economic importance of those relationships [Yagodin V.N., Nikitin A.B., Koshelenko G.A., 1985: 319].

Thus, the large tribal alliances of Iranian-speaking nomads populating the interfluve area between the Ural and the Volga rivers ensured stable functioning of trade communications which stretched for hundreds of kilometers and linked individual districts and regions of the Middle Asia, the Caucasus and the Northern Black Sea region by means of a steppe route which circumvented the Caspian Sea from the north [Bezrukov A.V., 2005: 119-121].

§ 2. TRADE AND ECONOMIC RELATIONSHIPS IN THE VOLGA AND THE KAMA RIVERS REGION IN THE 2ND C. BC – 7TH C. AD

The routes of significant length which crossed the vast Eurasian territories acted as political, trade and cultural links of various regions, probably, since the middle of the 1st millennium BC. It can be fully traced by reviewing the process of emergence, existence and functioning of the Great Silk Road which connected China with the Fore-Asia and the Mediterranean countries already in the last centuries BC. Besides, in the author's opinion, "the 5th-6th centuries were a special "trouble" period in the history of Eurasian steppes, and from that period one can talk about emergence of a certain united nomadic civilization" [Botalov S.G., 2009a: 443].

The name "The Great Silk Road" should be interpreted as a system of a fairly large number of caravan roads extending for many thousands of kilometers and connecting the most remote nations and states of the East and the West. The term "Silk" is rather conventional because the route was used not only for silk trade. Besides, we should never forget that the route functioned in both directions.

It was a special era for the nomads of the Eurasian steppes when, in the fair opinion of V.P.Budanova, a completely new stage of the history began, i.e. "The Great Transmigration of Peoples being a significant stage of historical development, both in terms of length (II-VII c.) and coverage (Europe, Asia, Africa), as the most intensive phase of interactions between the barbarism and the civilization, is a unique phenomenon of the world history. Some differentiate "great transmigrations of peoples" as a metaphor for chaos and the highest rise of migration activity and "the Great Transmigration of Peoples" in Europe and in Asia as a special transition stage between the Ancient Times and the Medieval Period when for the first time the migration processes became a part of the complex, diverse and dynamic interactions between the barbarism and the civilization reaching the most intensive phase in the confrontation of the center of civilization and its barbarian periphery. [V.P. Budanova, 2009: 139-140].

The regular functioning of this route began when in 138 BC Zhāng Qiān travelled and discovered cities and states which were not known to the Chinese before. In addition to this route, there were a few branches deviating from the main road, and naturally, we are particularly interested in the so-called "Northern Road" which was used for transportation of Chinese goods and products of the Asian centers to Europe via today's North-Western Kazakhstan, South Cisurals and the Lower Volga region – the so-called "Caspian steppe corridor", while the eastern regions, especially, the interfluve area of the Ural river and its tributaries until recently remained poorly studied [Moshkova M.G., 1982: 80].

The earliest source which tells us about the Northern Road is *Hanshu*, the historical book of the Han dynasty authored presumably by Ban Gu Гу (32-95 AD). From this book we learn that the Northern Road begins at Turfan oasis, then runs along the Northern mountains (Tian Shan) and the river (Tarim) to the west till Sule (Kashgar); further to the west the Northern Road crosses Tsung-Ling (Pamir) and Dayuan (Fergana valley), Kangju (Transoxiana) and Yancai (South Cisurals and Lower Volga region) [Lubo-Lesnichenko E.I., 1994: 232]. Describing Yancai, Zhāng Qiān writes that "it lies some 2,000 li northwest of Kangju. The people are nomads and their customs are generally similar to those of the people of Kangju. The country borders a great shoreless lake, perhaps what is now known as the Northern Sea" [Bichurin N.Ya., 1950: 150].

In this regard, the researchers highlight the north-western expansion of Kangju which could include attachment of Yan and Yancai dominions located on one of the areas of the Northern Road [Zadneprovsky Yu.A., 1998: 82]. Probably, their convenient geographical and strategically important location on the international trade route was one of the reasons for Kangju's expansion into these lands, although, the modern studies do not confirm S.P.Tolstov's concept about the existence of a powerful Kangju union with the center in Khorezm in the last centuries BC [Yagodin V.N., Nikitin A.B., Koshelenko G.A., 1985: 319-320].

Thus, the evidences of the ancient and medieval authors register the existence and functioning of the Northern Road during a relatively lengthy chronological period from the 2nd c. BC till the early medieval period.

As we see it, such a long international trade route emerged mostly due to intensification of activities of various Sarmatian tribes which dominated in the steppes from the Danube in the west to the individual regions of the Middle Asia in the east.

M.G. Moshkova identified three phases in the traditional links of the Sarmatians of Cisurals with the Aral Sea region tribes and the settled and cultivator nations, stating that in the third phase (2nd c. BC – 4th c. AD) there was undoubtedly a migration of some Cisurals tribes to the Middle Asia, and in the Late Sarmatian period reverse migration was also observed [Moshkova M.G., 1978: 106-107]. B.F. Zhelezchikov sticks to a similar opinion suggesting that in the 3rd-2nd c. BC a part of the Sarmatians of Cisurals migrated to the Middle Asian oases, and in the Lower Volga region and in the South Cisurals we observe standardization of burial rites and grave goods [Zhelezchikov B.F., 1988: 61-63]. Taking into account the latest data, there is no more support for the opinion that Cisurals did not depend on Khorezm, but Khorezm was subordinate to the Sarmatian peoples which conquered the Middle Asia in the 2nd c. BC or was politically dependent on them [Obelchenko O.V., 1992: 225].

The first finds of objects of Chinese production discovered in the Middle Sarmatian burials of the region under review relate to that period. Mirrors were one of the mostly spread and quite numerous categories of imported items of Chinese origins found in the Middle Sarmatian burials of the Volga region and Cisurals.

The earliest artifacts of this kind are mirrors with inscription "yìtǐzì" found in kurgan E 25 (grave 19) at Staraya Pol-tavka village in the Lower Volga river region [Sinitsin I.V., 1946: 92, fig. 26; Guguev V.K., Treister M.Yu., 1995: 147; Mielczarek M., 1997: 134] and in the former Samara province [Lubo-Lesnichenko E.I., 1994: 243-245]. Similar mirrors were found in the Lower Don region at Vinogradny village [Kosyanenko V.M., Maksimenko V.E., 1989: fig. 1, 4; Guguev V.K., Treister M.Yu., 1995: 147], in the Kuban region [Medvedev A.P. and Yfimov K. Y., 1986: 84; Mielczarek M., 1997: 134], near Vladikavkaz and in kurgan Klin-Yar III close to Stavropol [Lubo-Lesnichenko E.I., 1994: 245]. The researchers believe that the mirrors of this type were produced in the late 2nd c. BC – early 1st c. BC.

Obviously, at present these are the earliest Chinese artifacts which reached so far west. Their distribution geography points at the Northern Road as the most probable route for delivery of such mirrors to Cisurals, the Volga region and further to the Lower Don region and to the Kuban region [Bezrukov A.V., 2000: 151]. This is quite in line with the statement of Zhāng Qiān who wrote that the first data about the Eastern Mediterranean and the Greek colonies of the Northern Black Sea region were brought to the Han Empire via the Northern Road [Lubo-Lesnichenko E.I., 1994: 242].

Another group of Chinese bronze mirrors discovered on the hypothetical route of the Northern Road relates to a later period and is mainly dated to the turn of 1st – 2nd c. AD. Three Chinese mirrors of flat disk shape with the reverse side decorated with a relief arch ornamentation forming an octagon were found in Bashkiria in kurgans 3, 4 of Temyasovo group and in kurgan 3 of the 4th Komsomolsk group [Pshenichnyuk A.H., 1983: 124], they are dated to the turn of the 1st-2nd c. AD. The mirror from Lebedevka burial site in Western Kazakhstan belongs to the TLV mirror type and is dat-ed to the same period [Moshkova M.G., 1982: 82; Berlizov N.E., 1993: 30]. The Han mirrors belonging to different variants of the same type which was in wide use in China in the Western Han period were found in the burials of kur-gans 1, 10 of Kobyakovo burial site and in burial 1 of kurgan 10 in the Tanais necropolis [Guguev V.K., Treister M.Yu., 1995: 143-144]. Similar finds are known in the Kuban region. Like the mirrors from the South Cisurals burials, they are dated to the turn of the 1st-2nd c. AD. The researchers point at the fact that all three mirrors originating from the Lower Don region were found in the Tanais necropolis and in the neighboring necropolis of Kobyakovo settlement, thus, in their opinion, these mirrors could be brought to that region at the same time [*ibidem*: 147].

As of today, the finds of the Han mirrors in the Middle Asia, in the Ural, the Kama and the Volga regions and further in more than thirty locations, and the associated mapping of the finds allowed to reconstruct one of the directions of the Great Silk Road: from Fergana and Tian Shan (Talas valley and Ketmen-Tyube), via Tashkent oasis and the lower Syrdarya river to the South Cisurals, the Lower Volga region and further to Tanais for more than 3000 km [Zadneprov-sky Yu.A., 1998: 79-80].

This route served for delivery of metals, glass, Roman fabrics from the West and of decorations made of precious and semi-precious stones and silk fabrics from the East [Shilov V.P, 1983, p. 35]. There is no doubt that mirrors and silk reached the Ural, the Kama, the Volga regions and the Northern Black Sea region directly by the Northern Road [Gor-bunova I.G., 1992: 191-192]. We cannot deny completely that the nomads could receive some imported objects of Chi-nese origin as tribute or gifts or as a result of rampaging of the Middle Asian oases, taking into account the relations with the settled and agricultural peoples which were not always peaceful. It is not occasional that in additions to those items some other oriental imported goods were found in the rich graves of the Middle Sarmatian nobles.

The hypothesis of penetration of oriental goods, including those of Chinese origin, as a result of trade contacts on the Northern Road is supported by the finds of silk fabric fragments in the Late Sarmatian burial at Sovetskoe village (former Mariental) in the Lower Volga region [Rau P., 1927: 68].

Probably, along with fabrics and mirrors, this route was used for delivery of precious and semi-precious stones from India and Ceylon to the workshops of Chersonesos and Olbia which somehow catered the Aorsi who were potential customers and intermediaries. In the South Ural during excavations of Solonchanka I cemetery dated to the 5th– first half of the 6th c. AD there were discovered garnet inserts in a plate from a quiver; according to A.D. Tairov, the garnet was mined in India or Ceylon and then brought to Iran via an Indian trade center for semi-precious stones; the garnet was processed in Iran and inserted into the golden plate which decorated the quiver [Bushmakin A.F., Tairov A.D., 1999: 96].

Some researchers propose that, in addition to the finds of Chinese bronze mirrors, silk fabrics, Roman bronzeware, glassware and silverware, the existence of the Northern branch of the Great Silk Road is confirmed by a series of ancient coins and their imitations of diverse origins (both oriental and occidental) found in Uzbekistan, Georgia, Azerbaijan, the Northern Black Sea region and Ukraine, a part of which could reach these territories only by the northern route controlled by the Sarmatian tribal unions [Mielczarek M., 1997: 131-136].

In the opinion of N.E. Berlizov, the finds of generic oriental objects were made at locations spread mostly on the route which began in the Eastern Turkestan, passed through Fergana, along the Zeravshan, the Amudarya and the Uzboy rivers, further to the lower Bolshoy and Maly Uzen rivers, Samarskaya Luka and in the steppes of Trans-Volga till Volgograd, then the road crossed the Volga river, went down to the Don river, then across the Kuban region, the Eastern Trans-Kuban region arrived either in Sangar mountain pass or from the Lower Don region westwards to the Danube river to the north-eastern borders of the Roman Empire [Berlizov N.E., 1993: 33].

For transportation of the goods camels could be used, since a small quantity of their bones was found in Olbia, Panticapaeum and Phanagoria, but the majority thereof originates from the excavations of Tanais [Kropotkin V.V., 1964: 226]. Perhaps, the rare and expensive horses of a Middle Asian breed depicted, for instance, on the stela of Afenius, gravestones of Julius Patius and others in Bosporus, arrived in Bosporus from the Middle Asia together with the Sarmatian tribes which controlled this route [Desyatchikov M.Yu., 1972: 72-76].

The chronology of arrival of the main volume of oriental imported objects into the territories controlled by individual Sarmatian tribal unions is dated to the second half of the 1st c. BC – early 1st c. AD and the turn of the 1st-2nd c. AD.

A.S. Skripkin believes that, to a greater extent, "with the intermediation of the Sarmatians in the first centuries of our era the innovations of oriental origin reach the Central and Western Europe and integrate into the culture of the local peoples" [Skripkin A.S., 2000: 29].

Thus, both waves of oriental imports are quite correlated with the period of movement of Chinese caravans in 36–23 BC and in 74-122 AD and relate to the activities of Chinese mechants on this branch of the Great Silk Road [Berlizov N.E., 1993: 31-33].

But as we see it, the majority of Chinese merchants swapped the goods somewhere in the Middle Asian oases and did not move beyond that region. That is why we should not exaggerate the role of the Chinese merchants on the route or explain penetration of oriental imports to South Cisurals, the Lower Volga region and the Don region by the commercial activities of the Chinese [Bezrukov A.V., 2000: 151]. Besides, despite the change of the political and ethnical situation in the steppes among the tribes participating in the trade on the Silk Road, the commercial activity could decline and even be suspended, but on the whole, the trade communications stayed in use, maybe, not for their entire length, but on separate sections.

The archaeological materials of the Late Sarmatian period from the South Cisurals and North-Western Kazakhstan provide quite a reliable evidence of the route functioning during that period. The contents of Lebedevka burial site consisting of imported occidental and oriental articles: Asia Minor amphorae, beads, Roman enameled swivel fibulae, Khorezm pottery, Han mirrors etc. – show that the route with an exit to Tanais existed in the 2nd-3rd c. AD, and the cemetery is apparently a remnant of a large tribal union which controlled the caravan routes from the cities of Sogdiana via the Syrdarya river basin to the Northern Black Sea region crossing the Volga and reaching Tanais [Moshkova M.G., 1990: 37].

A similar combination of oriental and occidental articles is also characteristic for the hoard found in the south-western Kazakhstan on the east shore of Batyr lake which contained silk and products from the Black Sea region and the Caucasus (a chalcedony part of a finial, a golden cup which has analogies among the pottery from Kalinovka and Berezhnovka burials in the Volga region, as well as in Kertch and Myrmekion) [Skalon K.M., 1961: 116-124].

In this territory we need to mention the finds of sapphirine-chalcedony disks which were obviously used by the Late Sarmatians as finials of knives and daggers, while the concurrent chalcedony beads could be used for decoration of tassels and thongs [Kolobov A.V., Melnichuk A.F., Kulyabina N.V., 1999: 51-52]. Probably, the Sarmatians, and namely, the Aorsi had nomadic camps in summer in the Belaya river area and influenced the Ugric tribes of the Azelin and Mazunin cultures; thus, we can identify the routes of migration of the ancient Sarmatian tribes which remained the main intermediaries in spreading of the classical world influence in the remote peripheral lands [Melnichuk A.F., Vylegzhanina M.V., 2004: 80-81].

The presented materials, from our perspective, support the hypothesis of penetration of a significant part of imported articles of both oriental and occidental origin via the South Cisurals and the Lower Volga region. This is evidenced by the finds of finials made of chalcedony, paste, amber, glass, rock crystal and other materials widely distributed in Bosporus in the Late Sarmatian period and known in large numbers (compared to the neighboring regions) in the Ural and the Volga rivers region [Moshkova M.G., 1982: 81-83].

In the Early Medieval period the Byzantine chronicles mentioned a road which coincided with the itinerary of this route. In the middle of the 6th c. AD this road was used by a few embassy missions: Sogdian and Byzantine. Like in the previous period, the silk commerce held one of the leading positions in the trade and economic links between the Far East and the Central Asian countries and the Byzantine Empire. Ammianus Marcellinus writes that "they make sericum, formerly for the use of the nobility, but nowadays available even to the lowest without any distinction" [Amm. Marc., XXII, 15, 67].

The wide distribution of silk is confirmed by archeological data. In the 6th c. AD silk raising and weaving was developed in Sogd, and since the late 6th c. AD, and, as per some data, even earlier the Turkic rulers of Sogd started to search for sales markets for their silk weaving products [Ierusalimskaya A.A., 1967: 72]. Probably, that period saw the renewal of traffic on the route connecting the Middle Asia and Byzantium via the South Cisurals and the Lower Volga region, i.e., along the northern coast of the Caspian Sea.

In the first centuries of our era the trade route connecting the Northern Black Sea region via Tanais with the Volga, the Ural and the Kama regions remained in active use. From the Lower Don region and the Kuban region via the Volga-Don route the imported articles were brought either to the steppe interfluve area of the Volga and the Ural rivers or along the Volga route to the Middle Volga river region and further to the woody Kama region; this is evidenced by the finds of Roman bronzeware and provincial Roman fibulae of AVCISSA type. Obviously, Tanais received a large part of imported Roman articles from Panticapaeum and Phanagoria.

There also existed a steppe road which bypassed Tanais and ran from Pannonia along the Danubian trade route which was used for bringing some categories of Roman imported articles unknown in Bosporus, but found in Mesia, the Lower Danube region, in Olbia and in the interfluve area between the Volga and the Ural rivers. Thus, their distribution should be related to the regions of the Dnieper, the Azov Sea and the Don from where they reached the Volga region and Cisurals [Shelov D.B., 1965: 251-274; Shilov V.P., 1974: 60]. It is quite possible that one of the ways of penetration of imported objects was a more convenient route via the forest-steppe zone from the territory of the Middle Dnieper region via the Volga river to the Volga Luka in the shortest and most convenient route along the Desna and the Oka rivers, "always remaining within the familiar forest-steppe zone" [Shramm G., 1997: 90-91].

This hypothesis looks quite credible, considering the fact that the goods exchange between the nomads and the settled and agricultural peoples could occur in the forest-steppe belt which acted as a sort of a neutral zone. For instance, in the Early Iron Age the southern regions of the forest-steppe belt and the steppe Trans-Volga were populated by nomads – Sauromatian and Sarmatian tribes, and the woody Kama region was inhabited by Ananino tribes, while the major part of the forest-steppe territory was "neutral" because the Ananino tribes did not live there fearing the nomads, and for the nomads this land was not convenient for nomadic livestock raising [Vasiliev I.B., 1995: 215; Tairov A.D., 1995: 43].

So, in this chronological period the nations of the Ural and the Volga rivers region and Cisurals establish strong commercial contact with the ancient states of the South taking the most active part in the trade activities on the Northern branch of the Great Silk Road. This is evidenced by the finds of a significant number of imported objects of both occidental and oriental origin in the sepulchral complexes of the above chronological period.

As a result, we face a natural question: how can we explain presence of a quite significant number of imported objects in Cisurals, the Volga region and the Kama region both in terms of quantity and variety, and what could attract merchants to such remote regions making them travel for such long distances?

Probably, one of the reasons for presence of such diverse imports (in terms of composition and origin) is the geographical location of the region which occupies a border position on the frontier between Europe and Asia; this region was crossed by strategically (commercially) important routes which connected the largest states and empires of the West and the East in different epochs. The advantageous geographical position, functioning of large river and land trade communications in the course of a long chronological period mainly provided for that qualitative and quantitative diversity of imported objects found in the regions under review which represented samples of artisan production of the biggest states and production centers of the ancient times.

Thus, since the ancient times the South Ural region was one of the largest suppliers of copper ore and metals, both in the Ural region and in the Volga region [Kruglov E.A., 2002: 237], and copper ore was obviously used as an essential exchange item in the rudimentary process of intertribal trade which included long-distance journeys; it was an important factor for establishment of close ties of the region with the ancient states in the subsequent periods [Bezrukov A.V., 2001: 146-147].

In the Scythian period, as some researchers believe [Grakov B.N., 1947: 36; Smirnov K.F., 1964: 28], the main objective of the Scythian and Greek merchants was to obtain gold, copper and furs, since no other region could compel the Scythians to travel for such long distances. Besides, it looks quite possible that the furs were supplied from the Urals to the faraway lands; this can be proven by the finds made in the Semibratny IV kurgan and in the Artyukhov crypt [Kruglov E.A., 2002: 237].

The imported goods brought via the caravan route were apparently swapped for gold since its deposits and ancient mines were found in the South Ural region.

Like in the precedent period, ore and metals, copper and gold remain the main equivalents for the intertribal barter trade; furs become an important article of the local exports. In a later period one proper evidence shed light on the objectives of the risky long-distance breakthrough of the Goths to the Volga: among the northern peoples enslaved by Hermanaricus, according to Iordannis, there were "inhabitants of the Volga river banks" and "people who possessed gold", obviously, localized in the South Ural region. Apparently, only taking into account the exclusive value of gold and furs, we can understand why the Goths dared to undertake such a mission [Shramm G., 1997: 91]. It looks quite probable that the local tribal elite could arrange gold production locally, in the Ural mines [Sunchugashev Ya.I., 1975: 134].

In addition to gold and other precious metals, the Ural region avails of precious stones. Pliny writes that:

"…quamquam Scythcorum Aegyptiorumque duritia tanta est, ut non queant volnerari… Genera eorum duodecim: nobilissimi Scythici, ab ea gente, in qua reperiuntur, appellati." [Plin., 37, 64-65].

The smaragdi of Scythia and Egypt are so hard as to be unaffected by blows. There are twelve kinds of 'smaragdus'. The most notable is the Scythian, so called from the nation in whose territory it is found. Probably, some of the emeralds mentioned by Pliny originate from the Ural deposits, although, with one exception, the ancient stones did not have inclusions typical for the Ural deposits; it is also possible that in the ancient times some amethysts were extracted also in the Urals, in addition to other famous deposits [Treister M.Iu., 1993: 89; Ogden J., 1982: 94, 148: 105-106].

The intensity of such contacts between the southern countries and the northern regions along the Volga, the Kama and the Ural rivers for a long period is explained, as we see it, by a combination of a few circumstances which made a significant contribution in development of trade links of the region with the ancient states:

Like for the Greeks, the Romans [Pseudo-Arrianus, 1940: 264-281], the Scythians and later for the Goths, this route served as one of the sources of valuable furs; also for the ancient Chinese the northern route was the "fur road." In the Han empire there were especially appreciated sable furs from Yan, a country located in the South Ural region and in the Kama basin to the north of Yancai [Lubo-Lesnichenko E.I., 1994: 243].

So, it is not occasional that in the Han China there was adopted the name "fur road" which was used for bringing furs from the country of Yan located on the South Urals and in the Kama basin [Mamleeva L.A., 1999: 53-61]. In both Asian and European markets the most popular were sable furs, especially, of black colour; sable hunting was practiced mainly in the taiga areas between the Nothern Cisurals, the Ural and the Ob rivers.

According to G.A. Mukhamadiev, the information contained in the dynasty chronicle "Hou Hanshu" which said that "Yan territories are dependent on Kangju which pays in skins of micelike animals" – is the first written evidence of furs export (no later than the 3rd c. AD) from the Kama river region and Cisurals, which is also confirmed by finding of early forms of money [Mukhamadiev A. G, 1984: 219-222; *ibidem,* 1990: 26]. Makdisi (946/7 – ca. 1000) and other Arabic geographers and travelers of past times list furs of sables, ermines, ferrets, weasels, martens, foxes, beavers etc. among the goods arriving from Bulgaria [Leshchenko V.Yu., 1971: 253]. It is quite possible that a significant part of these furs originated from the regions of the woody Cisurals and the Kama region abundant in furs.

Thus, the exceptionally advantageous geographical and strategic position of the region, the richness of natural resources (copper, gold, and probably, precious stones), availability of valuable furs determined the interest of the ancients in this region, the activity and continuity of the trade routes in the course of a lengthy chronological period connecting the region with various parts of the ancient world.

CONCLUSION

For the conclusion we would like to highlight a few fundamental factors relating to the routes and ways of the ancient imports distribution in the peripheral lands, barder trade formats and main trends in the quantitative and qualitative composition of the imported products.

The nomadic people were in constant contact with the settled tribes (in the south – nomadic tribes and settled agricultural nations of the Middle Asia, in the north – Ananino tribes, in the west – settlements of the Scythians, the Meotes, the Greek cities of the Northern Black Sea region), and the particularities of their economy provide for continuous barter trade between them and for search of the most optimum and convenient format of barter.

Certainly, we cannot neglect the military and political history of the Sarmatian tribes and the associated numerous conquests, internal wars, participation of individual Sarmatian tribes as mercenaries in the armies of ancient cities and states, migrations and massive movements of certain population groups which were not linked to the nomadic routes. However, as we see it, the guiding role in the historical, cultural and economic processes belonged to the external and internal cultural, economic and political ties and interactions determined by the pastoral nomadic system of the people of the interfluve area between the Ural and the Volga rivers with all the relevant features.

A large part of objects of Roman origin, products of artisan workshops of the Greek colonies of the Northern Black Sea region, as well as the products from the Don and Kuban centers were found in the Lower and Middle Volga region where the major part of rich Middle Sarmatian burials were located, as well as in the Kama region. To a lesser extent, this is characteristic for the South Cisurals where almost no rich Middle Sarmatian graves were found due to the migration of the major part of nomads because of overpopulation of the region or worsening of climatic conditions. A significant number of them were discovered in the regions which were obviously used for overwintering of large Sauromatian and Sarmatian tribal unions (Orsk plateau, steppes of East-Kazakhstan region, eastern territories of Saratov, Volgograd and Astrakhan regions).

The topic about the routes which could connect the described regions with ancient cities and states in the south and with the tribes of the forest and forest-steppe areas in the north was profoundly analysed in the previous chapters of this paper. We just need to note that almost all of them were located along the valleys of the Volga, the Kama and the Urals basins and, thus, ran along the watersheds of their numerous tributaries.

In this regards, obviously, the route from the Kuban region to the Lower Don region (Tanais) and via the Volga-Don interfluve area to the Volga was the most convenient road from the Northern Black Sea region which crossed the Lower Volga region, the South Cisurals and then proceeded to the east. The road further crossed the rivers of the Bolshoy and the Maly Uzen, the Kushuma or the Chagana and headed to the basins of the Samara and the Bolshoy Irgim rivers, after that to the interfluve area of the headwaters of the Ural, the Belaya, the Sakmara, the Uy and on the watersheds of the Emba, the Or, the Ilek rivers across Ust-Urt plateau to reach the Middle Asia.

The composition of imported articles analysed in the research, as we can see, is quite diverse and includes both Italic and Byzantine articles and products of Roman provincial workshops, mainly, Gallic, including artisan products of the ancient cities of the Northern Black Sea region. The sets of imported articles discovered in Cisurals, the Volga region and the Kama region are, in general, typical for other barbarian territories (the Don region, the Kuban region), meaning that probably there were similar mechanisms of economic links and ways of ancient imports distribution among the tribes which occupied the steppe and forest-steppe belts of the territory of the Eastern Europe.

In terms of quantity, diverse decorations certainly prevail. Also popular are pottery and red-varnish ceramics, Italic and Gallic-Roman bronze utensils, Roman and Byzantine silver vessels, mirrors, coins, while there were almost no Italic ceramics, decorations, weapons or armature objects.

Relatively inexpensive imported objects which were brought to the Ural, the Volga and the Kama regions were obviously used by the local population in their daily life to satisfy their natural needs (beads, fibulae, ceramics, bronze utensils).

However, as we noted, the commercial interrelationships were not always explained by natural needs only; the imported articles made of precious metals were used mainly in the sphere related to satisfaction of the spiritual needs of the society, and sometimes the society gave greater attention to the symbolic parts of its life with its luxury, exotic and ritual actions. This hypothesis is confirmed by the numerous finds of diverse silver vessels of Byzantine origin discovered in Cisurals and in the Kama region.

The imported objects of both occidental and oriental origin shown in the paper belong to diverse categories and, in our view, evidence that the intertribal barter trade process involved the broad strata of the nomadic population of the region and individual tribes of the forest-steppe and forest areas. Large foreign trade operations some of which could be carried out with direct participation of foreign merchants without any intermediaries were controlled by the tribal nobles who ran all the international trade gaining the major part of the profit.

Meanwhile, still one of the most arguable topics is related to the ways of the objects coming into possession to the local tribes – which objects were obtained through direct barter trade and which ones were gained in the conflicts with the Roman squadrons on the borders of the Empire or as gifts for participation in the internal wars of the Bosporan tsars which is extremely difficult to identify. The prevaling idea is that there dominated multistage intertribal barter trade and acquisition of imported articles in transit trade, while the proper gifts and military trophies represent a smaller part. To a larger extent, this is relevant, in our opinion, for the previous highly-artistic silver and gold articles, weapons and expensive decorations.

More evidences to this hypothesis are expressed in the fact that some objects of Roman origin were found at significant distances from large trade routes, that is why it is quite doubtful that these objects related to the commerce which was carried out through the large international trade roads. At the same time, we cannot deny the possibility of penetration of imported articles in connection with movement of a part of the nomadic tribes to the north in the period of activization of migrations, commercial and cultural contacts in the age of the Great Transmigration of people. It is absolutely obvious that the Sarmatians could possess a part of imported objects as tribute imposed on trade caravans which were crossing their territory.

The peak inflow of imported goods of Roman origin was seen in the 1st–2nd c. AD – the period of the most active barter trade between the ancient cities and states, on the one hand, and the nations inhabiting the Ural, the Volga and the Kama regions, on the other hand, when the Roman empire and, therefore, the international trade were flourishing, and relative stability was observed in the steppes.

We can confidently state that the main trend in development of the Greek-Roman-Barbarian ties until the middle of the 3rd c. AD had a slow, but continuous growth. Possibly, direct relations were interrupted from time to time due to military conflicts, migrations of tribes and the general unstable political situation in the steppes, but as soon as the situation got stable, the trade routes resumed their functioning immediately, because, first of all, it was in the interests of the tribal elite.

The overall reduction of the imported goods inflow from the West is clearly registered immediately after the Gothic invasion in the 30–40-s of the 3rd c. AD and the destruction of Tanais when the city lost its dominant position in the trade with the barbarians, and since then other routes for purchasing of imported goods were in use, bypassing the Northern Black Sea region. The destruction of the ancient centers of the Northern Black Sea region and consequent pirate raids on the entire Black Sea coast led to a significant reduction of the international trade volume, although it did not cease completely, but switched to exchange in kind in a greater extent than in the 1st–2nd c. AD. Once of secondary importance, the trade roads from Gaul, Dacia and Pannonia started to play a more important role.

The almost complete cessation of inflow of imported articles to the Ural, the Volga and the Kama regions from the Roman Empire in the 4th c. AD had a few causes.

Firstly, the invasion of the Huns followed by destruction of the Bosporan cities which were traditional intermediaries in the trade between the Roman Empire and the barbarians – unprecedented in the history of the Greek colonies of the Northern Black Sea region.

Secondly, the overall socioeconomic and political crisis in the Roman Empire.

Thirdly, shifting of the centers of the large Sarmatian tribal unions to the west, therefore, the Volga region and Cisurals turned to quite remote peripheral lands.

Thus, the overall unstable situation in the steppes could not further contribute to development of the trade contracts. In a large extent, it can be explained by the fact that the Sarmatians as the stabilizing military and political power in the steppes of the Northern Black Sea region have lost their dominating position, except the strong Alanian tribal union, and the epoch of dominance of the Iranian-speaking nomads came to an end. That period saw the rise of the numerous Turkic peoples and tribes on the historical scene.

Summing up, we need to note that the general ethnical base (Srubnaya-Andronovo cultural and historical community) which provided for affinity in the material culture of the tribes of Cisurals and the Volga region, has initially ensured favorable opportunities for establishment of traditionally strong ties with the neighboring nomadic and settled agricultural centers which were later materialized by the Sarmatians. Absolutely, starting from the 4th–2nd c. BC and till the early medieval period the Sarmatians were actively promoting the development of those contacts with regard to barter trade relationships with the neighboring tribes and the largest states of the ancient times and the early medieval period.

ABBREVIATIONS

IK	– Археологические исследования Калмыкии (Arkheologicheskie issledovaniia Kalmykii. – *Archaelogical Studies of Kalmykia*) – Elista.
AIKSP	– Античная история и культура Средиземноморья и Причерноморья (Antichnaia istoriia i kultura Sredizemnomoria i Prichernomoria – *Ancient History of the Mediterrannean and the Black Sea Littoral*). – Leningrad.
AS	– Археологический сборник (Arkheologicheskii sbornik – *Archaeological Digest*). – Moscow.
AS	– Археологический съезд (Arkheologicheskii syezd – *Archaeological Convention*). – Moscow.
AO	– Археологические открытия (Arkheologicheskie otkrytiia – *Archaeological Discoveries*). – Moscow.
AEB	– Археология и этнография Башкирии (Arkheologiia i etnografiia Bashkirii – *Archaelogy and Ethnography of Bashkiria*). – Ufa.
AO U i P	– Археологические открытия Урала и Поволжья (Arkheologicheskie otkrytiia Urala i Povolzhia – *Archaelogical Discoveries of the Ural and the Volga Regions*).
AGSP	– Античные государства Северного Причерноморья (Antichnye gosudarstva Severnogo Prichernomoria – *Ancient States of the Northern Black Sea Region*). – Moscow, 1984
ASGE	– Археологический сборник Государственного Эрмитажа (Arkheologicheskii sbornik Gosudarstvennogo Ermitazha – Archaeological Digest of the State Hermitage Museum). – Leningrad.
BS	– Боспорский сборник (Bosporskii sbornik – *Bosporan Digest*. – Moscow.
VDI	– Вестник древней истории (Vestnik drevnei istorii – *Ancient History Bulletin*). – Moscow.
ZOAO	– Записки Одесского Археологического Общества (Zapiski Odesskogo Arkheologicheskogo Obshchestva – *Notes of Odessa Archaeological Society*).
ZOOID	– Записки Одесского общества истории древностей (Zapiski Odesskogo obshchestva istorii drevnostei – *Notes of Odessa Ancient History Society*).
IAK	– Известия Императорской Археологической Комиссии (Izvestiia Imperatorskoi Arkheologicheskoi Komissii – *News of Imperial Archaelogical Committee*). – St. Petersburg.
IAN KazSSR	– Известия Академии наук Казахской ССР (Izvestiia Akademii nauk Kazakhskoi SSR – *News of Academy of Science of Kazakh SSR*). – Almaty.
IGAIMK	– Известия Государственной Академии истории материальной культуры (Izvestiia Gosudarstvennoi Akademii istorii materialnoi kultury – *News of State Academy of Material Culture History*). – Moscow.
INVIK	– Известия Нижне-Волжского института краеведения (Izvestiia Nizhne-Volzhskogo instituta kraevedeniia – *News of Lower Volga Regional Ethnography Institute*). – Saratov.
IROMK	– Известия Ростовского областного музея краеведения (Izvestiia Rostowskogo oblastnogo muzeia kraevedeniia – *News of Rostov Regional Ethnography Museum*). – Rostov-na-Donu.

KSIA – Краткие сообщения Института Археологии АН СССР (Kratkie soobshcheniia Instituta Arkheologii AN SSSR – *Briefings of Archaeology Institute of USSR Academy of Sciences*). – Moscow.

KSIIMK – Краткие сообщения Института Археологии материальной культуры (Kratkie soobshchenia Instituta Arkheologii materialnoi kultury – *Briefings of Material Culture Archaelogy Institute*). – Moscow.

LOIA – Ленинградское отделение Института Археологии (Leningradskoe otdelenie Instituta Arkheologii – *Leningrad branch of Archaeology Institute*). – Leningrad.

MAR – Материалы по археологии России (Materialy po arkheologii Rossii – *Materials on Russian archaeology*). – St. Petersburg.

MAAE – Материалы Анапской археологической экспедиции (Materialy Anapskoi arkheologicheskoi ekspeditsii – *Materials of Anapa Archaeological Expedition*). – Krasnodar.

MAIET – Материалы по Археологии, Истории и Этнографии Тавриды (Materialy po Arkheologii, Istorii i Etnografii Tavridy – *Materials on Archaeology, History and Ethnography of Taurida*). – Simferopol.

MIA – Материалы и исследования по археологии СССР (Materialy i issledovaniia po arkheologii SSSR – *Materials and Research of USSR Archaeology*). – Moscow – Leningrad.

NIIIALIE – Научно-исследовательский институт языка, литературы, истории, этнографии (Nauchno-issledovatelskii institut iazyka, literatury, istorii, etnografii – *Scientific Research Institute of Linguistics, Literature, History, Ethnography*). – Saransk.

NE – Нумизматика и эпиграфика (Numizmatika i epigrafika – *Numismatics and Epigraphics*). – Moscow.

OAK – Отчет Археологической комиссии (Otchet Arkheologicheskoi komissii – *Report of Archaeological Committee*). – St. Petersburg.

PAV – Петербургский археологический вестник (Peterburgskii arkheologicheskii vestnik – *St. Petersburg Archaeological Bulletin*). – St. Petersburg.

PIFK – Проблемы истории, филологии и культуры (Problemy istorii, filologii, kul'tury – *Problems of History, Philology and Culture*), Moscow – Magnitogorsk.

RA – Российская археология (Rossiiskaia arkheologiia – *Russian Archaeology*), Moscow.

SA – Советская археология (Sovetskaia arkheologiia – *Soviet Archaeology*). – Moscow.

SAI – Свод археологических источников (Svod arkheologicheskikh istochnikov – *Collection of Archaeological Sources*). – Moscow.

SGMII – Сообщения Государственного музея изобразительных искусств им. А. С. Пушкина (Soobshcheniia Gosudarstvennogo muzeia izobrazitelnykh iskusstv im. A. S. Pushkina – *News of Pushkin National Artistic Museum*). – Moscow.

SGE – Сообщения Государственного Эрмитажа (Soobshcheniia Gosudarstvennogo Ermitazha – *News of State Hermitage Museum*). – Leningrad.

TGE – Труды Государственного Эрмитажа (Trudy Gosudarstvennogo Ermitazha – *Papers of State Hermitage Museum*). – Leningrad.

TR AS – Труды Археологических съездов (Trudy Arkheologicheskikh syezdov – *Papers of Archaeological Conventions*). – Moscow.

TR GIM – Труды Государственного Исторического Музея (Trudy Gosudarstvennogo Istoricheskogo Muzeia – *State Historical Museum Papers*). – Moscow.

Tr. SU – Труды Среднеазиатского государственного Университета (Trudy Sredneaziatskogo gosudarstvennogo Universiteta – *Papers of Middle Asian State University*). – Tashkent.

OIPKGE — Труды Отдела Истории Первобытной культуры Государственного Эрмитажа (Trudy Otdela Istorii Pervobytnoi kultury Gosudarstvennogo Ermitazha – *Papers of History Department of Primordial Culture Institute*). – Leningrad.

TSA RANION – Труды секции археологии Российской ассоциации научно-исследовательских институтов общественных наук (Trudy sektsii arkheologii Rossiiskoi assotsiatsii nauchno-issledovatelskikh institutov obshchestvennykh nauk – *Papers of Archaeological Section of Russian Association of Scientific Research Institutes for Social Sciences*).

ANRV — Aufstieg und Niedergang der romischen Welt. – Berlin.

ESA — Eurasia septentrionalis antique. – Helsinki.

RN — Revue Numismatique francaise.

REFERENCES

Herodotus, 1972. – Геродот. История в девяти книгах (Istoriia v deviati knigakh) / Translation and comments by G.A. Stratonovsky, chief editor S.L. Utchenko. – Moscow.

Justinian, 1984. – Дигесты Юстиниана. Избранные фрагменты (Digesty Iustiniana. Izbrannye fragmenty) / Translation and comments by I.S. Peretersky. – Moscow.

Diodorus of Sicily, 1774–1775. – Диодор Сицилийский: Историческая библиотека (Diodor Sitsiliiskii: Istoricheskaia biblioteka) / Translated from Greek by I. Alekseev. – St. Petersburg.

Marcellinus Ammianus, 1906–1908. – Марцеллин Аммиан. История (Istoriia) / Translated from Latin by Yu.S. Kulakovsky and A.Sonni, № 103. Kiev.

Pliny the Elder, 1946 – Плиний Старший. Естественная история: вопросы техники (Estestvennaia istoriia: voprosy tekhniki) // VDI, № 3.

Polybius, 1994–1995 – Полибий. Всеобщая история (Vseobshchaia istoriia) / Translated from Greek by F.G. Mishchenko. – St. Petersburg.

Pseudo-Arrianus, 1940 – Псевдо-Арриан. Плавание вокруг Эритрейского моря (Plavanie vokrug Eritreiskogo moria) // VDI, № 2.

Ptolemy Claudius, 1948. Географическое руководство (Geograficheskoe rukovodstvo) // VDI, № 2.

Strabo, 1994 – Страбон. География (Geografiia) / Translation, article and comments by G.A. Stratanovsky, chief editor S.L. Utchenko. – Moscow.

CYRILLIC BIBLIOGRAPHY

Abramzon M.G., Maslennikov A.A., 1999 – Абрамзон М.Г., Масленников А.А. Золотые монеты Феодосия II из Восточного Крыма (*Zolotye monety Feodosia II iz Vostochnogo Kryma*) // In: ВДИ (*VDI*). – № 4.

Akbulatov I.M., 1999 – Акбулатов И.М. Экономика ранних кочевников Южного Урала (*Ekonomika rannikh kochevnikov Yuzhnogo Urala*). – Ufa.

Akbulatov I.M., Obydennov M.F., 1984 – Акбулатов И.М., Обыденнов М.Ф. Погребения кочевников начала нашей эры из зоны Иштугановского водохранилища (*Pogrebeniia kochevnikov nachala nashei ery iz zony Ishtuganovskogo vodokhranilishcha*) // In: Памятники кочевников Южного Урала (*Pamiatniki kochevnikov Yuzhnogo Urala*). – Ufa.

Alekseeva E.M., 1982 – Алексеева Е.М. Античные бусы Северного Причерноморья (*Antichnye busy Severnogo Prichernomoria*) // In: SAI G1–12. – Moscow.

Alekseeva E.M., Arsenieva T.M., 1966 – Алексеева Е.М., Арсеньева Т.М. Стеклоделие Танаиса (*Steclodelie Tanaisa*) // In: SA. № 2.

Ambroz A.K., 1966 – Амброз А.К. Фибулы юга Европейской части СССР II в. до н.э. – IV вв. н.э. (*Fibuly yuga Evropeiskoi chasti SSSR II v. do n.e. – IV vv. n.e.*) // In: SAI. D1 – 30.

Anfimov N.V., 1951 – Анфимов Н.В. Меото-сарматский могильник (*Meoto-sarmatskii mogilnik*) // In: MIA, № 52.

Arakelian B.N., 1953 – Аракелян Б.Н. Значение раскопок в Гарни для изучения культуры Древней Армении (*Znachenie raskopok v Garni dlia izucheniia kultury Drevnei Armenii*) // In: VDI, № 3.

Akhmerov R.B., 1958 – Ахмеров Р.Б. Стеклянный сосуд из Уфимского погребения (*Stekliannyi sosud iz Ufimskogo pogrebeniia*) // SA. № 3.

Bagrikov G.I., Senigova T.M., 1968 – Багриков Г.И., Сенигова Т.М. Открытие гробниц в Западном Казахстане (II-IV и XIV вв.) (*Otkrytie grobnits v Zapadnom Kazakhstane (II-IV i XIV vv.)*) // In: Известия АН Казахской ССР (*Izvestiia AN Kazakhskoi SSR*). № 2.

Bader O.N., 1951 – Бадер О.Н. О восточном серебре и его использовании в древнем Прикамье (*O vostochnom serebre i ego ispolzovanii v drevnem Prikamie*) // In: На Западном Урале (*Na Zapadnom Urale*). №1.

Bader O.N., Smirnov A.P., 1954 – "Серебро Закамское" первых веков нашей эры (*"Serebro Zakamskoe" pervykh vekov nashei ery*) // TGE. №13.

Bank A.V., 1966 – Банк А.В. Византийское искусство в собраниях Советского Союза: Альбом. (*Vizantiiskoe iskusstvo v sobraniah Sovetskogo Soyuza: Albom)* – Leningrad.

Bezrukov A.V., 1999 – Безруков А.В. Римская бронзовая посуда на территории Урала, Поволжья и Прикамья (по материалам археологических комплексов I в. до н.э. – IV в. н.э.) *(Rimskaya bronzovaya posuda na territorii Urala, Povolzhya i Prikamya (po materialam arheologicheskih kompleksov I v. do n.e. – IV v. n.e.)*/ In: А.В. Безруков // Проблемы истории, филологии, культуры (*A.V. Bezrukov// Problemy istorii, filologii, kul'tury*), Magnitogorsk. Issue VIII.

Bezrukov A.V., 2000 – Безруков А.В. Сарматы Южного Приуралья и Нижнего Поволжья на Великом шелковом пути (*Sarmaty Yuzhnogo Priuralia i Nizhnego Povolzhya na Velikom shelkovom puti*)/ In: А.В. Безруков //Проблемы истории, филологии, культуры (*A.V. Bezrukov// Problemy istorii, filologii, kul'tury*), Magnitogorsk. Issue IX.

Bezrukov A.V., 2001 – Безруков А.В. Импортные изделия в археологических комплексах Урала и Прикамья второй половины I тыс. до н.э. – первые века н.э. (к проблеме развития обмена и торговли) *(Importnye izdelia v arheologicheskih kompleksah Urala i Prikamya vtoroi poloviny I tys. do n.e. – pervye veka n.e. (k probleme razvitiya obmena i torgovli)* / In: А.В. Безруков //Проблемы истории, филологии, культуры *(A.V. Bezrukov// Problemy istorii, filologii, kul'tury)*, Magnitogorsk. Issue XI.

Bezrukov A.V., 2003 – Безруков А.В. К вопросу о торговых коммуникациях в Южном Приуралье по данным письменных и археологических источников (VI-IV вв. до н.э.) *(K voprosu o torgovyh kommunikatsiyah v Yuzhnom Priuralie po dannym pismennyh i arheologicheskih istochnikov (VI-IV vv. do n.e.)/* In: А.В. Безруков //Проблемы истории, филологии, культуры *(A.V. Bezrukov// Problemy istorii, filologii, kul'tury)*, Magnitogorsk. Issue XIII.

Bezrukov A.V., 2005 – Безруков А.В. К вопросу о характере взаимоотношений кочевников Южного Приуралья и Ахеменидского Ирана в VI-IV вв. до н.э. *(K voprosu o haraktere vzaimootnoshenii kochevnikov Yuzhnogo Priuralya i Ahemenidskogo Irana v VI-IV vv. do n.e.)* / In: А.В. Безруков //Проблемы истории, филологии, культуры *(A.V. Bezrukov// Problemy istorii, filologii, kul'tury)*, Magnitogorsk. Issue XV.

Bezrukov A.V., 2008 – Безруков А.В. Торгово-экономические связи Волго-Камья по данным письменных и археологических источников (VI в. до н.э. – VII в. н.э.) *(Torgovo-ekonomicheskie svyazi Volgo-Kamya po dannym pismennyh i arheologicheskih istochnikov (VI v. do n.e. – VII v. n.e.)* / In: А.В. Безруков //Проблемы истории, филологии, культуры *(A.V. Bezrukov// Problemy istorii, filologii, kul'tury)*, Magnitogorsk, №1.

Bezrukov A.V., 2011 – Безруков А.В. Роль монеты в межплеменной торговле народов Волго-Камья *(Rol monety v mezhplemennoi torgovle narodov Volgo-Kamya)./* In: А.В. Безруков //Проблемы истории, филологии, культуры *(A.V. Bezrukov// Problemy istorii, filologii, kul'tury)*, Magnitogorsk, №1.

Berlizov N.E., 1993 – Берлизов Н.Е. Сарматы на Великом шелковом пути *(Sarmaty na Velikom shelkovom puti)* //In: Античная цивилизация и варварский мир: Материалы III-го археологического семинара Ч I. Новочеркасск, 1992 *(Antichnaia tsivilizatsiia i varvarskii mir: Materialy III-go arheologicheskogo seminara Ch. I. Novocherkassk, 1992)*. – Novocherkassk.

Berlizov N.E., 1996 – Берлизов Н.Е. К интерпретации ахеменидского импорта в сарматских курганах Южного Приуралья и Прикубанья *(K interpretatsii ahemenidskogo importa v sarmatskih kurganah Yuzhnogo Priuralya i Prikubanya)* // In: Мат-лы V-го археологического семинара *(Materialy V-go arheologicheskogo seminara)*. – Novocherkassk.

Berhin I.P., 1961 – Берхин И.П. О трех находках позднесарматского времени в Нижнем Поволжье *(O trekh nahodkakh pozdnesarmatskogo vremeni v Nizhnem Povolzhie)* // ASGE. № 2.

Bichurin N.Ia., 1950 – Бичурин Н.Я. Собрание сведений о народах, обитавших в Средней Азии в древние времена *(Sobranie svedenii o narodakh, obitavshikh v Srednei Azii v drevnie vremena)*. – Moscow – Leningrad.

Blavatskii V.D., 1953 – Блаватский В.Д. История античной расписной керамики *(Istoriia antichnoi raspisnoi keramiki)*. – Moscow.

Bongard-Levin G.M., Grantovskii E.A., 1983 – Бонгард-Левин Г.М., Грантовский Э.А. От Скифии до Индии *(Ot Skifii do Indii)* – Moscow.

Bondar N.N., 1955 – Бондарь Н.Н. Торговые сношения Ольвии со Скифией в VI-V вв. до н.э. *(Torgovye snosheniia Olvii so Skifiei v VI–V vv. do n.e.)* // SA. № XXIII.

Botalov S.G., 2009a – Боталов С.Г. Гунны и тюрки (историко-археологическая реконструкция) *(Gunny i tyurki (istoriko-arheologicheskaya rekonstruktsiya)* // South Ural State University. – Chelyabinsk.

Botalov S.G., 2009b – Боталов С.Г. Кочевая цивилизация Евразии *(Kochevaia tsivilizatsiia Evrasii)* // In: Проблемы истории, филологии, культуры *(Problemy istorii, filologii, kul'tury)*, № 3 – Moscow-Magnitogorsk-Novosibirsk.

Botalov S.G., Ivanov A.A., 2012 – Боталов С.Г., Иванов А.А. Новый комплекс кочевой аристократии гунно-сарматского времени в Южном Зауралье *(Novy kompleks kochevoi aristokratii gunno-sarmatskogo vremeni v Yuzhnom Zauralie)* // In: Проблемы истории, филологии, культуры *(Problemy istorii, filologii, kul'tury)*, № 4 – Moscow-Magnitogorsk-Novosibirsk.

Budanova V.P., 1982 – Буданова В.П. Передвижение готов в Северном Причерноморье и на Балканах в III в. н.э. (по данным письменных источников) (*Peredvizhenie gotov v Severnom Prichernomorie i na Balkanakh v III v. n.e. (po dannym pismennykh istochnikov)* // VDI. № 2.

Budanova V.P., 2009 – Буданова В.П. Время и безвременье Великого переселения народов (*Vremya i bezvremenie Velikogo pereselenia narodov*) // In: Темпоральность исторического пространства (*Temporalnost istoricheskogo prostranstva*) – Moscow.

Bulatova N.M.. Dvornichenko V.V., Zilivinskaia I.D., Fedorov-Davydov G.A., 1989 – Булатова Н.М.. Дворниченко В.В., Зиливинская И.Д., Федоров-Давыдов Г.А. Сокровища сарматских вождей и древние города Поволжья (*Sokrovishcha sarmatskikh vozhdei i drevnie goroda Povolzhia*). – Moscow.

Bushmakin A.F., Tairov A.D. – Бушмакин А.Ф., Таиров А.Д. Гранат из могильника Солончанка I (Южный Урал) (*Granat iz mogilnika Solonchanka I (Yuzhnyi Ural))* // In: Курган с "усами" Солончанка I. Сб. науч. тр. (*Kurgan s "usami" Solonchanka I. Sb. nauch. tr.*). – Chelyabinsk.

Vadetskaia E.V., 1992 – Вадецкая Э.Б. Античные бусы в Южной Сибири (*Antichnye busy v Iuzhnoi Sibiri*) // In: Античная цивилизация и варварский мир: Материалы III-го археологического семинара Ч I. Новочеркасск, 1992 ((*Antichnaia tsivilizatsiia i varvarskii mir: Materialy III-go arkheologicheskogo seminara Ch. I. Novocherkassk, 1992*). – Novocherkassk).

Vasqul I.O., 1987 – Васкул И.О. Курганное погребение эпохи переселения народов у с. Иб в Коми АССР (*Kurgannoe pogrebenie epohi pereseleniia narodov u s. Ib v Komi ASSR*) //In: Новые археологические исследования на территории Урала. Межвузовский сб. науч. тр. (*Novye arkheologicheskie issledovaniia na territorii Urala. Mezhvuzovskii sb. nauch. tr.)* – Ishevsk.

Vasiliev V.N., Saveliev N.S., 1983 – Васильев В.Н., Савельев Н.С. Ранние дахи Южного Урала по письменным источникам (*Rannie dahi Yuzhnogo Urala po pismennym istochnikam*). – Ufa.

Vasiliev I.B., 1973 – Сарматский курган на северо-западе Башкирии (*Sarmatskii kurgan na severo-zapade Bashkirii*) // In: SA. № 4.

Vasiliev I.B., 1995 – Васильев И.Б. К проблеме взаимодействия индо-европейских и финно-угорских культур (*K probleme vzaimodeistviia indo-evropeiskikh i finno-ugorskikh kultur*) //In: Древние культуры лесостепного Поволжья (к проблеме взаимодействия индо-европейских и финно-угорских культур) (*Drevnie kultury lesostepnogo Povolzhia (k probleme vzaimodeistviia indo-evropeiskikh i finno-ugorskikh kultur)*). – Samara.

Veselovskii N.I., 1902 – Веселовский Н.И. Отчет о раскопках в Кубанской области 1902 г. (*Otchet o raskopkakh v Kubanskoi oblasti 1902 g.*) // In: OAK.

Veselovskii N.I., 1905 – Веселовский Н.И. Курганы Кубанской области в период римского владычества на Северном Кавказе (*Kurgany Kubanskoi oblasti v period rimskogo vladychestva na Severnom Kavkaze)* // In: TR. XII AS.

Vinogradov Iu.G., 1994 – Виноградов Ю.Г. Очерк военно-политической истории сарматов в I в. н.э. (*Ocherk voenno-politicheskoi istorii sarmatov v I v. n.e.*) // In: VDI. № 2.

Volkovich A.M., 1941 – Волкович А.М. К южным связям Прикамья в последние века до нашей эры – первые века нашей эры (*K iuzhnym sviaziam Prikamia v poslednie veka do nashei ery – pervye veka nashei ery*) // In: TR OIPKGE.

Garustovich G.N., Ivanov G.A., 2010 – Гарустович Г.Н., Иванов Г.А. Уникальное произведение позднеантичной торевтики из погребения на Южном Урале (*Unikalnoe proizvedenie pozdneantichnoi torevtiki iz pogrebenia na Yuzhnom Urale*)//In: Проблемы истории, филологии, культуры (*Problemy istorii, filologii, kultury*), № 3 – Moscow-Magnitogorsk-Novosibirsk.

Goldina R.D., Kananin V.A., 1993 – Голдина Р.Д., Кананин В.А. Средневековые памятники верховьев Камы (*Srednevekovye pamiatniki verhoviev Kamy.*). – Izhevsk, 1993.

Goldina R.D., Vodolago N.V., Volkov S.R., 1994 – Голдина Р.Д., Водолаго Н.В., Волков С.Р. Исследования в Березовском районе Пермской области (*Issledovaniia v Berezovskom raione Permskoi oblasti*) // In: Археологические Открытия Урала и Поволжья (*Arkheologicheskie Otkrytiia Urala i Povolzhia*). – Syktyvkar.

Goldobin A.V., Lepihin A.N., Melnichuk A.F., 1991 – Голдобин А.В., Лепихин А.Н., Мельничук А.Ф. Исследование святилищ железного века в Пермском Прикамье (*Issledovanie sviatilishch zheleznogo veka v Permskom Prikamie*) // In: Археологические Открытия Урала и Поволжья (*Arkheologicheskie Otkrytiia Urala i Povolzhia*). – Izhevsk.

Grakov B.N., 1947 – Граков Б.Н. Чи мала Ольвія торговелні зносини с Поволжям і Приураллям в архаічну і классичну епохи (*Chi mala Olviia torgovelni znosini s Povolzhiam i Priuralliam v arhaichnu i classichnu epohi*) // In: Археологія (*Arkheologiia*). Kiev.

Guguev V.K., Treister M.Iu., 1995 – Гугуев В.К., Трейстер М.Ю. Ханьские зеркала и подражания им на территории юго-восточной Европы (*Hanskie zerkala i podrazhaniia im na territorii iugo-vostochnoi Evropy*) // In: RA. № 3.

Gurevich A.Ya., 1984 – Гуревич А. Я. Категории средневековой культуры. (*Kategorii srednevekovoy* kultury), 2nd edition. – Moscow.

Gushchina I.I., 1971 – Гущина И.И. О сосудах в Юго-Западном Крыму (*O sosudakh v Iugo-Zapadnom Krymu*) // In: SA. № 1.

Gushchina I.I., Moshkova M.G., 1990 – Гущина И.И., Мошкова М.Г. Курганы у с. Харьковка в Заволжье (раскопки Б.Н. Гракова и П.С. Рыкова в 1925, 1926 гг.) (*Kurgany u s. Harkovka v Zavolzhie (raskopki B.N. Grakova i P.S. Rykova v 1925, 1926 gg.*)) // In: Проблемы скифо-сарматской археологии (*Problemy skifo-sarmatskoi arkheologii*). – Moscow.

Gushchina I.I., Moshkova M.G., 1999 – Гущина И.И., Мошкова М.Г. Раскопки Б.Н. Гракова в Заволжье у сел Блюменфельд и Кано в 1925 г. (*Raskopki B.N. Grakova v Zavolzhie u sel Bliumenfeld i Kano v 1925 g.*) // In: Евразийские древности. 100 лет Б.Н. Гракову: архивные материалы, публикации, статьи (*Evraziiskie drevnosti. 100*

Darkevich V.P., 1976 – Даркевич В.П. Художественный металл Востока (*Hudozhestvennyi metall Vostoka*). – Moscow.

Desiatchikov Iu.M., 1972 – Десятчиков Ю.М. Катафрактарий на надгробии Афения (*Katafraktarii na nadgrobii Afeniia*) // In: SA. № 4.

Dudarev S.L., Fomenko V.A., 1996 – Дударев С.Л., Фоменко В.А. Новые данные о связях Центрального Предкавказья с Поволжьем в эпоху раннего железа (*Novye dannye o sviaziakh Centralnogo Predkavkazia s Povolzhiem v epohu rannego zheleza*). – Armavir.

Elnitskii L.A., 1961 – Ельницкий Л.А. Знания древних о северных странах (*Znaniia drevnikh o severnykh stranakh*). – Moscow.

Elnitskii L.A., 1970 – Ельницкий Л.А. Скифские легенды как культурно-исторический материал (*Skifskie legendy kak kulturno-istoricheskii material*) // In: SA. № 2.

Zhelezchikov V.F., 1988 – Железчиков Б.Ф. Степи Восточной Евразии в VI-II вв. до н.э. (*Stepi Vostochnoi Evrazii v VI-II vv. do n.e.*) // In: Проблемы скифо-сарматской археологии и истории (*Problemy skifo-sarmatskoi arkheologii i istorii*). Azov.

Zhelezchikov V.F., Piatykh G.G., 1981 – Среднесарматские погребения I Сорочинского могильника (Оренбургская обл.) (*Srednesarmatskie pogrebeniia I Sorochinskogo mogilnika (Orenburgskaia obl.)*) // In: SA. № 2.

Zadneprovskii Iu.A., 1960 – Заднепровский Ю.А. Археологические памятники южных районов Ошской области (*Arkheologicheskie pamiatniki iuzhnykh raionov Oshskoi oblasti*). – Frunze.

Zadneprovskii Iu.A., 1998 – Заднепровский Ю.А. Древние номады Центральной Азии (*Drevnie nomady Centralnoi Azii*) // In: Степи Восточной Европы во взаимосвязи Востока и Запада в Средневековье. Тезисы докладов.

Донецк, 1992 *(Stepi Vostochnoi Evropy vo vzaimosviazi Vostoka i Zapada v Srednevekovie. Tezisy dokladov. Donetsk, 1992.)*. – St. Petersburg.

Zaikovskii B.V., 1926 – Зайковский Б.В. Из монетной летописи Нижне-Волжского края (*Iz monetnoi letopisi Nizhne-Volzhskogo kraia*) //In: Труды Нижне-Волжского областного научного общества краеведения. Вып. 35, ч. 1 (*Trudy Nizhne-Volzhskogo oblastnogo nauchnogo obshchestva kraevedeniia. Vyp. 35, ch. 1*) – Saratov.

Zasetskaia I.P., 1979 – Засецкая И.П. Савроматские и сарматские погребения Никольского могильника в Нижнем Поволжье (*Savromatskie i sarmatskie pogrebeniia Nikolskogo mogilnika v Nizhnem Povolzhie*) // In: TGE. XX.

Zasetskaia I.P., 1994 – Засецкая И.П. Культура кочевников южнорусских степей в гуннскую эпоху (конец IV – V вв.) (*Kultura kochevnikov iuzhnorusskikh stepei v gunnskuiu epohu (konets IV – V vv.)*). – St. Petersburg.

Zaharov A.A., 1928 – Захаров А.А. Геммы и античные перстни Государственного исторического Музея (*Gemmy i antichnye perstny Gosudarstvennogo istoricheskogo Muzeia*) // In: TSA RANION. III.

Zbrueva A.V., 1946 – Збруева А.В. Древности Урала и Прикамья (*Drevnosti Urala i Prikamia*) // In: VDI. № 3.

Zeimal E.V., 1962 – Зеймаль Е.В. Клад римских монет из Таджикистана (*Klad rimskikh monet iz Tadzhikistana*) // In: NE. III.

Zograf A.N., 1951 – Зограф А.Н. Античные монеты (*Antichnye monety*) // In: MIA. № 15.

Zubar V.M., 1982 – Зубарь В.М. Некрополь Херсонеса Таврического I-IV вв. н.э. (*Nekropol Khersonesa Tavricheskogo I-IV vv. n.e.*) – Kiev/*et B.N. Grakovu: arhivnye materialy, publikatsii, statii*). – Moscow.

Ivanov A.Iu., Myshkin V.N., 1991 – Иванов А.Ю., Мышкин В.Н. Раскопки курганного могильника у с. Политотдельское в Волгоградской области (*Raskopki kurgannogo mogilnika u s. Politotdelskoe v Volgogradskoi oblasti*) // In: Археологические открытия Урала и Поволжья (*Arkheologicheskie otkrytiia Urala i Povolzhia*). – Izhevsk.

Ivanchik A.I., 1987 – Иванчик А.И. О киммерийцах Аристея Проконесского (*O kimmeriitsakh Aristeia Prokonesskogo*) // In: Античная Балканистика (*Antichnaia Balkanistika*). – Moscow.

Ierusalimskaia A.A., 1967 – Иерусалимская А.А. О северокавказском "шелковом пути" в раннем средневековье *(O severokavkazskom "shelkovom puti" v rannem srednevekovie)* // In: SA. № 2.

Iessen A.A., 1952 – Иессен А.А. Ранние связи Приуралья с Ираном (*Rannie sviazi Priuralia s Iranom*) // In: SA. XVI.

Kazamanova L.N., 1957 – Казаманова Л.Н. Бартымский клад византийских серебряных монет VII века (*Bartymskii klad vizantiiskikh serebrianykh monet VII veka*) // In: Tr. GIM. XXVI.

Knipovich T.N., 1941 - Книпович Т.Н. Некрополь на территории Ольвии (*Nekropol na territorii Olvii*) // KSIIMK. X. – M-L.

Knipovich T.N., 1955 – Книпович Т.Н. Художественная керамика в городах Северного Причерноморья (*Hudozhestvennaia keramika v gorodakh Severnogo Prichernomoria*) // In: Античные города Северного Причерноморья. Очерки истории и культуры (*Antichnye goroda Severnogo Prichernomoria. Ocherki istorii i kultury*). – Moscow – Leningrad. I.

Kolobov A.V., 2000 – Колобов А.В. Династическая пропаганда на знаменах и боевых наградах римских легионов (первый век империи) (*Dinasticheskaia propaganda na zmanenah i boevyh nagradah rimskih legionov (perviy vek imperii)*) //In: Проблемы истории, филологии, культуры VIII (*Problemy istorii, filologii, kultury VIII*)

Kolobov A.V., Melnichuk A.F., Kulyabina N.V., 1999 – Колобов А.В., Мельничук А.Ф., Кулябина Н.В. Римская фалера из Пермского Приуралья (*Rimskaya falera is Permskogo Priuralya*) (4653)// In: ВДИ (*VDI*). № 1

Kopylov V.V., 1994 – Копылов В.В. О транспортных сухопутных путях, проходивших через дельту Дона в скифское время (*O transportnykh suhoputnykh putiakh, prohodivshikh cherez deltu Dona v skifskoe vremia*) //

In: Проблемы скифо-сарматской археологии Северного Причерноморья. Тезисы докладов международной конференции, посвященной 95-летию со дня рождения проф. Б.Н. Гракова. Запорожье, 1994 (*Problemy skifo-sarmatskoi arkheologii Severnogo Prichernomoria. Tezisy dokladov mezhdunarodnoi konferentsii, posviashchennoi 95-letiiu so dnia rozhdeniia prof. B.N. Grakova. Zaporozhie, 1994*). – Zaporozhie.

Kosianenko V.M., Maksimenko V.E., 1989 – Косяненко В.М., Максименко В.Е. Комплекс вещей из сарматского погребения у хут.Виноградный на Нижнем Дону (*Kompleks veshchei iz sarmatskogo pogrebeniia u hut.Vinogradnyi na Nizhnem Donu*) // In: SA. № 1.

Krivtsova – Grakova O.A., 1955 – Кривцова – Гракова О.А. Степное Поволжье и Причерноморье (*Stepnoe Povolzhie i Prichernomorie*) // In: MIA. № 46.

Kropotkin V.V., 1961 – Кропоткин В.В. Клады римских монет на территории СССР (*Klady rimskikh monet na territorii SSSR*) // In: SAI. G4 – 4. Moscow.

Kropotkin V.V., 1962 – Кропоткин В.В. Клады византийских монет на территории СССР (*Klady vizantiiskikh monet na territorii SSSR*) // In: SAI E4 – 4. Moscow.

Kropotkin V.V., 1964 – Кропоткин В.В. Караванные пути в Восточной Европе (*Karavannye puti v Vostochnoi Evrope*) // In: Кавказ и Восточная Европа в древности (*Kavkaz i Vostochnaia Evropa v drevnosti*). Moscow.

Kropotkin V.V., 1967 – Кропоткин В.В. Экономические связи Восточной Европы в I тыс. н.э. (*Ekonomicheskie sviazi Vostochnoi Evropy v I tys. n.e.*). – Moscow.

Kropotkin V.V., 1969 – Кропоткин В.В. Римские импорты из Андреевского кургана в Мордовской АССР (*Rimskie importy iz Andreevskogo kurgana v Mordovskoi ASSR*) // In: KSIA. №119.

Kropotkin V.V., 1970 – Кропоткин В.В. Римские импортные изделия в Восточной Европе (II в. до н.э. – V в. н.э. (*Rimskie importnye izdeliia v Vostochnoi Evrope (II v. do n.e. – V v. n.e.)* // In: SAI. D1 – 27. – Moscow.

Kropotkin V.V., 1984 – Кропоткин В.В. О некоторых находках римских монет в Среднем Поволжье и Прикамье (*O nekotorykh nahodkakh rimskikh monet v Srednem Povolzhie i Prikamie*) // In: Древности Евразии в скифо-сарматское время (*Drevnosti Evrazii v skifo-sarmatskoe vremia*). – Moscow.

Kropotkin V.V., Obydennov M.F., 1985 – Кропоткин В.В, Обыденнов М.Ф. Находка античных монет в погребении кочевника на Южном Урале (*Nahodka antichnykh monet v pogrebenii kochevnika na Yuzhnom Urale*) // In: SA. № 2.

Kruglikova I.T., Tsvetaeva G.A., 1963 – Кругликова И.Т., Цветаева Г.А. Раскопки в Анапе (*Raskopki v Anape*) // In: KSIA. №95.

Kruglov E.A., 2002 – Круглов Е.А. К вопросу об уральском экспорте на Боспоре (*K voprosu ob uralskom eksporte na Bospore*) // In: Боспорский феномен: погребальные памятники и святилища. Материалы международной научной конференции. (*Bosporskii fenomen: pogrebalnye pamiatniki i sviatilishcha. Materialy mezhdunarodnoi nauchnoi konferentsii.*) – St. Petersburg.

Kuznetsova T.M., 1990 – Кузнецова Т.М. Торговые или священные пути греков? (*Torgovye ili sviashchennye puti grekov?*)// In: Проблемы скифо-сарматской археологии (*Problemy skifo-sarmatskoi arkheologii*). – Moscow.

Kuznetsova T.M., 1991 – Кузнецова Т.М. Этюды по истории Скифии *(Etiudy po istorii Skifii)*. Moscow.

Kuznetsova T.M., 2001 – Кузнецова Т.М. Все зеркала, зеркала... (*Vse zerkala, zerkala...*) // In: Материалы по археологии Волго-Донских степей. Сборник научных статей. Вып. 1. (*Materialy po arkheologii Volgo-Donskikh stepei. Sbornik nauchnykh statei. Vyp. 1.*) – Volgograd.

Kuzminykh S.V., 1983 – Кузьминых С.В. Металлургия Волго-Камья в раннем железном веке (*Metallurgiia Volgo-Kamia v rannem zheleznom veke*). – Moscow.

Kuklina I.V., 1971 – Куклина И.В. Античная литературная традиция о древних племенах на территории СССР (*Antichnaia literaturnaia traditaiia o drevnikh plemenakh na territorii SSSR*). Moscow.

Kuftin V.A., 1949 – Куфтин Б.А. Материалы к археологии Колхиды (*Materialy k arkheologii Kolhidy*) // Tbilisi.

Lebedeva E.Iu., 1990 – Лебедева Е.Ю. Экономические связи Римской империи с Индией (*Ekonomicheskie sviazi Rimskoi imperii s Indiei*) – Moscow.

Levchenko M.V., 1940 – Левченко М.В. История Византии (*Istoriia Vizantii*). – Moscow – Leningrad.

Leshchenko V.Iu., 1971 – Лещенко В.Ю. Восточные клады на Урале в VII-XIII вв. (по находкам художественной утвари) (*Vostochnye klady na Urale v VII-XIII vv. (po nahodkam hudozhestvennoi utvari)*) – Leningrad.

Leshchenko V.Iu., 1976 – Лещенко В.Ю. Использование восточного серебра на Урале (*Ispolzovanie vostochnogo serebra na Urale*) // In: Даркевич В.П. Художественный металл Востока (*Darkevich V.P. Hudozhestvennyi metall Vostoka*). – Moscow.

Litvinskii B.A., 1973 – Литвинский Б.А. Украшения из могильников Западной Ферганы (*Ukrasheniia iz mogilnikov Zapadnoi Fergany*). – Moscow.

Livshits V.A., Lukonin V.G., 1964 – Лившиц В.А., Луконин В.Г., Среднеперсидские и согдийские надписи на произведениях торевтики (*Srednepersidskie i sogdiiskie nadpisi na proizvedeniah torevtiki*) // In: ВДИ (*VDI*) № 3.

Lopatin V.A., 1997 – Лопатин В.А. Позднесарматское захоронение из степного Заволжья (*Pozdnesarmatskoe zahoronenie iz stepnogo Zavolzhia*) // In: Археологическое наследие Саратовского края. Охрана и исследования в 1996 году. Вып 2 (*Arkheologicheskoe nasledie Saratovskogo kraia. Okhrana i issledovaniia v 1996 godu. Vyp 2*). – Saratov.

Lubo-Lesnichenko E.I., 1988 – Лубо-Лесниченко Е.И. "Великий шелковый путь". Восточный Туркестан в древности и раннем средневековье (*"Velikii shelkovyi put". Vostochnyi Turkestan v drevnosti i rannem srednevekovie*). – Moscow.

Lubo-Lesnichenko E.I., 1994 – Лубо-Лесниченко Е.И. Китай на Шелковом пути. Шелк и внешние связи древнего и раннесредневекового Китая (*Kitai na Shelkovom puti. Shelk i vneshnie sviazi drevnego i rannesrednevekovogo Kitaia*). – Moscow.

Lukiashko S.I., 1984 – Лукьяшко С.И. О караванной торговле аорсов (*O karavannoi torgovle aorsov*) // In: Древности Евразии в скифо-сарматское время (*Drevnosti Evrazii v skifo-sarmatskoe vremia*). – Moscow.

Lunin B.V., 1940 – Лунин Б.В. Серебряная чаша с рельефными изображениями и греческой надписью и стеклянная чаша из находок у ст. Даховской (*Serebrianaia chasha s reliefnymi izobrazheniiami i grecheskoi nadpisiiu i stekliannaia chasha iz nahodok u st. Dahovskoi*) // In: IROMK. II.

Lvova Z.A., Marshak B.I., 1998 – Львова З.А., Маршак Б.И. Последнее пополнение Перещепинского сокровища его владельцем (*Poslednee popolnenie Pereshchepinskogo sokrovishcha ego vladeltsem*) // In: MAIET. VI.

Magomedov M.G., 1983 – Магомедов М. Г. Образование Хазарского каганата (*Obrazovanie Khazarskogo kaganata*). – Moscow.

Maksimov E.K., 1957 – Максимов Е.К. Сарматское погребение у с. Большая Дмитриевка Саратовской области (*Sarmatskoe pogrebenie u s. Bolshaia Dmitrievka Saratovskoi`oblasti*) // In: SA. № 4.

Maksimov E.K., 1969 – Максимов Е.К. Ново-Липовские курганы (*Novo-Lipovskie kurgany*) // In: AO.

Manandian Ia.A., 1954 – Манандян Я.А. О торговле и городах Армении в связи с мировой торговлей древних времен V в. до н.э. – XV в. н.э. (*O torgovle i gorodakh Armenii v sviazi s mirovoi torgovlei drevnikh vremen V v. do n.e. – XV v. n.e.*) – Erevan.

Markovin V.I., 1965 – Марковин В.И. Сердолик – "камень счастья" (*Serdolik – "kamen schastia"*) // In: MIA. № 130.

Masson M.E., 1951 – Массон М.Е. К вопросу о взаимоотношениях Византии и Средней Азии по данным нумизматики (*K voprosu o vzaimootnosheniiakh Vizantii i Srednei Azii po dannym numizmatiki*) // In: Tr. SU. XXIII, book 4.

Matveev A.V., Matveeva N.P., 1985 – Матвеев А.В., Матвеева Н.П. Саргатский могильник у д. Тютрина: По раскопкам 1981 г. (*Sargatsky mogilnik u d. Tyutrina: Po raskopkam 1981 g.*)// КСИА. Issue 184.

Machinskii D.A., 1971 – Мачинский Д.А. О времени первого активного выступления сарматов в Приднепровье по свидетельствам античных письменных источников (*O vremeni pervogo aktivnogo vystupleniia sarmatov v Pridneprovie po svidetelstvam antichnykh pismennykh istochnikov*) //In: ASGE. № 13.

Machinskii D.A., 1974 – Мачинский Д.А. Некоторые проблемы этногеографии восточноевропейских степей во II в. до н.э. (*Nekotorye problemy etnogeografii vostochnoevropeiskikh stepei vo II v. do n.e.*) // In: ASGE.

Mamleeva L.A., 1999 – Мамлеева Л.А. Становление Великого шелкового пути в системе трансцивилизационного взаимодействия народов Евразии (Stanovlenie Velokogo shelkovogo puti v sisteme transtsivilizatsionnogo vzaimodeistviya narodov Evrazii) // Vita Antiqua, № 2.

Matsulevich L.A., 1940 – Мацулевич Л.А. Византийский антик в Прикамье (*Vizantiiskii antik v Prikamie*) // In: MIA. № 1.

Melnichuk A.F., Vylegzhanina M.V., 2004 – Мельничук А.Ф. Вылегжанина М.В. Изделия из халцедона-сапфирина в восточной Европе как индикатор культурных связей населения Прикамья с сарматским миром в первой половине I тыс. н.э. (*Izdelia iz haltsedona-sapfirina v vostochnoy Evrope kak indicator kulturnih svyazei naselenia Prikamia s sarmatskim mirom v pervoi polovine I tys. n.e.*)// In: Новый Гиперборей. Межвуз. сб. науч. тр. (*Novy Giperborey. Mezhvuz. sb. nauch. tr.*) – Perm.

Meliukova A.I., 1962 – Мелюкова А.И. Сарматское погребение из кургана у с.Олонешты (*Sarmatskoe pogrebenie iz kurgana u s.Oloneshty*) // In: SA. № 1.

Meshcheriakov D.V., 1997 – Мещеряков Д.В. Впускные погребения сарматской культуры в курганах на р. Илек (*Vpusknye pogrebeniia sarmatskoi kultury v kurganakh na r.Ilek*) // In: Археологические памятники Оренбуржья (*Arkheologicheskie pamiatniki Orenburzhia*). – Orenburg.

Mordvintseva V.I., 1993 – Мордвинцева В.И. Среднесарматские погребения с краснолаковой керамикой (*Srednesarmatskie pogrebeniia s krasnolakovoi keramikoi*) // In: Древности Волго-Донских степей (*Drevnosti Volgo-Donskikh stepei*). 1993. № 3.

Mordvintseva V.I., Sergatskov I.V., 1995 – Мордвинцева В.И., Сергацков И.В. Богатое сарматское погребение у ст. Бердия (*Bogatoe sarmatskoe pogrebenie u st. Berdiia*) // In: RA. № 1.

Morozov V.Iu., 1996 – Морозов В.Ю. Пути проникновения сасанидских монет и художественных изделий в Поволжье и Прикамье (*Puti proniknoveniia sasanidskikh monet i hudozhestvennykh izdelii v Povolzhie i Prikamie*) // In: Евразийские степи в I тыс. н.э. (*Evraziiskie stepi v I tys. n.e.*) – Samara.

Moshkova M.G., 1956 – Мошкова М.Г. Производство и основной импорт у сарматов Нижнего Поволжья (*Proizvodstvo i osnovnoi import u sarmatov Nizhnego Povolzhia*) – Moscow.

Moshkova M.G., 1978 – Мошкова М.Г. Два позднесарматских погребения в группе "Четыре брата" на Нижнем Дону (*Dva pozdnesarmatskikh pogrebeniia v gruppe "Chetyre brata" na Nizhnem Donu*) // In: Вопросы древней и средневековой археологии Восточной Европы (*Voprosy drevnei i srednevekovoi arkheologii Vostochnoi Evropy*). – Moscow.

Moshkova M.G., 1981 – Мошкова М.Г. Комплекс находок с ритоном из Уральской области (*Kompleks nahodok s ritonom iz Uralskoi oblasti*) // In: SA. № 2.

Moshkova M.G., 1982 – Мошкова М.Г. Позднесарматские погребения Лебедевского могильника (*Pozdnesarmatskie pogrebeniia Lebedevskogo mogilnika*) //In: KSIA. №170.

Moshkova M.G., 1984 – Мошкова М.Г. Культовые сооружения Лебедевского могильника (*Kultovye sooruzheniia Lebedevskogo mogilnika*) // In: Древности Евразии в скифо-сарматское время (*Drevnosti Evrazii v skifo-sarmatskoe vremia*). – Moscow.

Moshkova M.G., 1989 – Мошкова М.Г. Краткий очерк истории савромато-сарматских племен (*Kratkii ocherk istorii savromato-sarmatskikh plemen*) // In: Археология СССР. Степи Евразии в скифо-сарматское время (*Arkheologiia SSSR. Stepi Evrazii v skifo-sarmatskoe vremia*). – Moscow.

Moshkova M.G., 1990 – Мошкова М.Г. Лебедевкий могильник и Великий Шелковый путь (*Lebedevsky mogilnik i Veliky Shelkovy put*) // In: Формирование и развитие трасс Великового шелкового пути в Центральной Азии (*Formirovanie i razvitie trass Velikogo Shelkovogo puti v Tsentralnoi Azii*), – Tashkent.

Moshkova M.G., 2000 – Мошкова М.Г. Фибулы из позднесарматских погребений Южного Приуралья: вопросы хронологии и производства (*Fibuly iz pozdnesarmatskih pogrebenii Yuzhnogo Priuralya: voprosy hronologii i proizvodstva*). //In: Нижневолжский археологический вестник (*Nizhnevolzhskiy arheologicheskiy vestnik*). Issue 3. – Volgograd.

Moshkova M.G., 2004 – Мошкова М.Г. Среднесарматские и позднесарматские памятники на территории Южного Прираля (*Srednesarmatskie i pozdnesarmatskie pamiatniki na territorii Yuzhnogo Priralia*). // In: Сарматские культуры Евразии: проблемы региональной хронологии. Доклады к 5-ой международной конференции "Проблемы сарматской археологии и истории" (*Sarmatskie kultury Evrazii: problemy regionalnoi khronologii. Doklady k 5-oi mezhdunarodnoi konferentsii "Problemy sarmatskoi arkheologii i istorii")* – Krasnodar

Muhamadiev A.G., 1984 – Мухамадиев А.Г. Бронзовые слитки – первые деньги Поволжья и Приуралья (*Bronzovye slitki – pervye dengi Povolzhia i Priuralia*) // In: SA. № 3.

Muhamadiev A.G., 1990 – Мухамадиев А.Г. Древние монеты Поволжья (*Drevnie monety Povolzhia*). – Kazan.

Myskov E.P., 1992 – Мыськов Е.П. Сарматские погребения из курганов у Волжского и Киляковки *(Sarmatskie pogrebeniia iz kurganov u Volzhskogo i Kiliakovki)* // In: Древности Волго-Донских степей (*Drevnosti Volgo-Donskikh stepei*). №2.

Nudelman A.A., 1982 – Нудельман А.А. Римская монета в междуречье Днестра, Прута и Дуная (*Rimskaia moneta v mezhdurechie Dnestra, Pruta i Dunaia*) // In: Нумизматика Античного Причерноморья (*Numizmatika Antichnogo Prichernomoria*). – Kiev.

Obelchenko O.V., 1992 – Обельченко О.В. Культура античного Согда (*Kultura antichnogo Sogda*). – Moscow.

Olgovskii S.Ia., 1982 – Ольговский С.Я. Цветная металлообработка в греческих городах Северо-Западного Причерноморья (*Tsvetnaia metalloobrabotka v grecheskikh gorodakh Severo-Zapadnogo Prichernomoria*). – Moscow.

Orbeli I.A., Trever K.V., 1935 – Орбели И.А., Тревер К.В. Сасанидский металл (*Sasanidskii metall*). – Leningrad.

Pigulevskaia N., 1951 – Пигулевская Н. Византия на путях в Индию. Из истории торговли Византии с Востоком в IV-VI вв. (*Vizantiia na putiakh v Indiiu. Iz istorii torgovli Vizantii s Vostokom v IV-VI vv.*) – Moscow – Leningrad.

Pletneva S.A., 1982 – Плетнева С.А. Кочевники Средневековья. Поиски исторических закономерностей (*Kochevniki Srednevekovia. Poiski istoricheskikh zakonomernostei*). – Moscow.

Pletneva S.A., 1991 – Плетнева С.А. Отношения восточно-европейских кочевников с Византией и археологические источники (*Otnosheniia vostochno-evropeiskikh kochevnikov s Vizantiei i arkheologicheskie istochniki*) // In: SA. № 3.

Pogrebova I.N., 1951 – Погребова И.Н. Позднесарматские города на Нижнем Днепре (городища Знаменское и Гавриловское) (*Pozdnesarmatskie goroda na Nizhnem Dnepre (gorodishcha Znamenskoe i Gavrilovskoe)*) // In: MIA. № 23.

Pshenichniuk A.Kh., 1983 – Пшеничнюк А.Х. Культура ранних кочевников Южного Урала. (*Kultura rannikh kochevnikov Yuzhnogo Urala.*) – Moscow.

Pshenichniuk A.Kh., Riazapov M.Sh., 1976 – Пшеничнюк А.Х, Рязапов М.Ш. Темясовские курганы позднесарматского времени на юго-востоке Башкирии (*Temiasovskie kurgany pozdnesarmatskogo vremeni na iugo-vostoke Bashkirii*) // In: Древности Южного Урала (*Drevnosti Yuzhnogo Urala*). – Ufa.

Piankov I.V., 1975 – Пьянков И.В. Общественный строй ранних кочевников Средней Азии по данным античных авторов *(Obshchestvennyi stroi rannikh kochevnikov Srednei Azii po dannym antichnykh avtorov)* // In: Ранние кочевники Средней Азии. Тезисы докладов конференции, ноябрь 1975 (*Rannie kochevniki Srednei Azii. Tezisy dokladov konferentsii, noiabr 1975*). – Leningrad.

Raev V.A., 1976 – Раев Б.А. К хронологии римского импорта в сарматских курганах Нижнего Дона (*K khronologii rimskogo importa v sarmatskikh kurganakh Nizhnego Dona*) // In: SA. № 1.

Raev V.A., 1993 - Раев Б.А. Бронзовая посуда позднего латена в Сарматии (*Bronzovaia posuda pozdnego latena v Sarmatii*) // In: Античный мир и археология. Проблемы истории и археологии древней ойкумены. Межвузовский сборник научных трудов. Вып 9 (*Antichnyi mir i arkheologiia. Problemy istorii i arkheologii drevnei oikumeny. Mezhvuzovskii sbornik nauchnykh trudov. Vyp. 9*). – Saratov.

Rostovtsev M.I., 1918a – Ростовцев М.И. Курганные находки Оренбургской области эпохи раннего и позднего эллинизма (с приложением П.К. Коковцова и С.И. Руденка) (*Kurgannye nahodki Orenburgskoi oblasti epohi rannego i pozdnego ellinizma (s prilozheniem P.K. Kokovtsova i S.I. Rudenka)*) // In: MAR. № 37.

Rostovtsev M.I., 1918b – Ростовцев М.И. Эллинство и иранство на Юге России (*Ellinstvo i iranstvo na Yuge Rossii*). – Petrograd.

Rostovtsev M.I., 1925 – Ростовцев М.И. Скифия и Боспор (*Skifiia i Bospor*). – Leningrad.

Rudenko K.A., Chizhevskii A.A., 1994 – Руденко К.А., Чижевский А.А. Раскопки Мурзихинского могильника (*Raskopki Murzihinskogo mogilnika*) // In: АО Урала и Поволжья (*AO Urala i Povolzhia*). – Syktyvkar.

Rykov P.S., 1925 – Рыков П.С. Сусловский курганный могильник (*Suslovskii kurgannyi mogilnik*). – Saratov.

Rykov P.S., 1927 – Рыков П.С. Отчет о раскопках в Нижнем Поволжье и Уральской губ. в 1926 и 1927 гг. (*Otchet o raskopkakh v Nizhnem Povolzhie i Uralskoi gub. v 1926 i 1927 gg.*) // Archive LOIA.

Savelieva T.M., Smirnov K.F., 1972 – Савельева Т.М., Смирнов К.Ф. Ближневосточные древности на Южном Урале (*Blizhnevostochnye drevnosti na Yuzhnom Urale*) // In: VDI. № 3.

Salnikov K.V., 1966 – Сальников К.В. Об этническом составе населения лесостепного Зауралья в сарматское время (*Ob etnicheskom sostave naseleniia lesostepnogo Zauralia v sarmatskoe vremia*) // In: SE. № 5.

Selivanova L.L., 1998 – Селиванова Л.Л. Индо-иранские мотивы дельфийской легенды об Аполлоне Гиперборейском (*Indo-iranskie motivy delfiiskoi legendy ob Apollone Giperboreiskom*) // In: Л.Л Селиванова // Проблемы истории, филологии, культуры (*L.L. Selivanova // Problemy istorii, filologii, kul'tury*), Magnitogorsk. Issue V. – P. 102-106.

Sergatskov I.V., 1989 – Сергацков И.В. Погребение среднесарматского времени у села Царев (*Pogrebenie srednesarmatskogo vremeni u sela Tsarev*) // In: SA. № 3.

Sinitsyn I.V., 1946 – Синицын И.В. К материалам по сарматской культуре на территории Нижнего Поволжья (*K materialam po sarmatsqoi`qul`ture na territorii Nizhnego Povolzhia*) // In: SA. VIII.

Sinitsyn I.V., 1947 – Синицын И.В. Археологические раскопки на территории Нижнего Поволжья (*Arkheologicheskie raskopki na territorii Nizhnego Povolzhia*). – Saratov.

Sinitsyn I.V., 1953 – Синицын И.В. Археологические работы в зоне строительства Сталинградской ГЭС (*Arkheologicheskie raboty v zone stroitelstva Stalingradskoi GES*) // In: KSIIMK. №50.

Sinitsyn I.V., 1959 – Синицын И.В. Археологические исследования Заволжского отряда (1953–1955) (*Arkheologicheskie issledovaniia Zavolzhskogo otriada (1953–1955)*) // In: MIA. № 60.

Sinitsyn I.V., 1960 – Синицын И.В. Древние памятники в низовьях Еруслана (*Drevnie pamiatniki v nizoviakh Eruslana*) // In: MIA. №78.

Sinitsyn I.V., 1961 – Синицын И.В. Ровненский курганный могильник (*Rovnenskii kurgannyi mogilnik*) // In: KSIA. №84.

Sinitsyn I.V., 1966 – Синицын И.В. Археологические памятники Саратовского Заволжья (*Arkheologicheskie pamiatniki Saratovskogo Zavolzhia*) // In: Археологический сборник (*Arkheologicheskii sbornik*). – Saratov.

Skalon K.M., 1961 – Скалон К.М. О культурных связях Восточного Прикаспия в позднесарматское время *(O kulturnykh sviaziakh Vostochnogo Prikaspiia v pozdnesarmatskoe vremia)* // In: Археологический сборник *(Arkheologicheskii sbornik)*. – Leningrad

Skrzhinskaia M.V., 1984 – Скржинская М.В. Зеркала архаического периода из Ольвии и Березани *(Zerkala arhaicheskogo perioda iz Olvii i Berezani)* // In: Античная культура Северного Причерноморья *(Antichnaia kultura Severnogo Prichernomoria)*. – Kiev.

Skrzhinskaia M.V., 1998 – Скржинская М.В. Скифия глазами эллинов *(Skifiia glazami ellinov)*. – St. Petersburg.

Skripkin A.S., 1974 – Скрипкин А.С. Позднесарматское катакомбное погребение из Черноярского района Астраханской области *(Pozdnesarmatskoe katakombnoe pogrebenie iz Chernoiarskogo raiona Astrahanskoi oblasti)* // In: KSIA. №140.

Skripkin A.S., 1977 – Скрипкин А.С. Фибулы Нижнего Поволжья *(Fibuly Nizhnego Povolzhia)* // In: SA. №2.

Skripkin A.S., 1978 – Скрипкин А.С. Позднесарматский комплекс из Нижнего Поволжья *(Pozdnesarmatskii kompleks iz Nizhnego Povolzhia)* // In: Вопросы древней и средневековой археологии Восточной Европы *(Voprosy drevnei i srednevekovoi arkheologii Vostochnoi Evropy)*. – Moscow.

Skripkin A.S., 1988 – Скрипкин А.С. Азиатская Сарматия: проблемы истории и культуры *(Aziatskaia Sarmatia: problemy istorii i kultury)* // In: Проблемы скифо-сарматской археологии и истории. Тезисы докладов конференции *(Problemy skifo-sarmatskoi arkheologii i istorii. Tezisy dokladov konferentsii)*. – Azov.

Skripkin A.S., 1990 – Скрипкин А.С. Азиатская Сарматия. Проблемы хронологии и ее исторический аспект *(Aziatskaia Sarmatia. Problemy khronologii i ee istoricheskii aspekt)*. – Saratov.

Skripkin A.S., 2000 – Скрипкин А.С. Новые аспекты в изучении истории материальной культуры сарматов *(Novye aspekty v izuchenii istorii materialnoi kultury sarmatov)*. //In: Нижневолжский археологический вестник *(Nizhnevolzhskiy arheologicheskiy vestnik)*. Issue 3. – Volgograd.

Skudnova V.M., 1962 – Скуднова В.М. Скифские зеркала из архаического некрополя Ольвии *(Skifskie zerkala iz arhaicheskogo nekropolia Olvii)* // In: TGE. №3.

Smirnov A.P., 1938 – Смирнов А.П. Прикамье в первом тысячелетии нашей эры *(Prikamie v pervom tysiacheletii nashei ery)* // In: TR GIM. VII. Moscow.

Smirnov K.F., 1959 – Смирнов К.Ф. Курганы у сел Иловатка и Политотдельского Сталинградской области *(Kurgany u sel Ilovatka i Politotdelskogo Stalingradskoi oblasti)* // In: MIA. № 60.

Smirnov K.F., 1964 – Смирнов К.Ф. Савроматы *(Savromaty)*. – Moscow.

Soboleva N.V., 1991 – Соболева Н.В. Раскопки Мокинского могильника *(Raskopki Mokinskogo mogilnika)* // In: Археологические открытия Урала и Поволжья *(Arkheologicheskie otkrytiia Urala i Povolzhia)*. – Izhevsk.

Sorokina N.P., 1969 – Сорокина Н.П. К вопросу об экономических связях государств Северного Причерноморья в I в. н.э. *(K voprosu ob ekonomicheskikh sviaziakh gosudarstv Severnogo Prichernomoria v I v. n.e.)* // In: Древности Восточной Европы *(Drevnosti Vostochnoi Evropy)*. – Moscow.

Sorokina N.P., 1961 – Сорокина Н.П. Стекло из раскопок Пантикапея 1949–1959 гг. *(Steklo iz raskopok Pantikapeia 1949–1959 gg.)* // In: MIA. № 103.

Sorokina N.P., 1965 – Сорокина Н.П. Стеклянные сосуды из Танаиса *(Stekliannye sosudy iz Tanaisa)* // In: Древности Нижнего Дона *(Drevnosti Nizhnego Dona)*. – Moscow.

Staviskii B.Ia., 1992 – Ставиский Б.Я. Средняя Азия и античное Причерноморье. Проблема контактов, их периодизация и характер *(Sredniaia Aziia i antichnoe Prichernomorie. Problema kontaktov, ikh periodizatsiia i harakter)* // In: Античная цивилизация и варварский мир: Материалы III-го археологического семинара Ч. I. Новочеркасск, 1992 *(Antichnaia tsivilizatsiia i varvarskii` mir: Materialy` III-go arkheologicheskogo seminara Ch. I. Novocherkassk, 1992)*. – Novocherkassk.

Starostin P.S., 1973 – Старостин П.С. Отчет о раскопках Рождественского могильника в 1973 г. (Otchet o raskopkah Rozhdestvenskogo mogilnika v 1973 g.) // In: Архив ИА, р-1, № 5140, № 3, 4, рис. 91. (Arhiv IA, r-1, № 5140, № 3, 4, ris. 91.).

Stepanov P.D., 1964 – Степанов П.Д. Андреевский курган (*Andreevskii kurgan*) // In: ТР НИИЯЛМЭ при Совете Министров Мордовской АССР. Вып. XXVII (*TR NIIIALME pri Sovete Ministrov Mordovskoi ASSR. Vyp. XXVII*). – Saransk.

Stepanov P.D., 1969 – Степанов П.Д. Южные связи племен Среднего Поволжья в I тысячелетии н.э. (*Yuzhnye sviazi plemen Srednego Povolzhia v I tysiacheletii n.e.*) // In: Древности Восточной Европы (*Drevnosti Vostochnoi Evropy*). – Moscow.

Sunchugashev Ia.I., 1975 – Сунчугашев Я.И. Древнейшие рудники и памятники ранней металлургии в Хакасо-Минусинской котловине (*Drevneishie rudniki i pamiatniki rannei metallurgii v Hakaso-Minusinskoi kotlovine*). – Moscow.

Symonovich E.A., 1964 – Сымонович Э.А. Стеклянные кубки из Журовки (*Stekliannye kubki iz Zhurovki*) // In: KSIA. №102.

Tairov A.D., 1993 – Таиров А.Д. Пастбищно-кочевая система и исторические судьбы кочевников урало-казахстанских степей в I тыс. до н.э. (*Pastbishchno-kochevaia sistema i istoricheskie sudby kochevnikov uralo-kazakhstanskikh stepei v I tys. do n.e.*) // In: Кочевники Урало-казахстанских степей (*Kochevniki Uralo-kazakhstanskikh stepei*). – Yekaterinburg.

Tairov A.D., 2004 – Таиров А.Д. Периодизация памятников ранних кочевников Южного Зауралья 7–2 вв. до н.э. (*Periodizatsiia pamiatnikov rannikh kochevnikov Yuzhnogo Zauralia 7–2 vv. do n.e.*) // In: Сарматские культуры Евразии: проблемы региональной хронологии. Доклады к 5-ой международной конференции "Проблемы сарматской археологии и истории" (*Sarmatskie kultury Evrazii: problemy regionalnoi khronologii. Doklady k 5-oi mezhdunarodnoi konferentsii "Problemy sarmatskoi arkheologii i istorii"*) – Krasnodar.

Teplouhov F.A., 1895 – Теплоухов Ф.А. Древности Пермской чуди из серебра и золота и ее торговые пути (*Drevnosti Permskoi chudi iz serebra i zolota i ee torgovye puti*) // Perm.

Tolstoi I.I., Kondakov N.P., 1854 – Толстой И.И., Кондаков Н.П.. Древности Боспора Киммерийского. Т. I–III. (*Drevnosti Bospora Kimmeriiskogo. T. I-III.*). St. Petersburg.

Tolstoi I.I., Kondakov N.P., 1890 – Толстой И.И., Кондаков Н.П. Русские древности в памятниках искусства (*Russkie drevnosti v pamiatnikakh iskusstva*) – St. Petersburg.

Tolstoi I.I., Kondakov N.P., 1899 – Толстой И.И., Кондаков Н.П. Русские древности в памятниках искусства (*Russkie drevnosti v pamiatnikakh iskusstva*) // St. Petersburg.

Tolstoi I.I., 1912–1914 – Толстой И.И. Византийские монеты. Вып. I-IX. (*Vizantiiskie monety. Vyp. I–IX*). St. Petersburg.

Treister M.Iu., 1991 – Трейстер М.Ю. Итальянские и провинциально-римские зеркала в Восточной Европе *(Italiiskie i provintsialno-rimskie zerkala v Vostochnoi Evrope)* // In: SA. № 1.

Treister M.Iu., 1993 – Трейстер М.Ю. Еще раз об ожерельях с подвесками в виде бабочек I в. н.э. из Северного Причерноморья (*Eshche raz ob ozhereliakh s podveskami v vide babochek I v. n.e. iz Severnogo Prichernomoria*) // In: PAV. № 4.

Uvarova P.S., 1899 – Уварова П.С. Бронзовая ручка из Недвиговского городища (*Bronzovaia ruchka iz Nedvigovskogo gorodishcha*) // In: AIZ. VII.

Uvarova P.S., 1900 – Уварова П.С. Могильники Северного Кавказа (*Mogilniki Severnogo Kavkaza*) // In: МАК. VIII.

Farmakovskii B.V., 1902 – Фармаковский Б.В. Памятники античной культуры, найденные в России (*Pamiatniki antichnoi kultury, naidennye v Rossii*) // In: IAK. №3.

Fasmer R.R., 1931 – Фасмер Р.Р. Завалишинский клад куфических монет VIII-IX вв. (*Zavalishinskii klad kuficheskikh monet VIII-IX vv.*) // In: Tr. IGAIMK. VII. №2.

Fersman A.E., 1920 – Ферсман А.Е. Самоцветы России (*Samotsvety Rossii*). Petrograd.

Fersman A.E. 1954 – Ферсман А.Е. Очерки по истории камня (*Ocherki po istorii kamnia*). V. 1. – Moscow.

Frolova N.A., 1982 – Фролова Н.А. О римско-боспорских отношениях в I – середине III в. н.э. по нумизматическим данным (*O rimsko-bosporskikh otnosheniiakh v I – seredine III v. n.e. po numizmaticheskim dannym*) // In: Нумизматика античного Причерноморья (*Numizmatika antichnogo Prichernomoria*). – Kiev.

Halikov A.H., 1971 – Халиков А.Х. Общие процессы в этногенезе башкир и татар Поволжья и Приуралья (*Obshchie protsessy v etnogeneze bashkir i tatar Povolzhia i Priuralia*) // In: AEB.

Tsalkin V.I., 1966 – Цалкин В.И. Древнее животноводство племен Восточной Европы и Средней Азии (*Drevnee zhivotnovodstvo plemen Vostochnoi Evropy i Srednei Azii*) // In: MIA. №135.

Chezhina E.F., 1989 – Чежина Е.Ф. Уникальная надпись на раннескифском псалии из Южного Приуралья (*Unikalnaia nadpis na ranneskifskom psalii iz Yuzhnogo Priuralia*) // In: SA. № 1.

Chernykh E.I., 1988 – Черных Е.И. Циркумпонтийская провинция и древнейшие индоевропейцы (*Tsircumpontiiskaia provintsiia i drevneishie indoevropeitsy*) // In: Древний Восток. Этнокультурные связи (*Drevnii Vostok. Etnokulturnye sviazi*). – Moscow.

Chlenova N.L., 1983 – Членова Н.Л. Предыстория "торгового пути Геродота" (из Северного Причерноморья на Южный Урал) (*Predystoriia "torgovogo puti Gerodota" (iz Severnogo Prichernomoria na Yuzhnyi Ural)*) // In: SA. № 1.

Shelov D.B., 1965 – Шелов Д.Б. Южноиталийские и западноримские изделия в торговле Танаиса первых веков нашей эры (*Iuzhnoitaliiskie i zapadnorimskie izdeliia v torgovle Tanaisa pervykh vekov nashei ery*) // Acta archaeologica Hungarika. XVII.

Shelov D.B., 1969 – Шелов Д.Б. Ольвийские монеты в Поволжье (*Olviiskie monety v Povolzhie*) // In: Древности Восточной Европы (*Drevnosti Vostochnoi Evropy*). – Moscow.

Shelov D.B., 1970 – Шелов Д.Б. Танаис и Нижний Дон в III-I вв. до н.э. (*Tanais i Nizhnii Don v III-I vv. do n.e.*) – Moscow.

Shelov D.B., 1972 – Шелов Д.Б. Танаис и Нижний Дон в первые века нашей эры (*Tanais i Nizhnii Don v pervye veka nashei ery*). – Moscow.

Shelov D.B., 1978 – Шелов Д.Б. Узкогорлые светлоглиняные амфоры первых веков нашей эры. Классификация и хронология (*Uzkogorlye svetloglinianye amfory pervykh vekov nashei ery. Klassifikatsiia i khronologiia*) // In: KSIA. №156.

Shelov D.B., 1983 – Шелов Д.Б. Римские бронзовые кувшины и амфоры в Восточной Европе (*Rimskie bronzovye kuvshiny i amfory v Vostochnoi Evrope*) // In: SA. № 3.

Shilik K.K., 1989 – Шилик К.К. Еще раз о "торговом пути Геродота" (*Eshche raz o "torgovom puti Gerodota"*) // In: Проблемы скифо-сарматской археологии Северного Причерноморья. Тезисы докладов областной конференции, посвященной 90-летию со дня рождения профессора Б.Н. Гракова (*Problemy skifo-sarmatskoi arkheologii Severnogo Prichernomoria. Tezisy dokladov oblastnoi konferentcii, posviashchennoi 90-letiiu so dnia rozhdeniia professora B.N. Grakova*). – Zaporozhie.

Shelov D.B., 1993 – Шелов Д.Б. Новые монетные находки в Танаисе (1961–1990 гг.) (*Novye monetnye nahodki v Tanaise (1961–1990 gg.)*) // In: Вестник Танаиса (*Vestnik Tanaisa*). №1.

Shilov V.P., 1956 – Шилов В.П. Погребения сарматской знати I в. до н.э. – I в. н.э. (*Pogrebeniia sarmatskoi znati I v. do n.e. – I v. n.e.*) // In: SGE. IX.

Shilov V.P., 1959a – Шилов В.П. Калиновский курганный могильник *(Kalinovskii kurgannyi mogilnik)* // In: MIA. №60.

Shilov V.P., 1959b – Шилов. В.П. Раскопки Елизаветовского могильника в 1954 и 1958 гг. *(Raskopki Eliza-vetovskogo mogilnika v 1954 i 1958 gg.)* // In: IROMK. № 13.

Shilov V.P., 1968 – Шилов В.П. Позднесарматское погребение у с. Старица *(Pozdnesarmatskoe pogrebenie u s. Staritsa)* // In: Античная история и культура Средиземноморья и Причерноморья (Antichnaia istoria i kultura). – Leningrad.

Shilov V.P., 1972 – Шилов В.П. Южноиталийские зеркала в волго-донских степях *(Iuzhnoitaliiskie zerkala v vol-go-donskikh stepiakh)* // In: SA. № 1.

Shilov V.P., 1973a – Шилов В.П. Металлические сосуды из кургана у села Большая Дмитриевка *(Metallicheskie sosudy iz kurgana u sela Bolshaia Dmitrievka)* // In: SA. №4.

Shilov V.P., 1973b – Шилов В.П. Южноиталийские сосуды Калиновского могильника *(Iuzhnoitaliiskie sosudy Kalinovskogo mogilnika)* // In: SGE. № 36.

Shilov V.P., 1974 – Шилов В.П. К проблеме взаимоотношений кочевых племен и античных городов Северного Причерноморья в сарматскую эпоху *(K probleme vzaimootnoshenii kochevykh plemen i antichnykh gorodov Severnogo Prichernomoria v sarmatskuiu epohu)* // In: KSIA. №138.

Shilov V.P., 1975 – Шилов В.П. Очерки по истории племен Нижнего Поволжья. – М.: Наука, 1975.

Shilov V.P., 1983 – Шилов В.П. Аорсы. (историко-археологический очерк) *(Aorsy. (istoriko-arkheologicheskii ocherk)* // In: История и культура сарматов *(Istoriia i kultura sarmatov)*. – Saratov.

Shkorpil V.V., 1910 – Шкорпил В.В. Отчет о раскопках в г.Керчи и его окрестностях в 1907 г. *(Otchet o raskopkakh v g.Kerchi i ego okrestnostiakh v 1907 g.)* // In: IAK. № 35.

Shramm G., 1997 – Шрамм Г. Реки Северного Причерноморья (историко-филологическое исследование их названий в ранних веках) *(Reki Severnogo Prichernomoria (istoriko-filologicheskoe issledovanie ikh nazvanii v rannikh vekakh)* // In: Взгляд издалека. Немецкие историки о прошлом Восточной Европы *(Vzgliad izdaleka. Nemetskie istoriki o proshlom Vostochnoi Evropy)*. – Moscow: Eastern communications.

Shtatman I.L., 1972 – Штатман И.Л. Волжский путь поступления византийских милиарисиев в Восточную Европу и Прибалтику в X веке *(Volzhskii put postupleniia vizantiiskikh miliarisiev v Vostochnuiu Evropu i Pribaltiku v X veke)* // In: История и культура славянских стран *(Istoriia i kultura slavianskikh stran)*. – Leningrad.

Shchukin M.B., 1989 – Щукин М.Б. Сарматы на землях к западу от Днепра и некоторые события I в. н.э. в Центральной и восточной Европе *(Sarmaty na zemliakh k zapadu ot Dnepra i nekotorye sobytiia I v. n.e. v Centralnoi i vostochnoi Evrope)* // In: SA. № 1.

Yablonskii L.T., 1999 – Яблонский Л.Т. Некоторые итоги работ комплексной Илекской экспедиции на юге Оренбургской области *(Nekotorye itogi rabot kompleksnoi Ilekskoi ekspeditsii na iuge Orenburgskoi oblasti)* // In: Евразийские древности. 100 лет Б.Н. Гракову: архивные материалы, публикации, статьи. *(Evraziiskie drevnos-ti. 100 let B.N. Grakovu: arhivnye materialy, publikatsii, statii.)*– Moscow.

Yagodin V.N., Nikitin A.V., Koshelenko G.A., 1985 – Ягодин В.Н., Никитин А.Б., Кошеленко Г.А. Хорезм *(Khorezm)*// In: Археология СССР: Древнейшие государства Кавказа и Средней Азии *(Arheologia SSSR: Drevney-shie gosudarstva Kavkaza i Sredney Azii)*. – Moscow.

Yanin V.L., 1956 – Янин В.Л. Денежно-весовые системы русского средневековья *(Denezhno-vesovye sistemy russ-kogo srednevekovia)*. – Moscow.

Yatsenko S.A., 1986 – Яценко С.А. Диадемы степных кочевников в Восточной Европе в сарматскую эпоху *(Dia-demy stepnykh kochevnikov v Vostochnoi Evrope v sarmatskuiu epohu)* // In: KSIA. №186.

BIBLIOGRAPHY

Abramzon M.G., Maslennikov A.A. Gold coins of Theodosius II from the East Crimea // Ancient Civilizations from Scythia to Siberia. 1999. 5.3. P. 207-213.

Bozi F. The Nomads of Eurasia in Strabo // The archaeology of the steppes methods and strategies. Papers from the International Symposium held in Naples, 9–12 November 1992. – Napoli. 1994.

Eggers H. J. Der romische Import in frien Germanien. Hamburg, 1951.

Ghirchman R. Iran: Parthians and Sasanians. London, 1962.

Goldina R.D., Nikitin A.B. New finds of Sasanian, Central Asian and Byzantine coins from the regions Perm, the Kama-Urals area //Silk Road Art and archaeology. Spesial Volume. 1997.

Medvedev A.P. and Yfimov K. Y. Sarmatian barrow with Roman and Chinese imports in the Middle Don Region // in B.A. Raev. Roman imports in the Lower Don Bassin. BAR Int Ser 278. Oxford. 1986. P. 34–47.

Mielczarek M. Ancient Greek coins found in Central, Eastern and Northern Europe //Academia scientiavum Polona. Bibliotheca antiqua. Vol. XXI. Wroclaw, 1989.

Mielczarek M. Remarks on the numismatic evidence for the northern Route: the Sarmatians and the trade route linking the northern Black Sea with Central Asia //Silk Road Art and archaeology. Spesial Volume. 1997.

Noonan Ih.S. Russia, the Near East, and the Steppe in the Early Medieval Period: An examination of the Sasanian and Byzantine finds from the Kama-Urals area //Archivum Eurasie Medii Aevi. Wiesbaden. V. II., 1982.

Ogden. J. Jewellery of the Ancient World. London: Trefoil Books, 1982.

Polanyi K. Ports of Trade in Early Societies // Journal of Economic History, 1963

Polanyi K. Primitive, Archaic and Modern Economies. Essays. Ed. By G. Dalton. Garden City, 1968.

Radnoti A. Die romische Bronze gefasse von Pannonien. Budapest. 1938.

Rashke M. New Studies in Roman Commerce with the East // ANRW. B. II: 9: 2., 1978 (Aufstieg und Niedergang der romischen Welt). Berlin.

Rau. P. Die Hugelgraber romischer Zeit an der unteren Wolga. Pokrovck, 1927.

Rau P. Prahistorische Ausgra bungen auf der Steppenseite des Deutschen Wolga – gebiets im jahre 1926. Pokrovsk, 1927.

Rostovtseff M.I. Iranians and Greeks in South Russia. Oxford, 1922.

Stralenberg E.I. Das Nord – und Ostliche Theil von Europa und Asia. Stocholm, 1730.

Willers H. Die romische Bronzee i mer von Hemmoor. Hannover, 1900.

GENERAL INDEX

Table I. Imported ceramic utensils

№	Place of finding	Year of finding	Description	Dating	Place of manufacturing	Source	Notes
1	Berezhnovka, Nikolaevsky district, Volgograd region	1954	Kurgan 44, Sarmatian grave. Red varnish pot with rounded body and outside-bent crown, on a ring tray, poor quality varnish. Vessel dimensions: height – 9 cm, opening diameter – 6,5 cm, bottom diameter – 5 cm.	2nd-3rd c. AD	Asia Minor	Sinitsin I.V., 1960: 50, fig.16, 8	
2	Berezhnovka, Nikolaevsky district, Volgograd region	1954	Kurgan 18, child's grave. Jug, the top part covered with varnish, varnish drips in the bottom part. Vessel dimensions: crown diameter – 12 cm, opening diameter – 5 cm, bottom diameter – 5 cm	2nd-3rd c. AD	Asia Minor	Kropotkin V.V., 1970: 18	
3	Bykovo Bykovsky district Volgograd region	1954	Kurgan 5, grave 3. Red varnish jug with reddish-brown varnish.	1st c. BC – 1st c. AD	Not defined	Smirnov K.F., 1960: 186, fig. 6, 13;	
4	Kalinovka Bykovsky district Volgograd region	1954	Red-clay balsamarium with red varnish traces on the neck, made of small-grain well-levigated pink clay, coated with cream engobe.	1st c. AD	Asia Minor (Pergam)	Shilov V.P., 1959: 469, fig. 53, 1	An absolutely identical vessel originates from grave 33 of Ust-Labinsky cemetery 2, dated to the 2nd c. AD. [Anfimov N.V., 1951: 196, fig. 17, 10]
5	Politotdelskoe Bykovsky district Volgograd region	1953	Hellinistic flask coated with brown varnish.	2nd c. BC.	Asia Minor	Smirnov K.F., 1959: 270, 321, fig. 25, 4	
6	Susly Sovetsky district Saratov region		Kurgan 2. Red varnish pot with two deep grooves on shoulders. Vessel dimensions: height – 9,6 cm, neck diameter – 8 cm, body diameter – 13 cm, bottom diameter – 5,8 cm.	1st c. BC – 1st c. AD	Asia Minor	Rykov P.S., 1925: 34	
7	Lebedevka Shyngyrlau district, West-Kazakhstan region		In a Late Sarmatian grave there was found a light-clay narrow-neck amphora with profiled handles	3rd c. AD	Tanais	Kropotkin V.V., 1970: 132	

Table II. Imported bronze utensils

№	Place of finding	Year of finding	Description	Dating	Place of manufacturing	Source	Notes
1	Kalinovka Bykovsky district Volgograd region	1954	In kurgan 55/8 the following bronze vessels were found: a) Bronze jug with flaring body.	2nd c. BC – 1st c. AD	Campania	Shilov V.P., 1956: 45	Jugs of this type or mugs with a biconical flaring body and an outside-bent crown, with a vertical handle which usually has a mask – or leaf-shaped attache at the bottom, the top end embraces the crown with two bows made as swan heads; such items are quite typical for all European collections of Italic bronze ware and are sometimes named vessels of the "Kelheim" type; two similar vessels were discovered in one of the graves of Kobansky cemetery [Uvarova P.S., 1900: 85, fig. 81] and among the grave goods at Dakhovskaya village in the Northern Caucasus [Lunin B.V., 1940: 33, 39]. The third vessel is, respectively, the jug from Kalinovka [Shelov D.B., 1983: 64]
			b) Bronze vessel with a ball-shaped body, two vertical handles and cap	1st c. BC – 1st c. AD	South Italy	Shilov V.P., 1959: 482	D.B. Shelov compares its shape features, handles fastening and decoration with the bronze vessels of South Italic production from the excavations of Pompeii, Boscoreale and Hildesheim hoard [Shelov D.B., 1972: 207]
2	Bolshaya Dmitrievka Shirokokaramyshsky district Saratov region	1887	In one of the kurgans a set of imported bronze vessels was found: a) Bronze riveted pot-shaped vessel with a soldered bottom and traces of repair.	1st c. BC – 1st c. AD	South Italy	Kropotkin V.V., 1970: 93	It belongs to the buckets of the so-called "Bargfeld" type or to the "vessels with a biconical body and outside-bent edge", as H.Willers names them [Willers H., 1900: 108 Radnoti A., 1938: 121-122]. They are dated to the 1st c. BC – 1st c. AD, but the traces of repair show that this vessel would rather belong to the late 1st c. AD, this is the most probable dating for the chronology of the entire

№	Place of finding	Year of finding	Description	Dating	Place of manufacturing	Source	Notes
							complex [Maksimov E.K., 1957:. 158]. In Europe they are found in the graves of the 1st c. BC – 1st c. AD.
			b) Bronze cast ladle with gilded external surface, a long flat handle with a semi-oval board on the edge. On the handle end there is a wide flat ring with a small hole, it is flat, on its external side there are embossed concentric circles. The ladle has a deep body, slightly convex walls and a slightly outside-bent edge.	second half of 1st c. AD	South Italy	Shelov D.B., 1965: 265-267	According to H.Eggers' typology, it belongs to type 140 and is dated to step BI (1-50 AD) [Eggers H.I., s: 172, taf. 12,140].
3	Susly Sovetsky district Saratov region	1913	Prior to the start of the excavations by P.S. Rykov, in a Sarmatian grave of the 2nd-3rd c. AD there was found a bronze bowl with a flat bottom decorated inside with carved concentric circles and an outside-bent board. Dimensions: diameter – 27 cm, height – 4,5 cm, board width – 2 cm.	1st c. BC	Italy	Shelov D.B., 1972: 208	
4	Rovnoe Rovnensky district Saratov region	1961	In a Sarmatian grave of Rovnensky kurgan cemetery a bronze cauldron with straight walls and rounded bottom was found.	1st-2nd c. AD	Gaul	Sinitsin I.V. 1961: 101	A similar bronze cauldron of Gaul-Roman production originates from a destroyed grave of one of Novo-Lipovsky kurgans (the Bolshoy Karaman river) [Maksimov E.K., 1969: 115].
5	Akhtial The Kama Region	1913	A well-preserved bronze ladle was found near the village, obviously, in a sepulcher of Pyanoborsk culture of the 3rd c. AD: the ladle had a ring-shaped handle ornamented with a triangle of six rounds. Dimensions: height – 8,9 cm, diameter – 15,6 cm,	1st c. AD	South Italy	Volkovich A.M., 1941: 255	The only similar object was found by I.A. Volkov in 1887 during excavations of one of the kurgan close to Bolshaya Dmitrievka [Kropotkin V.V., 1970: 93].

№	Place of finding	Year of finding	Description	Dating	Place of manufacturing	Source	Notes
			bottom diameter – 10 cm, handle length – 15 cm, ring diameter – 6,1 cm.				
6		early 20th c.	A bronze semi-spheric bowl on a ring tray, with two handles decorated with three embossed belts and flattened snake heads at the ends; on the inner side – a curved Latin mark – AFRICANSVF; the bowl was preserved in twelve fragments. Dimensions: diameter – 31 cm, height – 10,5 cm, bottom diameter – 9,8 cm.	1st-2nd c. AD	Italy (Capua)	*ibidem*: 230-233	In the paper by V.V.Kropotkin this bowl is considered a silver one, although we do not know the reasons for that [*ibidem*: 21, 86].
7	Nyrgynda Karakulinsky district, Udmurtia.	1898	Bronze ladle with a round body, flat bottom, concentric circles; the flat handle has an embossed ornament. Dimensions: diameter – 16,2 cm, bottom diameter – 9,3 cm, height – 8,2 cm, handle width at the end – 5 cm.	3rd c. AD	South Gaul (Lugdunum)	Shelov D.B., 1972: 210	
8	Lebedevka Shyngyrlau district, West-Kazakhstan region	1968	In a Late Sarmatian grave of kurgan 2 the following bronze vessels were found: a) Bronze jug with a high cylindrical neck and horizontal crown.	1st c. BC – 1st c. AD	South Italy	Bagrikov G.I., Senigova T.M.: 68 sl.	
9			b) Bronze oenochoe. This type of oenochoes is characterized by the ball-shaped body and a more stumpy general proportions. The shaped handle of the oenochoe from Lebedevka at the top has two bird heads which are located around the crown, below it has a raised shield with an image of Dionysos's bearded head.	1st c. AD	Capua	Shelov D.B., 1983: 65	

№	Place of finding	Year of finding	Description	Dating	Place of manufacturing	Source	Notes
10		1968	c) Bronze cauldron with vertical board, rounded bottom, embraced with an iron hop on the edge with two ring-shaped handles are fixed on both sides.	1st-2nd c. AD	South Italy	Bagrikov G.I., Senigova T.M., 1968: 68 sl.	
11		1968	d) Bronze kettle with rounded bottom, body slightly tapering to the top and horizontal board; bronze handle with a raised shield decorated with Dionysos's bearded head.	1st-2nd c. AD	South Italy	Bagrikov G.I., Senigova T.M., 1968, p. 68 sl.	

Table III. Imported silver articles

№	Place of finding	Year of finding	Description	Dating	Place of manufacturing	Circumstances of finding	Source
1	Alkino, Chisminsky district, Bashkortostan	1954	Silver platter	Not defined	Bysantium	On the Dema river – tributary of the Belaya river	Leshchenko V.Yu. 1971: 329
2	Bartym, Berezovsky district, Perm region	1925	Silver platter with an image of Venus at the Anchises's tent.	550	Bysantium	During plowing on a smooth slope on the right-hand bank of the Bartym river at the level of 2,5 m.	Matsulevich L.A., 1940: 150
3	Peshnigort former Solikamsk uezd. Perm region	1853	Silver ladle with a fishing image.	641-651	Bysantium	During plowing not far from the Inva river	Leshchenko V.Yu., 1971: 213, 217
4	Klimova Kudymkarsky district Perm region	1907	a) Silver platter with an image of a shepherd among the herd	527-565	Bysantium	At one verst from the village	*ibidem*: 304, 305
5			b) Silver platter with a niello image of a cross in a wreath.	602-610	Bysantium		
6			c) Silver platter AD with a cross, no marks	7th c.	Bysantium		
7	Maltseva Kudymkarsky district Perm region	1887	a) Silver platter depicting Silenus holding a skin with wine and images of maenads	613-629/630	Bysantium	At 1 km from the village on the left bank of the Kuva river – the left-hand tributary of the Ilva river – the right-hand tributary of the	Darkevich V.P., 1976: 23

№	Place of finding	Year of finding	Description	Dating	Place of manufacturing	Circumstances of finding	Source
						Kama on the bank of Kalganovka creek.	
8			b) Silver platter with niello image of a chrisscross in a wreath.	7th c.	Bysantium		
9			c) Fragment of a similar platter (bottom) with a chrisscross.	7th c.	Bysantium		
10	Bolshoy Palnik, Kochevsky district Perm region	1953	Silver platter with a rosette with a festooned edge.	651-688	Bysantium	Found in summer during plowing at 2 km from the desolate Martynova village where, apparently, an ancient sanctuary once existed	*ibidem*: 33
11	Pyatigory, Gainsky district. Perm region	1913	Silver platter with a cross on the front side	Not defined	Bysantium	On the right bank of the Kama river	
12	Sludka, Ilyinsky district Perm region	1780	a) Silver platter with an image of a horse under a tree.	527-565	Bysantium	On the right bank of the Kama river	Matsulevich L.A., 1940: 150; Leshchenko V.Yu., 1971: 213-217
13			b) Silver platter depicting the court proceedings on the litigation of Ajax and Odyssey for Achilles's armour.	VI в.	Bysantium		
14			c) Silver platter with a cross.	613-629/630	Bysantium	Not defined	
15			d) Silver platter depicting a maenad feeding a snake which rises from a cyst	VI в.	Bysantium		
16	Ust-Kishert, Kishertsky district. Perm region	1916	Profusely ornamented silver platter with brand marks on the bottom.	second quarter of 6th c. AD	Bysantium	Not defined	Matsulevich L.A., 1940:145, table II, 2, fig. 4-5
17	Cherdyn Perm region	1895	Large silver ladle depicting a nilometer.	491-518 гг.	Bysantium	Not defined	Bank A.V., 1966: 295
18	Tomyz, Glazov district Kirov region	1893	Silver platter with geometrical niello image on the front side in the center.	613–629/630 гг.	Bysantium	The hoard was discovered at 7 versts from the Kama river and at 2 versts from the Tomyz river – a left-hand tributary of the Kama.	Leshchenko V.Yu., 1971: 286

№	Place of finding	Year of finding	Description	Dating	Place of manufacturing	Circumstances of finding	Source
19	Turusheva, Omutninsky district Kirov region	1927	a) Silver platter with a rosette in the center.	629/630–641	Bysantium	Not defined	Matsulevich L.A., 1940: 142, fig. 3
20			b) Silver platter with a niello cross in an ivy wreath	641-651 гг.	Bysantium		
21			c) Silver platter with a cross.	7th c.	Bysantium		
22	Karasevo, Glazovsky district Kirov region	1890	a) Silver platter with a wavy board, no ornament.	middle of 7th c.	Bysantium	The hoard was found at the Zhaba river, a tributary of the Cheptsy river	Darkevich V.P., 1976: 13
23			b) Silver platter	6th c.	Bysantium		

Table IV. Coins of Greek cities of the Northern Black Sea Region

№	Place of finding	Time of finding	Coin description or definition	Coin dating	Circumstances of finding	Source
1	Selitrennoe Harabalinsky district Astrakhan region	unknown	Olbia – 2 pc. Chersonesos – 1 pc.	unknown	The coins were found on the bank of the Akhtuba river.	Kropotkin V.V., 1961: 46
2	Rovnoe Rovnensky district Saratov region	unknown	Panticapaeum – 1 pc.	unknown	The coins were found on the left bank of the Volga	Shelov D.B., 1970: 178

Table V. Roman coins

№	Place of finding	Time of finding	Coin description or definition	Coin dating	Circumstances of finding	Source
1	Selitrennoe Harabalinsky district Astrakhan region	unknown	copper coins – 2 pc.	4th c. AD	The coins were found after a storm on the bank of the Akhtuba river.	Kropotkin V.V., 1961: 40
2	Savinka Palassovsky district Volgograd region	1901	Hadrianus's large bronze coin minted in the Egyptian Alexandria.	117-138 AD	Found in vegetable soil at Shingarei farm at the conflux of the Torgun and the Vodyanka rivers	Zaikovsky B.V., 1926: 46:116
3	Staraya Poltavka Staro-Poltavkinsky district Volgograd region	1925	Alexander Severus's bronze coin minted in Nicomedia (Bithynia). Av.: emperor's bust in a laurel wreath to the right. Rv.: eight-point temple with a frontal on the basement.	222-235 AD	unknown	ibidem: 46:115
4	Dergachi Dergachevsky district Saratov region	1916	Vespasianus's sesterce with AETER NITAS type.	69-79 AD	During house construction at the depth of 1,4 m in a grave with a skeleton.	Kropotkin V.V., 1961, p. 46
5	Dergachi Dergachevsky district Saratov region	Before 1926	there were found silver coints of Hadrianus (117-138), Antoninus Pius (138-161), Faustina (138-141) and Lucius Verus (161-169).	2nd c. AD	On the dunes of the Altata river at 3 versts from the village	ibidem

№	Place of finding	Time of finding	Coin description or definition	Coin dating	Circumstances of finding	Source
6	Krasny Kut Krasnokutsky district Saratov region	1926	two silver coins of Gordianus III (238-244); bronze coin of Gallienus (253-268); bronze coin of Claudius II (268-270)	3rd c. AD	On the dunes of the Eruslan river	*ibidem*
7	Krasny Kut Krasnokutsky district Saratov region	about 1900	coins of Gordianus III – 8 pc.; Otacilia Severa (244-249) – 3pc.; Claudius II – 2 pc.; Gallienus – 1 pc.;	3rd c. AD	It is said that at the same place was found a hoard which consisted of golden and silver coins. The golden coins were not kept to date, the silver coins of Gordianus III (238-244) and Philippus Arabs (244-249) were dispersed. It was possible to collect 14 (fourteen) Antonian coins.	Zaikovsky B.V., 1926: 46:112
8	Rovnoe Rovnensky district Saratov region	1911	Roman republican denarius	135-134 BC	On the shoal of the Volga	*ibidem*: 43:30
9	Rovnoe Rovnensky district Saratov region	unknown	Roman republican denarius	109 BC	On the shoal of the Volga	*ibidem*: 43:29
10	Osinovy Gai Novo-Repinsky district Saratov region	unknown	Lucilla's denarius	161-169	On the dunes of the Altata river, a tributary of the Bolshoy Uzen river.	Kropotkin V.V., 1961, p. 47
11	Svintsovka Tatishchevsky district Saratov region	unknown	Faustina Jr.'s silver coin	130-176 AD	In a field	*ibidem*
12	Izhevsk Udmurtia	1975	Alexander Severus's bronze coin minted in Tomy, with a hole, poorly preserved.	222-235 AD	Occasional finding on a burial site.	*ibidem*: 49
13	Rozhdestveno, Laishevsky district Tatarstan	1973	Alexander Severus's sesterce Av.: emperor's bust to the right, circular legend: IMPSEVALEXADRAVG. Rv.: Victoria standing upright, head turned to the left, dressed, holds a wreath in the right hand and a palm branch in the left hand, circular legend: PMTRP [....] COS III Pp, field – SC. Satisfactory preservation state, a hole punched in the center.	222-235	During the excavations by P.S. Starostin in a child's grave there were found remnants of a wooden grivna banded with an iron rod, two appendant bronze roman coins were attached to the grivna.	Starostin P.S., 1973: № 3, 4, fig. 91; Kropotkin V.V., 1984: 137 – 140
			dupondius of Maximianus I Av.: emperor's bust to the right, circular legend: IMPMAXIMINUS PIVSA UG Rv.: Similar image of Victoria, at the left of her feet a prisoner is sitting, circular legend VICTORIA GERMANICI, field – SC. Coin preservation state is poor. A hole is punched in the center	235-238		

№	Place of finding	Time of finding	Coin description or definition	Coin dating	Circumstances of finding	Source
14	Kurgan Kurgan region	1907	well-preserved golden coin of Theodosius I. Av.: Theodosius's bust in a tiara to the right. RV.: emperor on the throne in a robe and a helmet with a globe in his hand.	379-395 AD	In the outskirts of the city. The finding is doubtful.	Kropotkin V.V., 1961: 45
15	Ufa Bashkortostan	1926	well-preserved golden coin of Theodosius I.	379-395	During digging of a ditch for a house foundation in a sepulcher with a horse and iron parts of horse harness.	*ibidem*: 48
16	Kargalinsky ore mine Orenburg region	1896	Traianus's bronze "medal" (98-117).	116 AD	During mine wall creeping	*ibidem*: 45

Table VI. Byzantine coins

№	Place of finding	Time of finding	Coin description or definition	Coin dating	Circumstances of finding	Source
1	Selitrennoe Harabalinsky district Astrakhan region	1899	Unclassified copper coins	unknown	The coins were found on the Saray mounting close to the village.	Kropotkin V.V., 1962: 40
2	Kanaevka Ivanteevsky district Saratov region	unknown	silver Byzantine coin: Av.: Christ's image; Rv.: three-line Greek inscription.	unknown	On the Irgiz river	*ibidem*: 28
3	Ust-Karaman Marxovsky district Saratov region	unknown	Justinus I's copper coin equal to forty nummia, minted in Constantinople.	518-527	Not defined	*ibidem*
4	Orsk Orenburg region	1922	Justinianus I's solid Av.: emperor's bust to the right, circular inscription [DNIVSTINIANVS]; Rv.: Nika standing, circular legend VICTORIA AVG.	527-565 AD	During construction of a dam there was found a hoard consisting of golden items and several coins. All the golden coins were not kept to date, except one coin.	*ibidem*: 27
5	Bartym Berezovsky district Perm region	1950	Heraclius's hexagrams of the same type minted in Constantinople – belonging to the early variant.	615-629	In a Sassanidian silver vessel there were found two hundred and sixty Byzantine silver coins. During a pit digging nearby there were also found twelve more coins.	Bader O.N., 1951, p. 19; Kazamanova N.L., 1957: 71, 72
6	Bartym Berezovsky district Perm region	1981	bronze coin – imitation of coins of the Byzantine Chesonesos of Heraclius's period	610-641	During the excavations by N.V. Vodolago in grave 5a of the second half of 7th c.	Goldina R.D., Nikitin A.B., 1997: 113, 114, № 56
7	Shestakovo Suksunsky district Perm region	1851	silver hexagrams of Heraclius and Hera-clius Constantinus –	7th c.	On the Irgen river a hoard with silver articles and coins was found: silver jug	Kropotkin V.V., 1962: 26

№	Place of finding	Time of finding	Coin description or definition	Coin dating	Circumstances of finding	Source
			11 pc.		of oriental production, weighing 1 kg, a silver twisted grivna with clips, silver pendants and earrings, fragments of golden signet rings, crystal and cornelian beads, Sassanidian coins.	
8	Suksunsky district Perm region		silver hexagrams of Heraclius and Heraclius Constantinus – 7 pc.	7th c.	In Ust-Sylvensky settlement (on the bank of the Sylva river) among the set of objects of Glyadenovo and Ananino cultures, presumably, on an early medieval sacrificial site with surface of about 1000 m.	Goldobin A.V., Lepikhin A.N., Melnichuk A.F., 1991: 40
9	Verkh-Sainskoe settlement Perm region	1982	bronze coin – imitation of Byzantine coins (Justinianus ?) equal to forty (40) nummia.	6th c.	During the excavations by N.V. Vodolago in a destroyed grave of the second half of 6th c. – early 7th c.	Goldina R.D., Nikitin A.B., 1997: 113, 114, № 47

Map I Finds of imported ceramic pottery

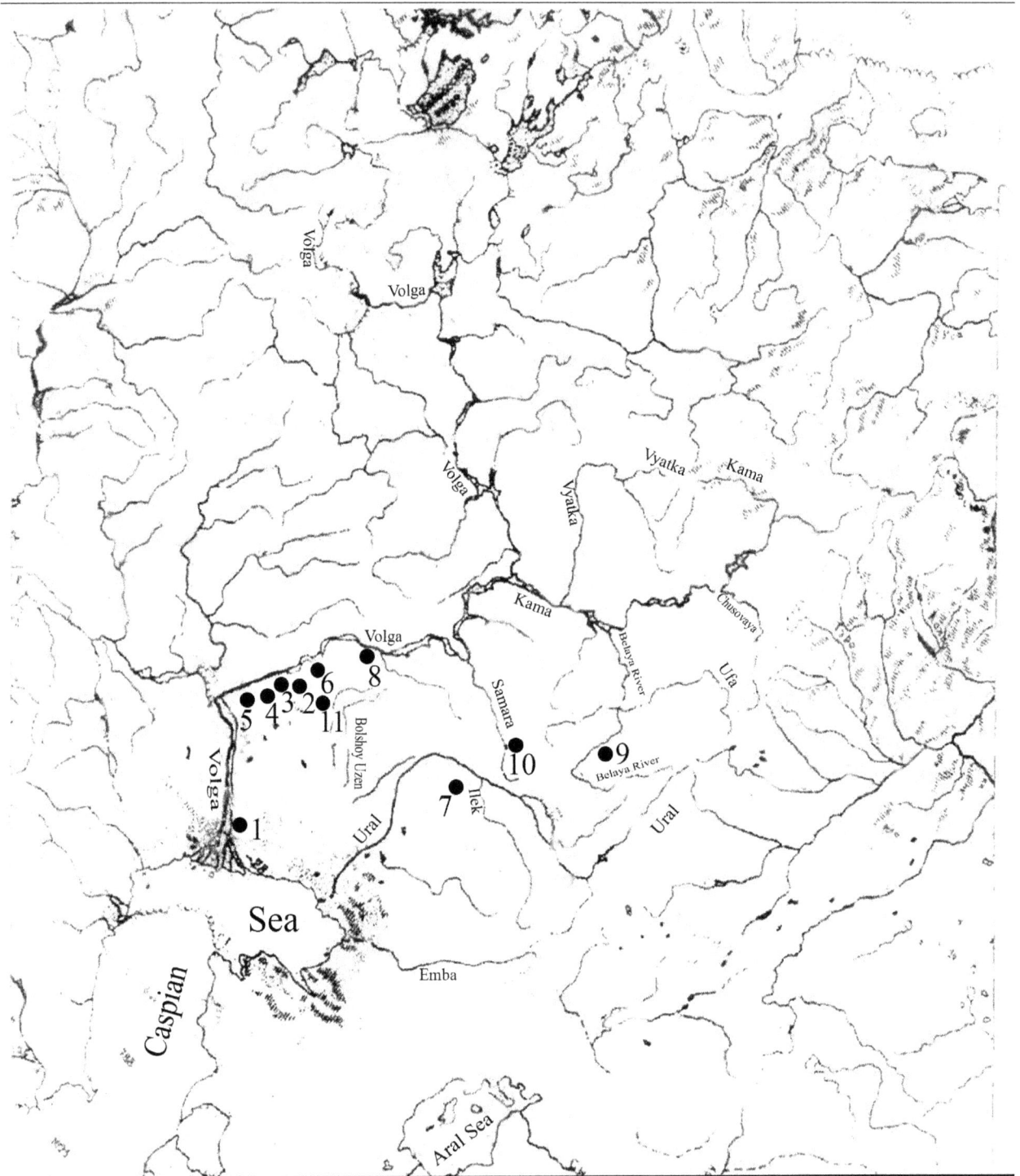

1. Krivaya Luka
2. Kalinovka
3. Berezhnovka
4. Bykovo
5. Politotdelskoe

6. Susly
7. Lebedevka
8. Tsarevo
9. Ishtuganovo
10. Sorochinsk

11. Staraya Ivantsovka

1: 20 000 000

Map II Finds of imported bronze utensils

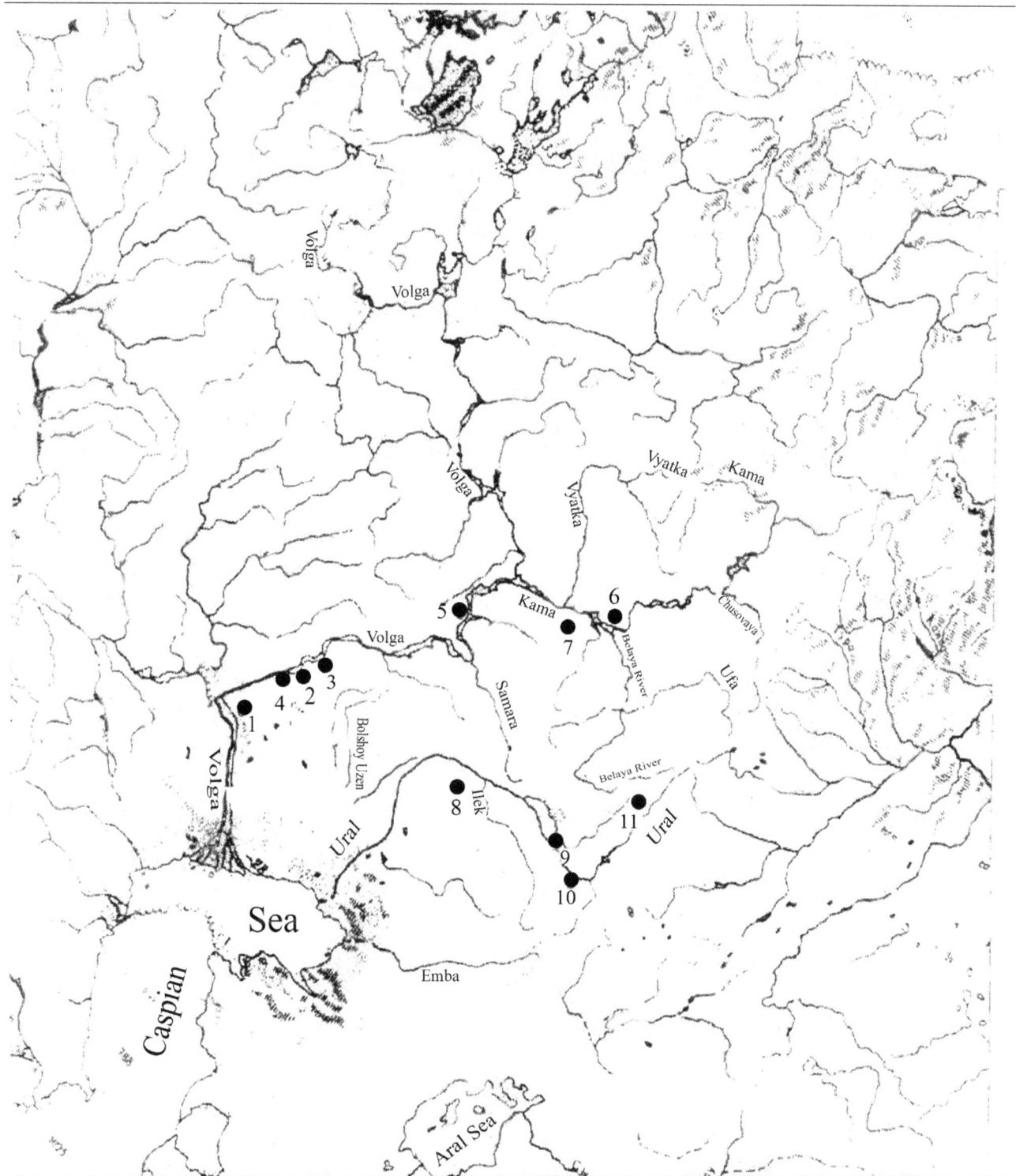

1. Kalinovka
2. Bolshaya Dmitrievka
3. Susly
4. Rovnoe
5. Ichalkovo

6. Nyrgynda
7. Akhtial
8. Lebedevka
9. Krasnogorsky
10. Akbulak

11. Magnitny

1: 20 000 000

Map III Finds of imported silverware

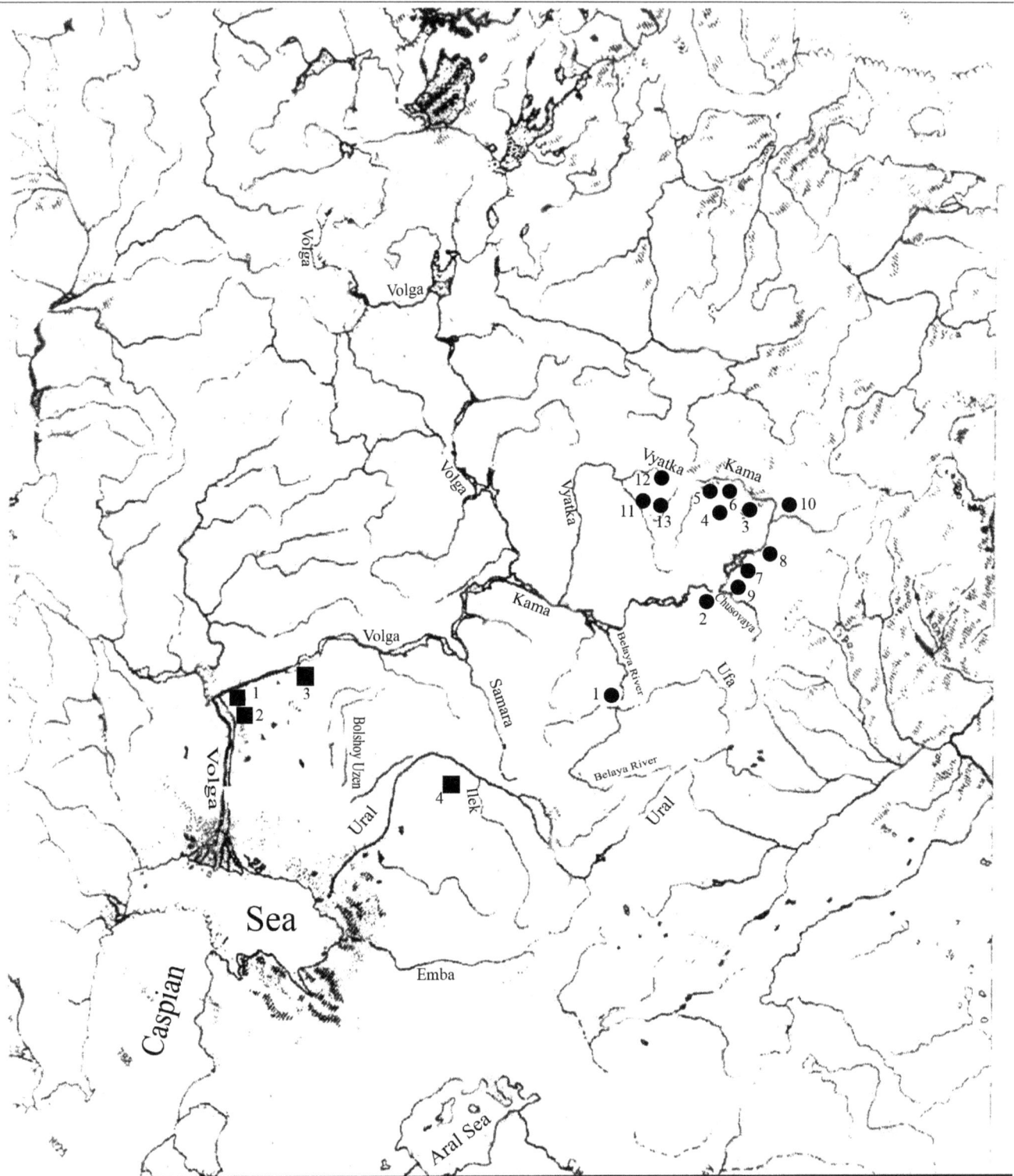

Map IV Finds of imported glassware

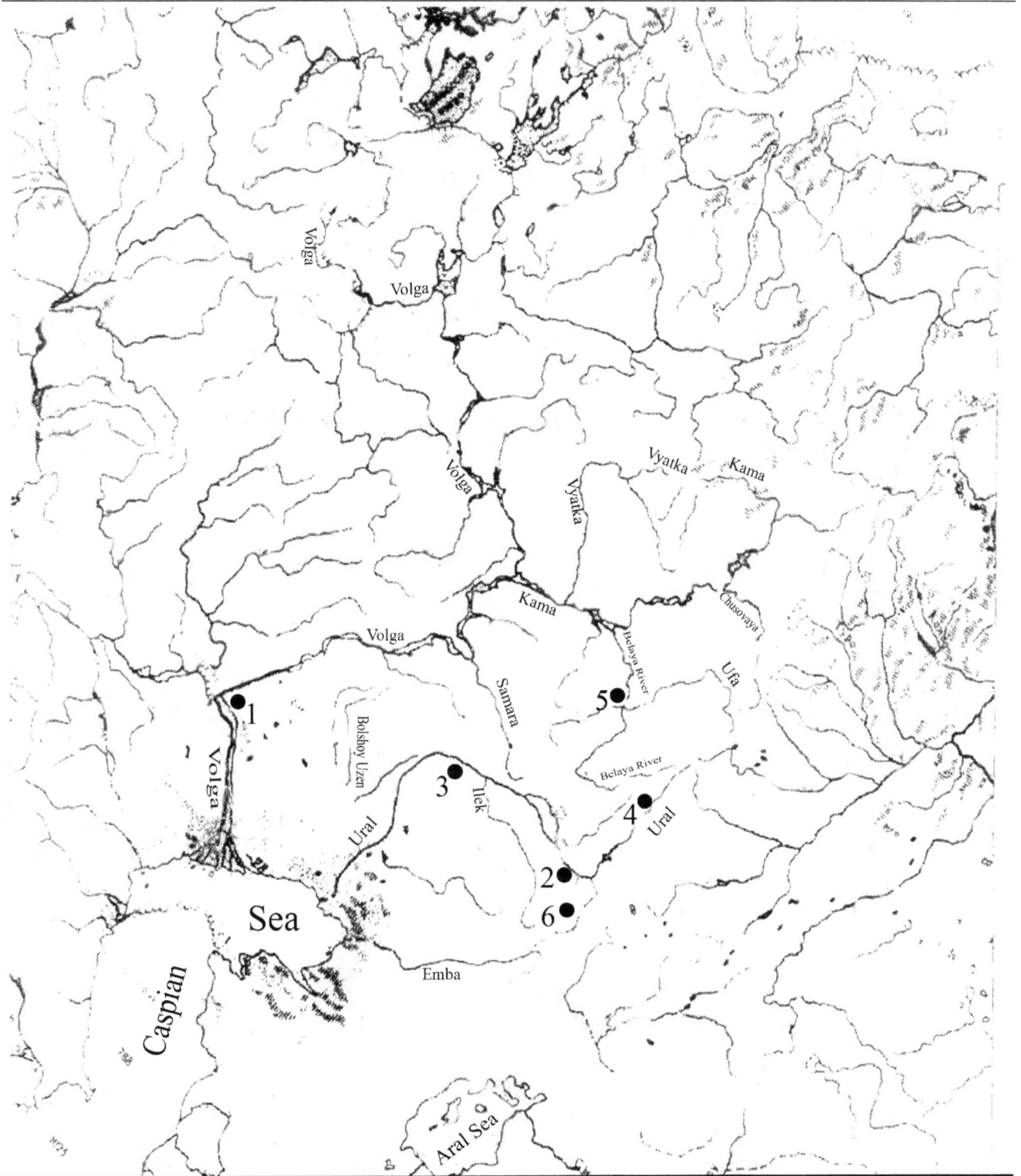

1. Kalinovka
2. Pokrovka
3. Lebedevka
4. Magnitny
5. Ufa
6. Kara-Agach

1: 20 000 000

Map V Finds of imported decorations

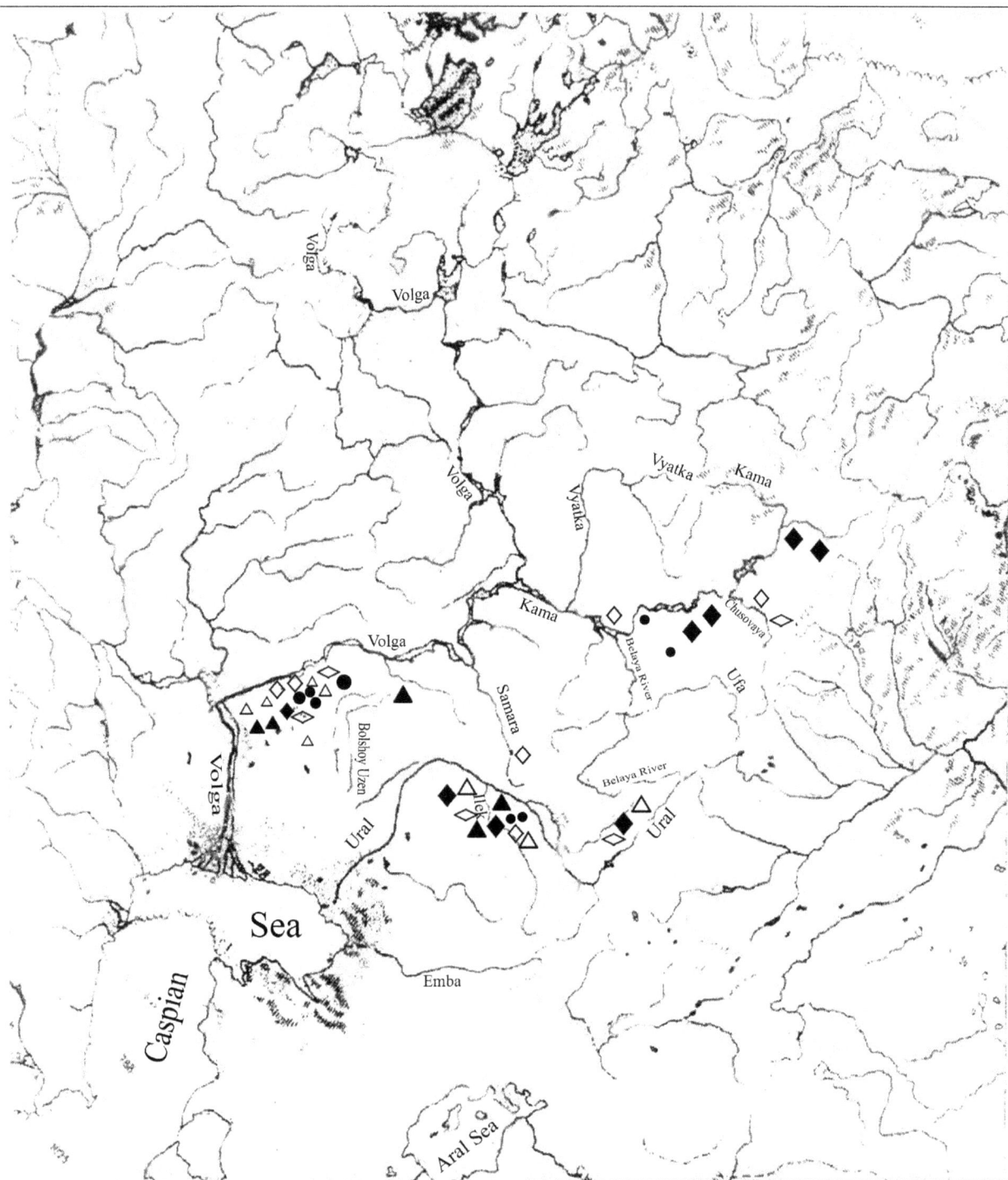

Map V Finds of imported decorations

Symbol	Legend
◇	a) Egyptian faience scarabaei and decorations
●	b) Coral and seashell decorations
◆	c) Decorations made of amber, semi-precious stones and minerals
⬦	d) Metallic decorations
△	e) Fibulae
▲	f) Toiletware and household items

2.Privolnoe
4. Atasovo
5. Berezhnovka
6. Susly
7.Usatovo
8.Novo-Molchanovka
9. Kama region

c)Decorations made of amber, semi-precious stones and minerals

1. Usatovo
2. Temyasovo
3. Lebedevka
4. Ilek kurgan
5. Lomovatovo
6. Verkh-Sainsk
7. Ust-Sylva
8. Kargort
9. Kalinovka

e)Fibulae
1. Kalinovka
2.Susly
3. Kano
4. Temyasovo
5.Lebedevka
6.Tselinny
7.Magnitny
8.Lipovka

f)Toiletware and household items
1.Alt-Weimar (now StarayaIvantsovka)
2.Berezhnovka
3.Susly
4.Berezhnovka
5. Rovnoe
6.Kalmykovo
7.Pokrovka

a)Egyptian faience scarabaei and decorations
1.Susly
2.Berezhnovka
3.Kalinovka
4.Zuevskie klutchi
5.Kharkovsky kurgan
6.Sorochinsk
7.Privolnoe

b)Coral and seashell decorations
1.Pokrovka

d)Metallic decorations
1.Berezhnovka
2.Temyasovo
3.Ust-Sylva
4. Lebedevka
5. Mokino

1: 20 000 000

Map VI Finds of coins of Greek cities of Northern Black Sea region

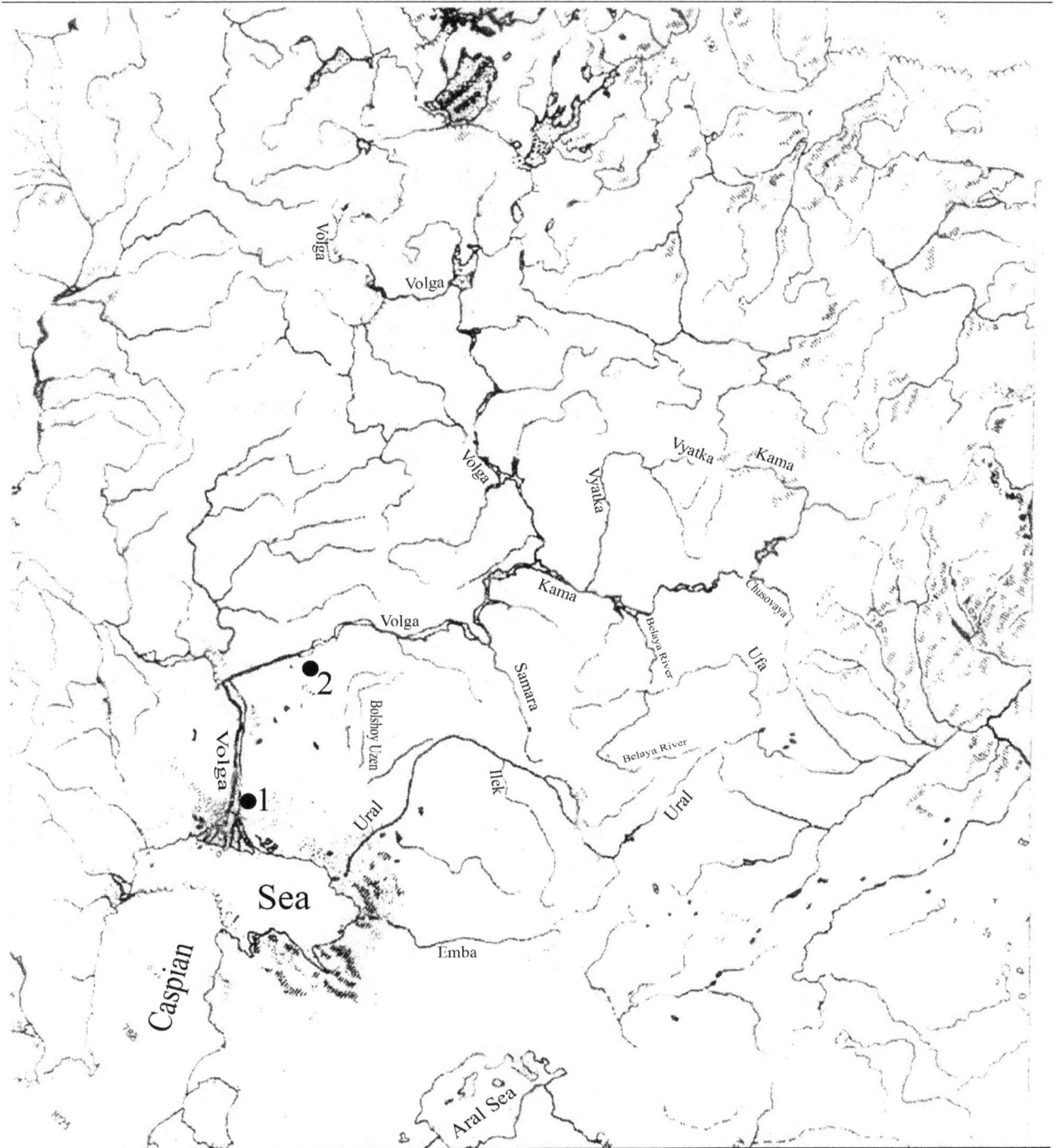

1. Selitrennoe
2. Rovnoe

1: 20 000 000

Map VII Finds of Roman coins

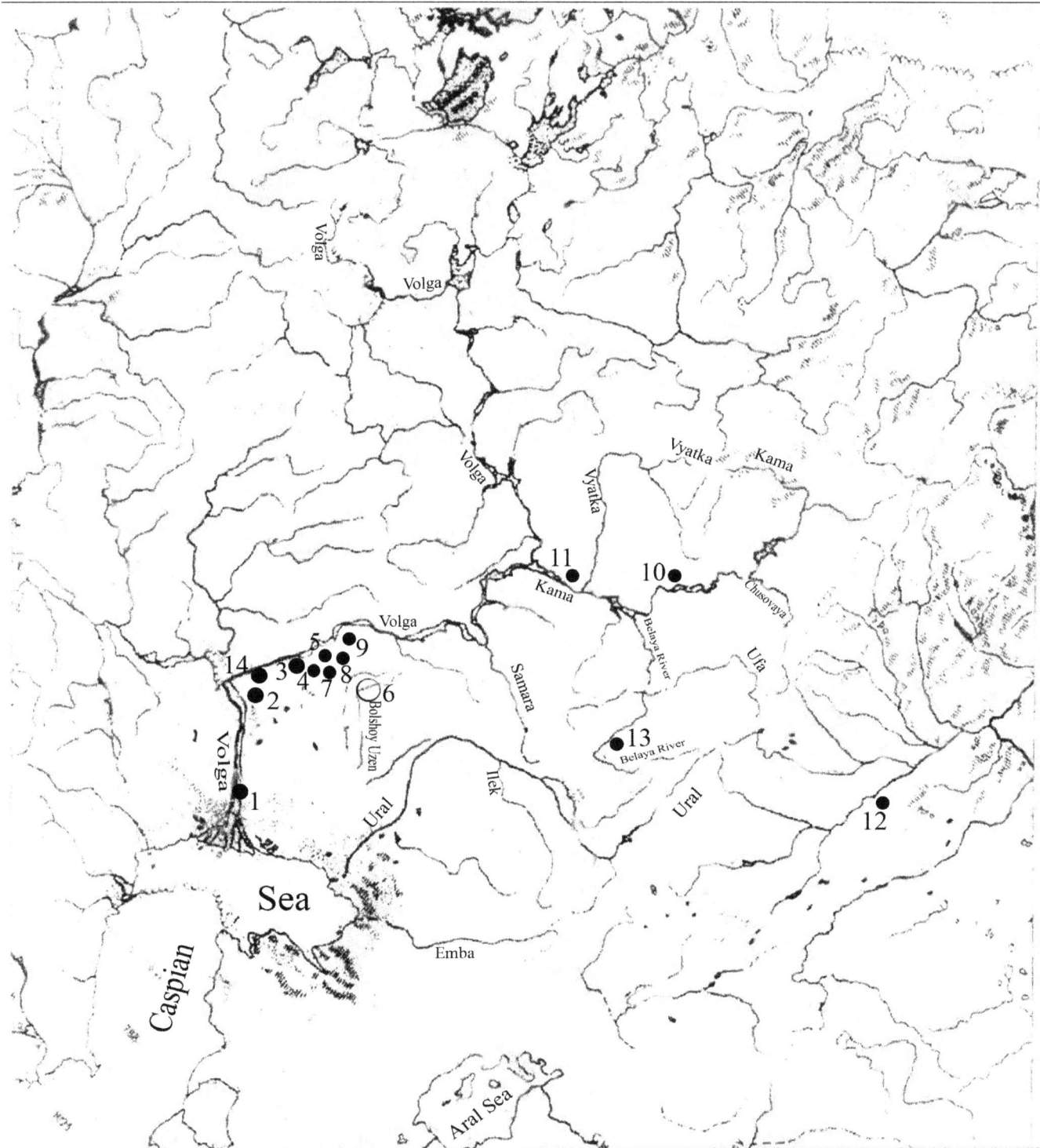

Map VII Finds of Roman coins

● Single finds
1. Selitrennoe
2. Savinka
3. StarayaPoltavka
4. Dergachi

7. Rovnoe
8. OsinovyGai
9. Svintsovka
10. Izhevsk
11. Rozhdestveno
12. Kurgan
13. Ufa
14. Kargalinsky ore mine

○ Hoards
6. Krasny Kut

1: 20 000 000

Map VIII Finds of Byzantine coins

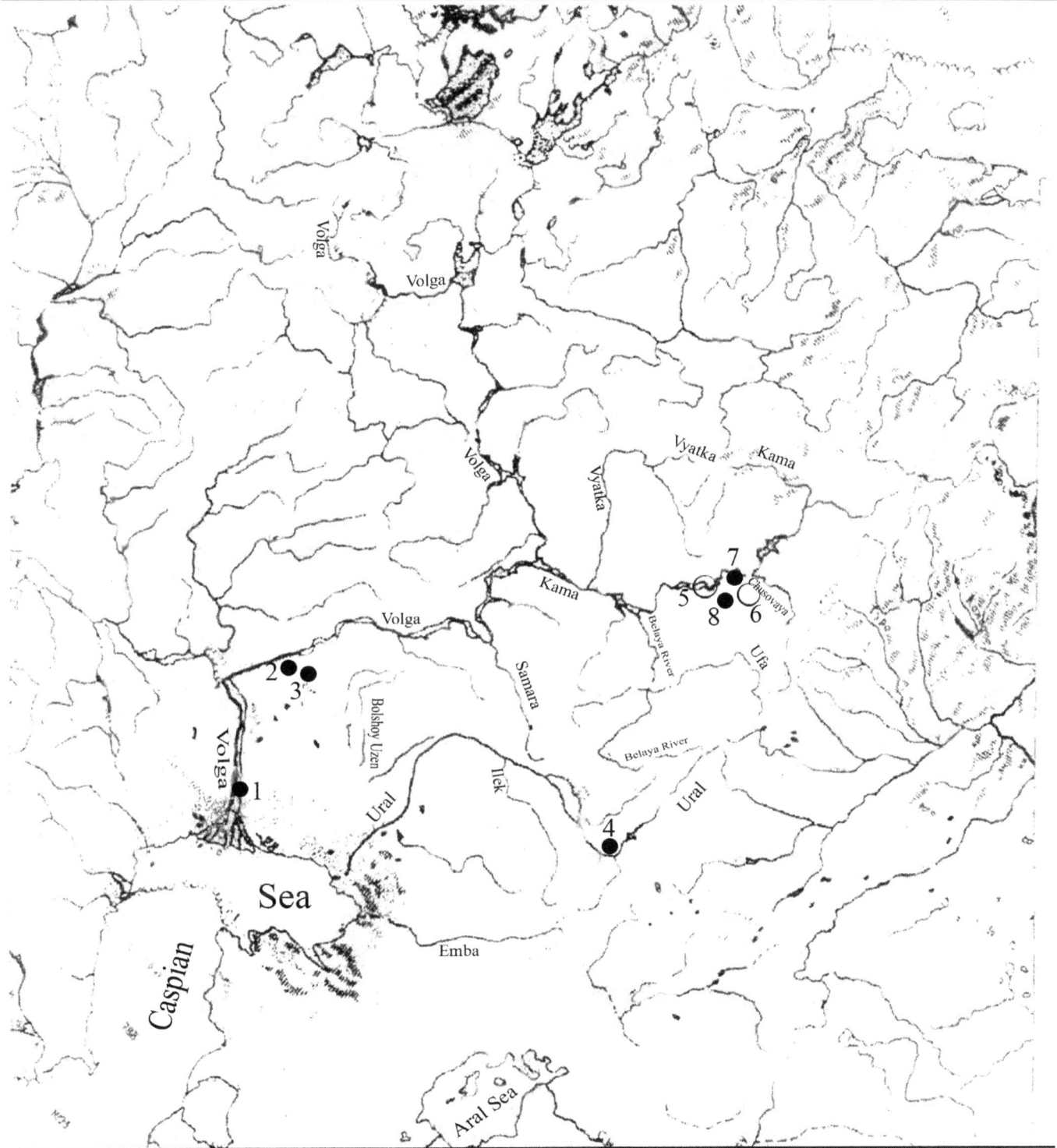

Map VIII Finds of Byzantine coins

● Single finds   ○ Hoards
  1.Selitrennoe   5.Bartym
  2.Kanaevka   6.Shestakovo
  3.Ust-Karaman
  4.Orsk
  7. Suksunsk
  8.Verkh-Sainsk

1: 20 000 000